Post-structuralist Joyce

Post-structuralist Joyce

Essays from the French

Edited by Derek Attridge and Daniel Ferrer

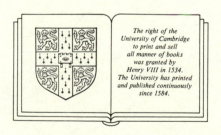

The right of the
University of Cambridge
to print and sell
all manner of books
was granted by
Henry VIII in 1534.
The University has printed
and published continuously
since 1584.

Cambridge University Press

Cambridge
London   New York   New Rochelle
Melbourne   Sydney

PR
6019
09Z78234
1984

Published by the Press Syndicate of the University of Cambridge
The Pitt Building, Trumpington Street, Cambridge CB2 1RP
32 East 57th Street, New York, NY 10022, USA
296 Beaconsfield Parade, Middle Park, Melbourne 3206, Australia

First published 1984

Printed in Great Britain at the University Press, Cambridge

Library of Congress catalogue card number: 84–4317

British Library Cataloguing in Publication Data
Post-structuralist Joyce.
  1. Joyce, James, 1882-1941—Criticism
and interpretation—Congresses
I. Attridge, Derek II. Ferrer, Daniel
823'.912 PR6019.09Z/
ISBN 0 521 26636 X hard covers
ISBN 0 521 31979 X paperback

49988

GG

Contents

À Suzanne, Véronique, et Juliette

Preface

This collection of newly translated essays has been brought together with two kinds of reader in mind (though any individual reader may well belong to both categories): those with an interest in Joyce, and those with an interest in literary theory. The combination of these two concerns is not something fabricated for this book, but is a matter of history, a history which the essays themselves exemplify: between the late 1960s and the early 1980s Joyce's writing was a stimulus, a focus, and a proving-ground for new modes of theoretical and critical activity in France, whose widespread impact has been one of the most striking features of the intellectual climate of recent years. Most of these essays first appeared in the Parisian journals – *Tel Quel, Poétique, Change* – which were the main forum for critical debate in this period, and all of them form part of the movement away from the structuralism that dominated intellectual discussion in the 1960s to what is now called (though not in France itself) 'post-structuralism'. Their authors come from different backgrounds and have somewhat different theoretical orientations, but they share a preoccupation with the mechanisms of textuality and their implications for the writing – and reading – subject. We have excluded both purely formalist and purely rhetorical studies, as well as pithy pronouncements unsubstantiated by a detailed reading of the texts. We have also decided not to include essays which assume familiarity with a very specific system of thought: for instance, an understanding of Lacan's seminar on Joyce requires, besides a good knowledge of topology and the mathematical theory of knots, a close acquaintance with Lacanian psychoanalytic concepts.

The first kind of reader mentioned above will find original and challenging accounts of Joyce's work from *Dubliners* to *Finnegans Wake*, while the second will find theoretical problems of continuing importance presented and discussed through close engagement with a writer who raises them in a peculiarly acute (but also peculiarly delightful) form. It is the hope of the editors that any reader who begins the book in one of these camps will finish it in both.

This book has been much more of a collaborative effort than is indicated by the title-page, and the close involvement of the contributors and translators (with one another and with the editors) has extended well beyond what is suggested by these limiting appellations. In particular, we wish to thank Jean-Michel Rabaté and Geoff Bennington, without whom the collection would have remained an idea dreamed up one hot Parisian summer. The French Ministry of Culture provided a generous grant towards the expenses of the translation, which we gratefully acknowledge. We are grateful, too, to David Bellos and Maud Ellmann for advice and assistance, to Norma Martin, Sheila James, and Jill Bennett for valuable secretarial help, and to Cambridge University Press for their concretely manifested faith in this cross-Channel project.

D.A., D.F.

Southampton–Paris
December, 1983

References and sources

Quotations from Joyce's writing are cited with page numbers from the following editions, using the abbreviations indicated where necessary:

Dubliners (*D*) and *A Portrait of the Artist as a Young Man* (*P*): *The Essential James Joyce,* ed. Harry Levin, Penguin Books, 1963.

Ulysses (*U*): Penguin Books, 1968, and Random House, 1961. Except where they are identical, page-references to both are given in this order.

Finnegans Wake (*FW*): Faber & Faber and The Viking Press, 1939. References are given in the standard form: II.4 is Book II, chapter 4; 345.25 is page 345, line 25.

Letters: Vol. I, ed. Stuart Gilbert (1957), Vols. II and III, ed. Richard Ellmann (1966), Faber & Faber and The Viking Press.

The original titles and the sources of the essays collected in this volume are as follows:

Hélène Cixous, 'Joyce, la ruse de l'écriture', *Poétique* 4 (1970), 419–32.

Stephen Heath, 'Ambiviolences: Notes pour la lecture de Joyce', *Tel Quel* 50 (1972), 22–43, and 51 (1972), 64–76.

Jacques Aubert, 'Riverrun', *Change* 11 (1972), 120–30.

Jean-Michel Rabaté, 'Lapsus ex machina', *Poétique* 26 (1976), 152–72.

André Topia, 'Contrepoints joyciens', *Poétique* 27 (1976), 351–71.

Daniel Ferrer, 'Circé, ou les regrès éternels', written in 1975; to be published in *Les Cahiers de l'Herne.*

Jacques Derrida, 'Deux mots pour Joyce', paper given at the Centre Georges Pompidou, Paris, 1982; to be published in *Les Cahiers de l'Herne.*

The essay by Hélène Cixous has been reprinted in her *Prénoms de personne* (Paris, 1974), and is translated by kind permission of Editions du Seuil.

1 Introduction: Highly continental evenements

DEREK ATTRIDGE AND DANIEL FERRER

Let us ran on to say oremus prayer and homeysweet homely, after fully realising the gratifying experiences of highly continental evenements.

(*FW* 398.11–13)

I Omelette on the belly

On the table at James Joyce's fifty-seventh birthday party (which also marked the publication of *Finnegans Wake*) there stood at one end a decanter shaped like the Eiffel Tower, at the other end a bottle in the form of Nelson's Pillar, and in between a mirror tray representing the English Channel; while silver paper did duty for the Seine on one side and the Liffey on the other.[1] Though Joyce knew many cities, two in particular wove themselves into his life and his writing; and if he never wholly left the one in which he spent his first twenty years, it could also be said that from an early age he was moving towards the one that became the focus of his last twenty years. If Dublin was 'homeysweet homely', an unfailing source of memories and material for Joyce's books, it was the 'gratifying experiences' of Paris that provided the environment and the audience which those books demanded. That the two cities were separated by much more than the English Channel – let alone a mirror tray – was part of their continuing importance for Joyce, who throve on the impossible fusion of polar opposites. The distance is extravagantly dramatized in a scene in the 'Circe' episode of *Ulysses*, provoked by what Bella Cohen takes to be Stephen's demand for unorthodox sexual satisfactions:

BELLA: None of that here. Come to the wrong shop.
LYNCH: Let him alone. He's back from Paris.
ZOE: (*Runs to Stephen and links him*) O go on! Give us some parleyvoo. [...].
STEPHEN: (*Gabbles, with marionette jerks*) Thousand places of entertainment to expenses your evenings with lovely ladies [...]. Perfectly shocking terrific of religion's things mockery seen in universal

1

world. All chic womans which arrive full of modesty then disrobe and squeal loud to see vampire man debauch nun very fresh young with *dessous troublants.* (*He clacks his tongue loudly*) *Ho, la la! Ce pif qu'il a!*

LYNCH: *Vive le vampire!*

THE WHORES: Bravo! Parleyvoo!

STEPHEN: [. . .] Caoutchouc statue woman reversible or lifesize tompeeptoms virgins nudities very lesbic the kiss five ten times. Enter gentlemen to see in mirrors every positions trapezes all that machine there besides also if desire act awfully bestial butcher's boy pollutes in warm veal liver or omelette on the belly *pièce de Shakespeare.*

BELLA: (*Clapping her belly, sinks back on the sofa with a shout of laughter*) An omelette on the . . . Ho! ho! ho! ho! . . . Omelette on the . . . [. . .]

THE WHORES: (*Laughing*) Encore! Encore!

(*U* 509–10/569–70)

One of the functions of this comic fantasy of Parisian perversion is to reassure the occupants of a Dublin brothel of their own healthy normality; and it offers itself to us as a parable, pointing to a recognizable pattern in responses to 'French excesses' since at least the Revolution of 1789. The publication of *Ulysses* itself – with passages such as this – no doubt fostered fantasies of French decadence among the guardians of decency in the English-speaking world: Paris was just the kind of place where one would expect to find a book like *that*. And the general pattern has been repeated in various ways more recently: fantasies about the Paris *événements* of May 1968 helped to strengthen British and American conservatism; and fantasies about the intellectual movements in Paris in the 1970s helped to keep Anglo-American literary criticism on its straight and narrow path. Fortunately, the pattern is now changing, in literary theory at least, but lest incomprehension and hostility be replaced by reductive assimilation, let us remember how much of Joyce's peculiar and explosive energy derived from the uncloseable gap between shocking Paris and shockable Dublin, and let us not condemn his domesticated ghost to traverse a safe, easy bridge across the Atlantic. Joyce's excesses, to which Paris has always been so receptive, can never be contained: no critical consensus will ever be able to control the rapturous and rupturing laughter provoked, inside and outside the text, by that outrageous omelette – *pièce de Shakespeare* – on the belly.

II   Come to the wrong shop

Literary criticism often presents itself as the humble servant of the work on which it comments, uncovering the text's meanings and structures and rewriting them in a more easily apprehensible form for the benefit of readers less intelligent, or less industrious, or less sensitive to literary techniques (or the subtleties of human experience) than the critic. Such servitude may, however, be a barely disguised form of mastery, functioning to elide, mask, or divert attention away from whatever in the text tends to move beyond the control of the reader, who operates necessarily within a horizon of inherited expectations and conventions. When a literary work is praised by a critic for revealing significant truths hidden deep within human affairs, this may be a way of saying that it is recuperable within the critic's existing presuppositions, and when a *critic* is praised for revealing significant truths hidden deep within a text, this may mean that the commentary has created a verbal envelope through which the recuperated text can be read. Each claims to have a secure position outside the object they are judging – critic outside the literary text, reader outside the critical text – and not to be in any way implicated in producing, or being produced by, the text they read. And both feel the satisfaction of 'discovering' truths in a text which coincide with those they have brought to it. The literary work which refuses this satisfaction, which does not yield to the prevailing critical strategies, whose proliferations go uncontrollably beyond established reading habits and threaten to obliterate the safe distance between text and reader, is put to one side, to await the critic who will be able to show that it is, after all, not so ferocious, but has merely been misunderstood. But the *critical* text which refuses the same satisfaction, and which neither professes to serve nor seeks to master, declining to stand clear of the text on which it comments, failing to unearth a buried human significance, and producing instead a further unmasterable proliferation of meaning, is permanently discarded.

   To present the business of criticism in this way is to sketch the outlines of a certain theoretical position, a position which has been powerfully argued during the past fifteen years and which has an obvious bearing on Joyce's writing and on the critical endeavours that surround it. The picture needs a great deal of finer brushwork to render it convincing to anyone who remains within the ideological framework it exposes (it is subject, that is to say, to its own logic); and the essays that follow offer the reader one way of tracing, in specific detail rather than in general theoretical argument, some of its justifications and implications. It is important, however, to make one qualification at the outset: the activity of assimilation, of providing readers with a manageable version of a threatening or perverse text, of *producing* meaning by analysis and commentary, is not something which can merely be dismissed or transcended once it has been acknowledged. It is the only way we possess of reading; it is, in fact, what reading *is*: we always, and inevitably, read through and by means of previous readings, both our own and other people's. Meaning is always produced in a social space filled with texts, not in a private encounter between the words on the page and the cleanly stripped mind. Moreover, changing historical conjunctures demand changing readings: the choices available for the reader of *Ulysses* in 1922 were vastly different from those available in 1983, and it is possible to argue that a reading which was valid and valuable in the former year is wholly invalid and inadequate now.

The power of criticism (by which we mean all commentary, formal and informal, in print or by word of mouth) to produce readings that will bring about the acceptance and enjoyment of a text has probably never been so crucial as it was with the major achievements of high modernism (it is only by virtue of the exercise of that power, after all, that they have acquired the epithet 'major'). Pound, Eliot, and Joyce were all well aware that their newborn literary offspring needed an incubator of supportive commentary in order to thrive in the world of publishers and purchasers, and did much, in their different ways, to encourage the production of such commentary, or to provide it themselves; and it was inevitable that until their writing was securely established within the portals of the canon most of that commentary should be devoted to the task of minimizing the challenge to the doxa which their work represented (without, of course, dimming the appeal of its 'novelty'). This is not the place to embark on a survey of Joyce criticism, but one might note two things in Eliot's early plug for *Ulysses* (in *The Dial*, November 1923): its suasive Lincolnian rhetoric − 'I hold this book to be the most important expression which the present age has found; it is a book to which we are all indebted, and from which none of us can escape' − and its reassuring emphasis on Joyce's use of a firm mythic structure as 'a way of controlling, of ordering, of giving a shape and a significance to the immense panorama of futility and anarchy which is contemporary history'.[2] Pound, at the same time, was finding (or producing) traditionalism within the innovation of *Ulysses* in a quite different way: for him it represented the finest flower of the realist line descending from Flaubert, the fulfilment of the early promise of *Dubliners*, 'a realistic novel *par excellence*', as he pronounced in the *Mercure de France* in June 1922.[3]

Thus the major strategies for the assimilation of Joyce's writing were laid down early, and soon enabled a large part of his output to be read without gross affront to the modes of interpretation and evaluation (and their ideological foundations) that continued to sustain the pre-modernist canon and the less demanding contemporary writers. It is true that the later chapters of *Ulysses* − apart from the final one − and virtually the whole of *Finnegans Wake* remained for a long time resistant to this enterprise, and can still hardly be said to be lodged comfortably within the accepted tradition, which is to say that considerably less than half of Joyce's work (whether one measures in terms of authorial time or finished length) has proved amenable; this has been a sufficient proportion, however, to assure for Joyce a distinguished place in the pantheon of 'world literature', as a glance at school and college syllabuses and textbooks – the most widely effective arena in which meanings are produced – will testify. Three main methods of assimilation – and it must be emphasized once more that this was an entirely necessary assimilation, and one in which Joyce himself was a busy participant – can be roughly distinguished, and all of them can be seen to spring from, and to reinforce, a recognizable ideology. Eliot's emphasis on symbol and myth, which we can call a 'transcendentalist' approach, has been echoed in many readings that trace patterns of imagery or allusion in Joyce's texts, usually relating the discovered pattern to some universalized and universalizing structure – the Trinity, the epic journey, the Romance quest, the nuclear family, the Oedipus complex, the historical cycle, the stages of human life; by this means the potentially explosive text is endowed with order and significance of a wholly traditional kind. Pound's contrasting delight in the realistic presentation of the texture of contemporary experience has been followed by more and more minutely detailed accounts of the referents of Joyce's writing (including the minutiae of his own biography), supporting what we might call an 'empiricist' reading. Both of these modes of interpretation have provided resources for 'moralizing' readings, which often draw on nineteenth-century notions of character and narrative to defend Joyce against accusations of misanthropy and nihilism and to resituate him in the 'Great Tradition' from which F. R. Leavis emphatically excluded him – so that Joyce, like Chaucer, Shakespeare, Congreve, or Austen, may be seen to espouse and celebrate 'humane' values, exhibiting an affirmative, tolerant stance towards the individual, a stance so evidently worthy that it would scarcely seem to require the length and complexity of a work like *Ulysses* to justify or to promote it. (Hugh Kenner sums up both the achievement and the limitation of this approach when he pigeonholes one of its most highly regarded exemplars with the comment: 'How *Ulysses* would read if it were a novel'.)[4] These supportive readings performed their task admirably, and without them we probably would not be reading Joyce at all today; but from the perspective of the present, there is more of value in some of the early *attacks* on Joyce which register the force of his challenge and feel no need to mitigate or disguise it. Wyndham Lewis's hostile chapter on *Ulysses* in *Time and Western Man* (1927) makes a number of points about Joyce's 'sardonic catafalque of the victorian world' (109) which lead directly to current preoccupations (their negative charge switched to positive), including his comments on the use of cliché (112–16), and the observation that 'what stimulates [Joyce] is *ways of doing things*, [. . .] and not *things to be done*' (106–7).[5] And Jung's almost equally notorious essay, '*Ulysses*: A Monologue' (1932), is an example of a wholly non-recuperative reading which, for all the naivety of its alternating despair and wonder over Joyce's 'brilliant and hellish monster-birth', marks the presence of a great deal in the text to which more accommodating readers have remained blind.[6]

None of these methods of domestication succeeded in making *Finnegans Wake* welcome in the house, however, in spite of the efforts of Joyce and his willing apostles. The collection of essays which he put together in an attempt to ease the reader's burden – *Our Exagmination Round his Factification for Incamination of Work in Progress* (1929) – failed in this task partly because he could not, understandably, allow the process of simplification and accommodation to go very far: the title would hardly have been reassuring, for a start, and many of the pieces imply that formidable intellectual attainments are a prerequisite for appreciation of the new work. In fact, the collection included an essay written by a naturalized Parisian which now stands as one of the most valuable introductions to the *Wake*, and which might be seen as a forerunner of the essays in this book: Samuel Beckett's 'Dante . . . Bruno. Vico . . Joyce', with its famous slogan (an echo of Lewis's comment on *Ulysses* of two years earlier): 'His writing is not *about* something; *it is that something itself*' (p. 14). It also contained an ancestor of the Anglo-American tradition in the shape of Stuart Gilbert's 'Prolegomena to *Work in Progress*', again clearly written with Joyce's help, in which a slight shift in the argument produces a totally different account of Joyce's writing (developed at length in Gilbert's immensely influential study of *Ulysses*): 'the fixing of the reader's mind on the subject-matter by every possible means, the exploitation of every potentiality of the language to create a complete harmony between form and content' (p. 56). But *Finnegans Wake* offered both too much and too little – too much to the symbol-hunter, the allusion-tracer, the pattern-builder, and too little to the seeker after narrative coherence, rounded character, moral wisdom – to respond very well to the treatment that had succeeded with *Ulysses*, and many of those who had laboured on behalf of the earlier novel, including Pound and Eliot, gave up the later one as still-born. It has remained, for most of those who pick it up, literally *unreadable*.

Not long after the enterprise of making Joyce's texts readable got off the ground, the first signs of a complementary undertaking became evident: the winning of cultural and academic esteem for Joyce (and for those who write about Joyce) by the operations of the increasingly powerful machinery of literary scholarship. Canonization was assured by the appearance of Richard Ellmann's formidably authoritative and powerfully orthodox biography in 1959 (a widely read book which helped to sustain the humanist and empiricist readings of Joyce), and firm entrenchment was secured by the publication of scrupulously edited letters and manuscripts, together with a string of compendious reference-books and discussions of Joyce's relation to this or that philosophical, religious, or literary tradition. (And here *Finnegans Wake* came into its own: it might not have been possible to *read* Joyce's last book, but it was certainly possible to track down its references, follow up its allusions, translate its languages, unpack its portmanteaux, and tabulate its verbal patterns.) The machinery was in full swing by the early 1960s, which saw the initiation of two journals specializing in Joyce studies; and in 1967 a James Joyce Foundation was established and the first in a series of International Symposia took place. Most of this activity has been based in the United States, where the necessary economic substructure exists, but there have also been significant contributions from other countries – including progress towards the long-awaited culminating scholarly accolade: a 'definitive' edition of the works.[7]

As a phenomenon of the 1960s, associated with an expanding programme of higher education and increasing professionalism in literary studies, this picture of devoted but unadventurous academic labour in the name of Joyce scholarship and criticism is hardly surprising; but if we turn to the present situation in Anglophone countries, after twenty years of upheaval and radical challenge within the intellectual and institutional structures that constitute the domain of literary studies, we find a remarkable absence of substantial change in what has become widely and disparagingly known as 'the Joyce industry'. The harvest of recent years includes a massive published archive of manuscript material, an Ellmann biography with even more detail, additional letters, further lexicons and annotations, a spate of introductions, and a growing pile of specialist studies – Joyce and Dante, Joyce and cities, Joyce and alchemy, Joyce and politics; and through all these endeavours run the same well-established critical stances, which we have termed transcendentalist, empiricist, and humanist, in various combinations and configurations. Much of this work is intrinsically fascinating, and offers immense scope to the dedicated Joycean (or the ideal insomniac); but one would have thought that the need to make Joyce readable and reputable had long since passed, and that the time had come to take the full measure of his literary revolution – to produce Joyce's texts in ways designed to challenge rather than comfort, to antagonize instead of assimilate.

It could be said, however, that the very multiplication of what already existed *has*, in spite of itself, produced a change. The academic machinery that once turned out useful information to guide the ordinary reader through the Joycean maze has become an uncheckable generator of endlessly proliferating secondary literature, revealing *in toto* something about Joyce's texts (and about all literary texts?) to which each individual contribution, in its attempt to arrive at final answers, is oblivious: the infinite productivity of interpretative activity, the·impossibility of closing off the processes of signification, the incessant shifting and opening-out of meaning in the act of reading and re-reading. The dream of final and total explication seems to be turning into a prospect of interminable accumulation – which can be experienced as a Borgesian nightmare of inescapable repetition or a Rabelaisian vision of infinite and comic fecundity. There is no doubt which view Joyce would have taken.

The realization that texts are unmasterable, and will return new answers as long as there are new questions, new questioners, or new contexts in which to ask questions, and that Joyce's texts display this characteristic more openly than most, is a thread that is barely visible in the vast library of scholarly and critical material that now overwhelms Joyce's two thousand published pages. And here we come to the paradox which is the occasion and the justification for this book: in France in the late 1960s and the 1970s Joyce's work provided a crucial impetus and focus for radical and widely influential shifts in literary theory and criticism, while in Britain and North America writing on Joyce remained virtually untouched by these intellectual changes, even when their effects were being strongly felt in many less obviously appropriate areas of literary studies. There were a few notable exceptions, but even these tended to make use of the most easily assimilable of the new ideas;[8] and some of those who referred to Derrida, Lacan, Deleuze, or Barthes appeared to do so on the basis of only slight acquaintance and comprehension, wielding continental formulae as new methods of controlling the unruly Joycean text. In 1978/9 a special number of the *James Joyce Quarterly* entitled 'Structuralist/Reader Response Issue' (the collocation in the title is itself revealing) drew attention to work on Joyce in France, and included essays with a flavour of current European theory, but gave little sense of the challenge which it represents to much of the critical work published by that journal since its inception. For the most part, American Joyce criticism has proceeded neither by assimilating nor by opposing the arguments of French critics, theorists, and philosophers of the last fifteen years (arguments which are in part the product of Joyce's revolutionary literary project), but by ignoring them – and ignoring equally the detailed readings of Joyce's texts which exemplify and support those arguments.

The situation in Britain is, perhaps, even stranger: on the one hand the British academic establishment has proved to be even less responsive to shifts in European thought than its North American equivalent, but on the other hand it includes a few writers working very closely with French critics and philosophers, for many of whom Joyce has been an important focus of attention. In the early 1970s, one of the contributors to the present volume, Stephen Heath, published important studies of Joyce and of new developments in literary theory not in English but in French;[9] and the same close involvement with French post-structuralist and psychoanalytic discourses informs Colin MacCabe's influential work on Joyce, while Maud

Ellmann's recent studies divert these currents into new and fertile critical channels.[10] In Ireland, as far as one can tell, the intellectual tremors of the 1960s are taking as long to be registered as Joyce's own literary earthquake did; Dublin remains a very long way from Paris.

III   Give us some parleyvoo

In October 1982, Editions Gallimard published a complete French translation of *Finnegans Wake*. Much to everyone's surprise,[11] the first edition was sold out in a few days. It seems that more than forty years after his death, and sixty years after he published *Ulysses* in Paris, Joyce is still very much a star in the eyes of the French public. Of course it could all be the result of one of those notoriously ephemeral Parisian fashions, but this is made unlikely by the fact that some of the most important French thinkers of the recent past have evidently considered Joyce's writing as crucial to their enterprise. Jacques Lacan spent part of his last years reading or re-reading the texts, drawing frequently on Jacques Aubert's vast Joycean erudition, opening the 5th International Joyce Symposium in the Great Amphitheatre of the Sorbonne, devoting a whole year of his Seminar to the *Portrait of the Artist*. It is also significant that although Jacques Derrida has just written his first essay on Joyce (included in this volume), he confirms in it that Joyce has been a central preoccupation for him over more than thirty years.

In order to understand the nature of this passionate interest, it is important to remember that there is no firmly entrenched French tradition of Joyce criticism (as there is in the case of Kafka, who has long been an important element in the French literary and philosophical debate, or in the case of Faulkner, who has found in France, from the time of Malraux and Sartre to the present day, some of his most able apologists and analysts). Although the reception of Joyce in Paris was favourable from the start,[12] for a long time very few critical studies were published, apart from the work of Joyce's own friends (Valery Larbaud, Louis Gillet) and the articles commissioned by Joyce himself for the launching of *Finnegans Wake* and *Ulysses* (see, for instance, one of the essays in *Our Exagmination*, Marcel Brion's 'The Idea of Time in the Work of James Joyce', *translated from the French*: its main point is a comparison between Joyce and Proust, 'the two greatest writers of the century' – and it is probably symptomatic of Joyce's status in France forty years later that Gilles Deleuze, in his *Proust et les signes*,[13] feels the need to define Proust in terms of Joyce).

For years Joyce's name was highly respected in France, but his work was probably not much read. He was mainly spoken of as the practitioner of the 'interior monologue', the crowning achievement – and ultimate resource[14] – of Realism and the Psychological Novel, so dear to the French heart. It was also partly on these grounds that the writers of the Nouveau Roman claimed him as an ancestor, but this had at least the advantage of indirectly involving his work in a series of intense critical controversies (about the Nouveau Roman, the Nouvelle Critique, Structuralism . . .). By the sixties, the literary landscape had changed as a result of those controversies, and it was becoming fashionable to mention Joyce's name in a very different context. Typically he would appear at the end of a list featuring Mallarmé, Lautréamont, Artaud, Bataille, Sade, and sometimes Rabelais. Very often this remained at the level of name-dropping, and many pronouncements made at the time revealed little better than a superficial acquaintance with the texts. But simultaneously a number of books and articles began to appear that combined a familiarity with the complexities of Joyce's work, an awareness of the results of Anglo-Saxon criticism, and a radically new approach – or rather a variety of new approaches.[15]

Since then, there has been a steady flow of such publications, and the affinity between Joyce and the theory of the Text and the Subject being elaborated in Paris is so close that it is not likely to dry up soon. The point is not that Joyce is the most perfect illustration for such a theory – for one of the convictions that the authors of the essays included in this book have in common (and this is probably the fundamental difference between them and the Structuralists) is that there is no metalanguage, there is no possible *application* of a theory to a text: the text reads the theory at the same time as it is read by it. This is particularly true of Joyce: any reader cannot but feel that the text constantly overreaches the landmarks established by the best critical constructions. It is impossible to exert any mastery over it, its *shifts* are such that you can never pin it down in any definite place – it always turns up again, laughing, behind your back. In fact, the aim is not to produce a *reading* of this intractable text, to make it more familiar and exorcise its strangeness, but on the contrary to confront its unreadability; not to produce an indefinite accumulation of its meanings (or search for the one authentic meaning) but to look at the mechanisms of its infinite productivity; not to explore the psychological depths of the author or characters, but to record the perpetual flight of the Subject and its ultimate disappearance; not to reconstruct the world presented by the text, but to follow up within it the strategies that attempt a deconstruction of representation. The endeavour is not to assimilate *Finnegans Wake* and the last chapters of *Ulysses* to the traditional elements present in the early works but to look at this apparently traditional writing in the light of the most radical aspects of the later texts. But this does not mean that the tradition is disregarded. It is not possible to dismiss altogether meaning, character, and referential value. The full strength of Joyce's text cannot be appreciated if one does not differentiate it from a psychotic shout or a poetical incantation. It acts from *within* the Great Tradition of narrative fiction, violently dragging that tradition out of itself. It is as the culmination of Western culture that it leads that culture irretrievably astray, far towards the limits of madness.[16]

For this reason, the new readings of Joyce are perhaps not as utterly divorced as one might think from some apparently more orthodox approaches, starting from a very different basis. It so happened that a leading Joyce scholar, with a well-earned reputation for many years of imaginative work, was present in Paris when Jacques Derrida delivered the paper included in this volume. He listened carefully and whispered afterwards with a mixture of disappointment and relief: 'But this is not so different from what we [meaning himself and a few other 'untheoretical' *Finnegans Wake* enthusiasts] have been doing for years . . .' He was right. The power of the Joycean text is such that it tends to lead its perceptive and unprejudiced readers, whatever their theoretical backgrounds, to similar procedures of reading. What is being attempted by Derrida and the French Joyceans is nothing more than a reflection on these procedures and an evaluation of their full import, literary and philosophical.

We believe that the English-speaking reader who is not wedded to a set of preconceptions about critical writing will find the texts included here relatively accessible. The various metaphors offered as models of the text – an extraordinarily advanced computer (Derrida), serial music (Rabaté), Freud's diagram of the psychic apparatus in the *Traumdeutung* (Ferrer) – are not meant to be taken too seriously, and should not be allowed to solidify and constrict the text once they have served their purpose. The occasionally aggressive *tone* of the essays is characteristic of the period to which they belong (they were all written in the late sixties or early seventies, except Derrida's piece, which is largely retrospective). So is perhaps a certain programmatic enthusiasm. It is significant that one of them deals with the first paragraph of the first story of *Dubliners* (Joyce's first published work of fiction); another with the first word of *Finnegans Wake*; that another claims to be simply arranging notes for a future reading, clearing the space for it. The implication would seem to be that the same treatment will be applied in the future to the rest of the *Wake*, to the whole of the Joyce canon; that it will be eventually possible to produce a (definitive) reading of Joyce. Of course this is nothing more than a fantasy, and it is now obvious that what Aubert calls 'an initial state of suspense' is not a transitory stage, and that, as Derrida puts it, 'this "not having begun to read" is [. . .] the most singular and active relationship' one can have to the work of Joyce. It is probably the reason why these essays have not been superseded in any way.

Notes

1. Richard Ellmann, *James Joyce*, rev. edn (New York: Oxford University Press, 1982), p. 715.
2. Eliot's review, entitled '*Ulysses*, Order and Myth', is reprinted in *Selected Prose*, ed. Frank Kermode (London: Faber, 1975), pp. 175–8, and in *James Joyce: The Critical Heritage*, ed. Robert H. Deming (London: Routledge, 1970), I, 268–71.
3. The French original of Pound's article, 'James Joyce et Pécuchet', is given in Forrest Read, *Pound/Joyce* (New York: New Directions, 1967), pp. 200–11; a translation by Fred Bornhauser appeared in *Shenandoah* 3 (Autumn, 1952), 9–20.
4. Hugh Kenner, *Ulysses* (London: Unwin Critical Library, Allen & Unwin, 1980), p. 177.
5. Wyndham Lewis. *Time and Western Man* (London: Chatto & Windus, 1927): 'An Analysis of the Mind of James Joyce', pp. 91–130.
6. C. G. Jung, '*Ulysses*: ein Monolog', *Europäische Revue* 8 (September, 1932), 548–68: translated by R. F. C. Hull in the *Collected Works*, vol. 15, 1966, pp. 109–32. (*The Critical Heritage* provides only a misleading fragment of this long essay.)
7. Such an edition of the works prior to *Ulysses* has now appeared in French translation in the Pléiàde collection under the editorship of Jacques Aubert (and deserves immediate translation into Joyce's own language); and a corrected text of *Ulysses* is imminent from Germany, edited by Hans Walter Gabler. The definitive *Finnegans Wake*, we are told, will take a little longer.
8. Valuable contributions were made in the 1970s by Margot Norris (*The Decentered Universe of 'Finnegans Wake'* (Baltimore: Johns Hopkins University Press, 1976)) and Jennifer Schiffer Levine ('Originality and Repetition in *Finnegans Wake* and *Ulysses*', *PMLA* 94 (1979), 106–20). More recently, books by Karen Lawrence (*The Odyssey of Style in Joyce's 'Ulysses'* (Princeton: Princeton University Press, 1981)), Brook Thomas (*Joyce's 'Ulysses': A Book of Many Happy Returns* (Baton Rouge: Louisiana State University Press, 1982)), and John P. Riquelme (*Teller and Tale in Joyce's Fiction: Oscillating Perspectives* (Baltimore: Johns Hopkins University Press, 1983)), have benefited from French work on narrative. Some of the many collections and special issues that marked the 1982 centenary also contain essays that bear witness to a serious engagement with structuralist and post-structuralist writing. (This is not to suggest that the degree of such influence is in any way a measure of value; some of the most enduringly fruitful studies of Joyce predate or complement the work which is our concern in this book – one might put Harry Levin, Hugh Kenner, Clive Hart, and Fritz Senn at the beginning of a longer list.)
9. Apart from the essay in this volume, see Stephen Heath's 'Trames de lecture (à propos de la dernière section de *Finnegans Wake*)', *Tel Quel* 54 (1973), 4–15; 'L'écriture spiralée (la socialité comme drame)', *Le Discours Social* 3–4 (1973), 9–21; and *Vertige du déplacement: lecture de Barthes* (Paris: Fayard, 1974). See also his 'Joyce in Language', in Colin MacCabe, ed., *James Joyce: New Perspectives* (Brighton: Harvester, 1982), pp. 129–48.
10. Colin MacCabe, *James Joyce and the Revolution of the Word* (London: Macmillan, 1979); Maud Ellmann, 'Disremembering Dedalus: *A Portrait of the Artist as a Young Man*', in Robert Young, ed., *Untying the Text: A Post-Structuralist Reader* (London: Routledge, 1981), pp. 190–205; and 'Polytropic Man: Paternity, Identity and Naming in *The Odyssey* and *A Portrait of the Artist as a Young Man*', in MacCabe, ed., *James Joyce: New Perspectives*, pp. 73–104.

11. This probably includes the publishers themselves, who had held the manuscript for years before finally deciding to print it. The translator, Philippe Lavergne, is not an academic but a telecommunications engineer, which sounds very promising. Unfortunately, the result of his heroic enterprise is disappointing in its lack of inventiveness (especially if it is compared with the Italian translation).
12. It was incomparably more favourable than was the case in London. Edmund Gosse wrote to Louis Gillet in 1924: 'There are no English critics of weight or judgement who consider Mr Joyce an author of any importance. If, as you tell me, "on fait grand bruit du nommé J. J. . . . à Paris" it must be among persons whose knowledge of English literature and language is scanty' (Ellmann, *James Joyce*, rev. edn, p. 528n). For an account of the English response see Patrick Parrinder, 'The Strange Necessity: James Joyce's Rejection in England (1914–30)', in MacCabe, ed., *James Joyce: New Perspectives*, pp. 151–67.
13. New edition, Paris: Presses Universitaires de France, 1971, pp. 168–70, 182–3.
14. 'It seems that what is persistently being called "interior monologue" is the most indomitable way in which an entire civilization conceives itself as identity, as organized chaos, and finally, as transcendence. Yet, this "monologue" probably exists only in texts that pretend to reconstitute the so-called physical reality of "verbal flux". Western man's state of "interiority" is thus a limited literary effect (confessional form, continuous psychological speech, automatic writing). In a way, then, Freud's "Copernican" revolution (the discovery of the split within the subject) put an end to the fiction of an internal *voice* by positing the fundamental principles governing the subject's radical exteriority in relation to, and within, language': Julia Kristeva, 'Word, Dialogue, and Novel', in *Desire in Language*, ed. Leon S. Roudiez (Oxford: Basil Blackwell, 1980), p. 90. (It is regrettable that so much of Kristeva's impressive work remains untranslated, as it represents the most systematic attempt at a theory of literature based on the work of Lacan, Derrida, and Barthes. Several of the essays included here quote her or reveal the direct or indirect influence of her writing.) It should by now be obvious that Joyce's 'monologue' is anything but *monological*, in the sense proposed by Bakhtin and developed by Kristeva. see André Topia's essay in this volume, and Hélène Cixous, 'D'un oeil en coin', in her *Prénoms de personne* (Paris: Editions du Seuil, 1974).
15. An important turning point was the publication of Hélène Cixous' *L'Exil de James Joyce* (Paris: Grasset, 1968) (translated by Sally A. J. Purcell, New York: David Lewis, 1972), with its seminal appendix, 'Thoth et l'écriture'.
16. Jacques Derrida quotes Joyce's comment on *Ulysses*, 'In any event this book was terribly daring. A transparent sheet divides it from madness', as an introduction to his essay 'Cogito and the History of Madness', in *Writing and Difference*, tr. Alan Bass (London: Routledge, 1978).

2   Joyce: The (r)use of writing

HÉLÈNE CIXOUS

Discrediting the subject

Joyce: 'I am the foolish author of a wise book.'
'The Catholic Church was built on a pun. It ought to be good enough for me.'

After a long theoretical disquisition on the engendering of writing, on paternity and maternity, on the relationship between Shakespeare's life and his work, and on the mythical kinship between Shakespeare, Hamlet, and the ghost of the dead father, Stephen Dedalus replies to the question posed by an irritated listener:

> – Do you believe your own theory?
> – No, Stephen said promptly.
> [. . .]
> I believe, O Lord, help my unbelief. That is, help me to believe or help me to unbelieve? Who helps to believe? *Egomen*. Who to unbelieve? Other chap.
> (*U* 213–14, 'Scylla and Charybdis' chapter)

Here begins a reading of Joyce which will point out by means of certain fragments of *Dubliners*, of *A Portrait*, or of *Ulysses* how Joyce's work has contributed to the discrediting of the subject; how today one can talk about Joyce's modernity by situating him 'on that breach of the self'[1] opened up by other writings whose subversive force is now undermining the world of western discourse; how his writing, which is justly famed for its system of mastering signs, for its control over grammar (including its transgressions and dislocations which cut across a language which is too much a 'mother' tongue, too alienating, a captive language which must be made to stumble), how this writing takes the risk of upsetting the literary institution and the Anglo-Saxon lexicon: by hesitating over the interpretation of signs, by the vitiation of metaphor, by putting a question mark over the subject and the style of the subject.

Joyce's work is crossed right through by a subject-waiting-for-itself which assumes the formal appearance of a quest, an apprenticeship, a journey, of all those literary genres where the advent of the self finds its niche and is

15

proclaimed — *Bildungsroman* or Dantesque path — with never a definitive way out, with no conclusion. Sudden appearance of the self continually announced, continually cancelled, in books made up of beginnings and exits on top of other beginnings and other exits.

Book of departure: 'That lies in space which I in time must come to, ineluctably' (*U* 217); departures from the Book of departure: 'I go to encounter for the millionth time the reality of experience and to forge in the smithy of my soul the uncreated conscience of my race' (*P* 252).

The penultimate note of the Artist's diary projects the image of the creator in the paternal figure of Daedalus, who melts into Icarus in the last sentence of the book: 'Old father, old artificer, stand me now and ever in good stead.' Cry of the son taking wing, the surge of the *created*, the flight of the work, with, between father and son, the same flesh of writing; and from the father to the son, the sea, the drowning; and from *A Portrait* to *Ulysses*: 'Fabulous artificer, the hawklike man. You flew. Whereto? Newhaven–Dieppe, steerage passenger. Paris and back. Lapwing. Icarus. *Pater, ait.* Seabedabbled.' (*U* 210).

Between Daedalus and Icarus: *Ulysses*. And: 'My will: his will that fronts me. Seas between' (*U* 217). From father unto son, via the mother, always, begun again. This delayed birth constitutes the movement of a work which playfully undermines gestation, the delay inscribing itself in the various falls, losses, repeated and unexpected exiles, which are all the more astounding in that the goal seems accessible, is named, puts itself forward, fascinates, is not hidden but rather pointed out (I, the Artist, the Word), is not forbidden but rather promised, and in that the subject, held in suspense, pursues it with the foolhardiness, the stubbornness, the perfidious will of a hero, with the weapons of the self (silence, exile, cunning), marking out its passage with theories, incorporated hypotheses of formalization: one or two ideas from Aristotle, a pinch of St Thomas; a chapter on poetics and literary history; several chapters on the problems of autobiography; and, in a pre-Freudian context, an implicit theory of the authorial unconscious, and of the textual unconscious, in a blasphemous analogy with the Arian heresy, showing in the Trinity the three-sided, divinely ordered production that allows the Father to see through the Son's eyes, where the Holy Spirit would be like the chain linking the Name of the Father to the Name of the Son, the scriptor to writing: the breath of the unconscious on the text. And all this reverberating from book to book, till lost from sight but held in memory, as an echo, a leitmotiv, a reiteration, for the greater glory of a Word whose power is elevated on the absence or decline of the notion of *a unified* subject. Quest, odyssey, with a plural hero, question whose answer is only ever what is already known in the questioning, question which, while not answering itself, has as an answer the answer's aberration and as effect the eternal revival of the question whose point will no longer know where to put itself, will no longer put itself.

Point which is looking for its departure point, whose invisible pointillage divides up *Finnegans Wake* into explosions and a crazy coalescence of the subject which undoes itself at the very moment when it constitutes itself in the new fragmentation of the word become word-tale or word-book, become one-plural.

In the passage to be discussed we shall grasp the first manifestation of the slide from One to the plural, from the disquieting plural of One, slipped between the narrator and the I subject, between the one and the other, between master of diction and master of interdiction, between pseudo-father (priest, initiator) and pseudo-son, between true words and bad words [*mots vrais et mauvais mots*]; the extract, chosen for its position on the border of the Joycean corpus, is the start of play in a discourse which presents its discontinuity as the uncertainty of the child narrator: a wily text precisely on account of its claim of naivety, naturally unclear, innocent at a first reading. But all the same . . .

This extract is the locus of a consciousness which censorship hardly separates from the unconscious which speaks in a dream a little later in the story. Scene of the decentering of the subject, as it immediately strikes the readers *of* the text (*in* the text): since a reading subject is present, and on the level of the text. Thus my reading is always preceded by the reading of the other-scriptor, which is preceded by the reading of the other-subject: and this reading is as (far from) innocent as the text which produces it, starting with signifiers which are privileged by their work in the writing, but whose immediate impact is multiplied by their return in other places,[2] so that for a retrospective reading it is necessary to make this text resound with its after-effects, to fray its innocence with its culpability.

The Sisters[3]

There was no hope for him this time: it was the third stroke. Night after night I had passed the house (it was vacation time) and studied the lighted square of window: and night after night I had found it lighted in the same way, faintly and evenly. If he was dead, I thought, I would see the reflection of candles on the darkened blind for I knew that two candles must be set at the head of a corpse. He had often said to me: 'I am not long for this world,' and I had thought his words idle. Now I knew they were true. Every night as I gazed up at the window I said softly to myself the word paralysis. It had always sounded strangely in my ears, like the word gnomon in the Euclid and the word simony in the Catechism. But now it sounded to me like the name of some maleficent and sinful being. It filled me with fear, and yet I longed to be nearer to it and to look upon its deadly work.[4] (*D* 354)

What the author said about his book:

Letter to C. P. Curran, a friend, 1904: 'I call the series *Dubliners* to *betray the soul* of that hemiplegia or *paralysis* which many consider a city.' (*Letters*, I, 55)

I emphasize: '*betray*', '*the soul*', '*paralysis*': to betray, by naming, to write in order to betray, to betray 'the soul' of / that paralysis / which many consider a city; reading the metonymic substitution of 'the sickness' for the sick body, the traditional dichotomy of soul (manifest in)/body, the substitutive reinforcement, a parodic mechanism, playing between sickness and city, the one for the other in inverse proportion to the expected order: Dublin is sick – Dublin is its sickness – *The* sickness *is*, Dublin is put in its stead. One becomes aware of limits beginning to dissolve in the perversion of signifiers.

Letter to Grant Richards, the editor, 1906:
[. . .] I believe that in composing my chapter of moral history [of my country] in exactly the way I have composed it I have taken the first step towards the spiritual liberation of my country. (20 May: *Letters*, I, 62–3)

Even if their author intended *Dubliners* to belong to the world of meaning and expression – Joyce insisting on what he *meant* to the very word ('in accordance with [. . .] the classical tradition of my art') – at least one sees how representation is immediately modulated, in so far as the discourse has less bearing on a concrete outside, on a reproducible real, than on the gaze directed at the referent (the Dubliners), on the nature of that gaze, and even on the name, the letter of that gaze: so initially there is only deferred representation, a perceptible hesitation on the surface to be inscribed.

One could modify the orders which Joyce gave himself by articulating them with certain declarations which seem to point towards the idea (a Freudian idea, and Joyce loathed Freud's thinking) of text as either pathbreaking or as substitutive formation: 'This race and this country and this life produced me, he said. I shall express myself as I am' (*P* 211). This statement, made by Stephen Dedalus, echoing similar statements by Joyce, could equally well be read, if there were a relaxing of the signifiers instead of 'expression', as the recognition that writing is a mode of production determined, beyond the biographical, by the socio-cultural system.

But there remains, lurking, that theological left-over instituted in the notion of the 'spiritual' which holds the text in front of the mirror. Spiritual mirror, spiritual chapter. Is not the 'spiritual liberation' in fact brought about via a liberation of signifiers, fraudulently crossing the 'classical' realist border, and that of its solemn double, symbolism? Is not the scene of writing, when only just set, already slipping, turning, and always decentered? A flirt beckoning at the same time as pushing away. Choosing to suffer from a confusion afflicting the ego, the it, the id, the subject, the signified and the sacred. Interrupting the strangeness of here and now with even more strangeness from elsewhere. Producing that *unheimlich* effect which sets up a play between the familiar, and the sudden breakdown of the familiar, between the home (*Heim*) and the hidden (*heimlich*), between my self and that which escapes me. Freud[5] has demonstrated that all this is aroused by doubt, by intellectual insecurity, acting as a screen for the fear of being blinded (a fear which is an indispensable axis crossing the Joycean space) which is itself a substitute for the fear of castration: fear which in its turn produces the other self, that kind of other which is kept handy in case the self should perish, which in literature becomes 'the double', a stranger to the self, or its indirect manifestations: doubling of the self, split self, and all those subversions of the subject, *visibly at work* in the excerpt quoted: where 'I' (the narrator) weigh up my strength, my existence, my grasp on reality, and my abdicating by examining the power of words.

(R)used writing, writing governed by ruse: which is therefore luxury writing, because in order to play tricks and to sow seeds, you have to produce wild-goose chases, you have to modify the traditional mode of the narrative which claims to offer a coherent whole, utilizable down to its smallest detail, the author being tacitly bound to produce an account of his expenditure. This is writing which is prodigal and therefore disconcerting because of its economy, which refuses to regulate itself, to give itself laws: sometimes restrained, finely calculated, strategic, intending by the systematic use of networks of symbols and correspondences to impose a rigid grid on the reader, to produce an effect of mastery; sometimes, on the other hand, within the same textual web, surreptitiously, perversely, renouncing all demands, opening itself up without any resistance to the incongruous, introducing metaphors which never end, hypnotic and unanswerable riddles, a proliferation of false signs, of doors crafted without keys: in other words (spoken in jest), it is an extraordinarily free game, which should shatter *any habits* of reading, which should be continually shaking the reader up, and thus committing this reader to a double apprenticeship: the necessary one which is reading–writing a text whose plurality explodes the painstakingly polished surface: and the one which is, in the very practice of a reading not condemned to linearity, an incessant questioning of the codes which appear to function normally but which are sometimes suddenly rendered invalid, and then the next moment are revalidated, and, in the inexhaustible play of codes, there slips in, indecipherable and hallucinatory by definition, the delirious code, a lost code, a kind of reserve where untamed signifiers prowl, but without the space of that reserve being delimited. We may expect to feel tricked, deceived, abandoned, and therefore enchanted (or exasperated) when, having thought that we heard a key turn, it is finally clear to us that the key had no door, and was supported only by its sound as a key. Thus in *Ulysses*, plumb in the middle of a majestic episode ('Nestor') which

bears the meaning of History, which resounds with the echoes of battles, with questions concerning a country's past and its political heritage, and in general with a weighty examination of the fate of humanity, there slips onto the scene of representation and into a network of correspondences tightly worked by the idea of historical causality, a riddle posed by Stephen.[6]

It is posed to his pupils at the end of a History lesson (the world of science and objectivity). The context forces the reader into a dumbfounded identification with the pupils; everything combines to make you 'take seriously' the existence of an answer: the very genre of the riddle, a literary and detective-story genre, which assumes as a fundamental convention that there should be a solution somewhere, the one who asks being in theory the one who possesses the knowledge. Stephen, as the one who asks, is indeed the master of knowledge: however, his answer reveals not a positive knowledge, but the gap in knowledge, the knowledge of non-knowledge, the author abandoning his rights over language, and thus the desacralization of reading in the sense that reading is implicitly the rite of passage into culture.

- This is the riddle, Stephen said.

> *The cock crew*
> *The sky was blue*:
> *The bells in heaven*
> *Were striking eleven.*
> *Tis time for this poor soul*
> *To go to heaven.*

- What is that?
- What, sir?
- Again, sir. We didn't hear.
Their eyes grew bigger as the lines were repeated. After a silence Cochrane said:
- What is it, sir? We give it up.
Stephen, his throat itching, answered:
- The fox burying his grandmother under a hollybush.
He stood up and gave a shout of nervous laughter to which their cries echoed dismay.

(*U* 32–3/26–7)

(Listen to the sound effects in the background of this passage: intensification, echo upon echo which calls to and then disappoints the ear; repetition of the puzzle which doubles the thickness of the lure, miming tension, − eyes − ears − open − the preciseness of the terms of the question, and the answer which apes scientificity or the absolute: eleven o'clock and not twelve. *The* fox and not a fox, his grandmother etc. And the play: poetic rhythm/silence/shout of laughter/ exclamations, which makes a sonorous commentary on his disturbing words. Privilege slipping from the cock to the fox, without any apparent reason to support it. There remains the untamed subject: the fox. That is all. Stephen's nervous laughter is indeed, provided that you listen to it, the laughter of the perverse text. But it is hard to bear, just as it is difficult to accept that frustration is normal, especially in the intellectual sphere, where it is experienced as the subterfuge of castration: yet it is at this point that you must stop demanding meaning. It is also at this point that academic discourse is brought to its limit, or its 'dismay' ('dismay' → according to the etymology, *dis* is privative, indicating division, dispersion in all directions; *may* (from *magnan* O.H.G.), to possess potency, the power to . . .; → discouragement, loss of heart, of moral fibre, of potency, in the face of danger or difficulty). The position of the critic, the reader whose reading is the received version for another reader, is in deep trouble here, unless there is a constant rethinking based on a continual calling back into question, and on a renunciation of all conclusions. There are two possible courses of action: the first trusting to the known facts about Joyce's work, particularly his intensive use of symbols, and his obsessive and often explicit concern to control word-order, thus prejudging the book as a 'full' text, governed by 'the hypostasis of the signified',[7] a text which conceals itself but which has something to conceal, which is findable. This reassuring position is in fact almost necessary, granted the conscious or unconscious fashion of pushing Joyce back into the theological world from which he wanted to escape, by squeezing him 'through the back door' (cf. the versions of Joyce as a Catholic, Medieval Joyce, Irish Joyce, Joyce the Jesuit in reverse and hence the right way round as well, etc.). On the other hand one can imagine a reading which would accept 'discouragement', not in order to 'recuperate' it by taking it as a metaphor for the Joycean occult (which would, by the way, be right but would only be taking account of the formal aspect of that effect of privation), but rather by seeing in that trap which confiscates signification the sign of the willed imposture which crosses and double-crosses the *whole* of Joyce's work, making that betrayal the very breath (the breathlessness) of the subject. Nothing will have been signified save the riddle, referral of a referral beneath a letter which, besides, is not beyond the pretence of having spirit. That fox worries us. And there are quite a few more of them in *Ulysses*.[8] He breaks (with his grandmother and with all that the simple relation animal + bond of kinship suggests, even on the level of the signifier) the circle of the 'readable',[9] of the causal chain which guarantees the continuation of metaphysics.

This farce of breaking-up which interferes directly with the order of *Ulysses*, indicating the vulnerability of that order, is easy to spot because it is isolated almost as a symptom in the extensive textual network in which thousands of apparently detached elements actually excuse their air of being *unemployed* by allusion, analogy, metonymy . . . or by being re-employed in motifs or figures: the unattached element is indirectly granted a transgressive violence which it does not possess in previous texts (*Dubliners, A Portrait*) in which a *gratuitousness* which is more discreet, if not less dangerous, comes to the surface and makes significance quiver as if it were the *nervous laughter of writing*. 'Laughter' which by its vocal outburst also stands in contrast to the horrible and silent smile of the corpse;[10] which is the inscription under the insidious sound 's'[11] of unspeakable vice, of sin which is suggested, 'murmured' but unfinished, of the perversion of relations between subject and object, between body and soul, life and death, sound and meaning [*son et sens*], work and magic, relations of reversal and overstepping as when the attributes of one term slip onto another in the direction of a terrifying materialization of the power of the letter; if you know that the narrator whose thoughts suggest these opening sentences is the disciple of a queer disappointed priest in whom 'there was something gone wrong', if you know that the priest, initiator, had taught the boy Latin, a tongue which is doubly foreign, dead, theological, magical, and also 'how complex and mysterious were certain institutions of the Church which I had always regarded as the simplest acts' (*D* 357), that the priest amused himself 'by putting difficult questions to him', then you sense the harrowing intensification of an examination which centres on the highest knowledge, below the decaying garments of the master and behind the mask of 'simplicity': there the master represents an unfathomable authority, and the scene is from the outset the sacred one, profaned by a highly 'incarnate' death: if there is complicity between the subjects such that the curiosity of the one regarding the other seems to announce some morbid identification, if the dead priest's smile parts the disciple's lips, it is because there is at stake between them the access to an object of desire, which in the end is perhaps nothing other than the very play of inscription in so far as certain signifiers can hollow out an 'other' place in the text, the sexual metaphor for which is given later: the narrator's dream reveals the secret, desirable[12] and fearsome nature of it: shows itself, moving, appealing, withdrawing, miming the exile of jouissance, displacing the prohibited place, which is never seen, where the priest's head, the grey *disembodied* face, has *something* secret to tell which is never told. Hidden recess receding in a sinister movement to vanish on the other side of soft curtains ('I remembered that I had noticed long velvet curtains and a swinging lamp of antique fashion' (*D* 358)), through the veils of perverted confession, summoned by the head, object-subject ('*it* smiled'), 'very far away' to 'some land where the customs were strange – in Persia, I thought . . . But I could not remember the end of the dream'; parodying the excentricity of the subject, the pursuit of *Where id was, there ego shall be*, where the id signals with dead tongue and disembodied head. Far, antique, strange, Persian, perverse, perdition, piercing, slipping, transgressing the occidental/oriental line, sending the sacred back to a desecration, continually emptying out speech, shifting the name for strangeness without representing the signified, the fleeing letter offering itself only in order to efface itself, drawing the subject further on, ever further, beyond the Church, beyond Persia, how far? on the dribbling trace of the other's halting words. So it goes along a metonymic chain where the other place always has its other place.

An 'other' place which cuts off meaning, as the head is cut off − the title of the story which, from the very first sentence, excludes the reader from meaning:

(1) *The Sisters: 'There was no hope for him this time: it was the third stroke'*. In this way the floating head(ing) (*The Sisters*) is inscribed as split off from the body of the text; it usurps the place of the subject right up to the end of the story.

A play on fixation is instituted, allowing the first sentence to be spoken, its elements arranged as follows:

(2) '*There was*': impersonal (neuter) type, the impersonal being announced as subject at the outset (chain: personalization of the subject/animation/death). The effect of the impersonal as subject is double: the consolidation of the personalization of a non-human, and the depreciation of the human. The personal subject is buried as complement to the object (*'for him'*). Hence the *waiting* for the subject (*'him'*) in as much as he is a person.

Is there a relationship between that waiting and repetition and time?

(3) '*There* was − *it* was': anaphora, the sign of repetition from the very first sentence: there has been a series, *involution*, closing up of repetition in identity (*'this time'*, *'third stroke'*, this time again, the third the same) instead of evolution. Closure from the beginning, suspended time.

The one who is speaking 'I', 'it', 'I', 'I', first person singular, third person neuter singular. Breach of the subject hidden in the heart of the text, but: in what distant time, more-than-finite, which designates its own finish. Where the statement winds on, that subject (*'him'*) does not speak. He remains a silent object →

(4) '*Paralysis*': this is the signifier which, with its foreign, savage grip, sucks up the text, invests it, immobilizes it in space and time: the whole of this extract converges in it and it stops the text. Sudden chill. Take-over. But its power is enigmatic, supported by an equally wild[13] set of replacements: '*gnomon*', '*simony*', '*catechism*'. Paralysis inscribes impotence in the kind of 'slip' in the text. The word *paralysis* inscribes the whole of the text as analysis − paralysis (relaxing of the muscles, play of opposites, stiffness/fixity/lack of control) like a text mined by the riddle which produces it in its involution. Speech which is exhausted in its pursuit of a meaning, and which comes up against the occlusion of an Elsewhere fixed there by an antique language (g − k − Euklid, KateKhism, Gnomon).

How does the word *paralysis* function in this text? As follows:

(5) '*No*': negation attacking the sentence, triggers off the play between being and non-being of which paralysis is the arbiter, paralysis being ultimately the non-being of being; paralysis because being and non-being cancel each other out; because desire + repression result in immobility. In this case neurosis, writing becomes perversion once beyond the velvet curtains.

(6) 'No *hope*': waiting, hope, space ahead: exit? '*No*'. No hope in this cancellation before the letter which from then on does violence to the very time of writing. A paradigm perhaps for the ear, hope/stroke, the one cutting across the other. The indefinite/the finite. The hope and the fear build up tension in the anticipation of the sacred which takes me as far as 'filled with fear', where fear fills up the hollow left empty by hope. But was there ever hope? That weighty impersonal which does not make me aware of being pitiable, does it not mark the uncrossable frontier between the signifier and the signified, '*hope*' detached from a subject which constitutes itself in an insane, empty absolute?

(7) '*It was the third stroke*': Absence – and juxtaposed: repetition: *the third stroke*, figure of repetition on the level of the signified, doubled by the repetition on the level of the signifier; multiplied by the reverberation of time which scores the text uninterruptedly ('*often*', '*every night*', '*night after night*') and which is reinscribed by an oblique projection of the space produced by the drive in its movement towards:
'*I longed*': where time and place are articulated by desire, a tension which makes the text quiver from '*hope*' to '*fear*'.
'*Stroke*': the sentence comes to an end with the death blow. 'Third' made fateful, as if the curse slipped in with the 3, for why would the third be more deadly than the second or the fourth? '*Third*' indicates some occult triangle which also creeps in with the punctuation–lure ':': surreptitiously the sign of the confrontation, never made more explicit, between rival subjects before the verb; there is manifestly, although it is imperceptible, an elliptical manoeuvre on the part of the scriptor who profits from his function as the subject of the utterance to cheat on the level of the signified.

Desire (a homosexuality which is only admitted in the dark folds of a confessional) is eclipsed here, so swiftly, almost unnoticed, by the desire to kill.

Let us make a tactical regrouping around the privileged signifiers ('*paralysis*', '*sinful*', '*word*' . . .) along axes which are literally visible; and audible.

Beginning with the visible:

The obvious play of light and shade is put in question by the text's uncertainty, vacillating, like all the logical pairs which function insubordinately in the grey margin of doubt (life/death, hope/fear, true/empty) ('*idle*': empty – then vain, without foundation; lacking;

lacking an occupation; unoccupied → not working). Doubtful light or shade, which presents the always deferred place of revelation: the trajectory of the question is guided by a system of '*faint*' signs, of reflectors, of filters (the reflection of candles, for there would be two candles at the head: the light seen from outside, returning to the inside . . .).

We shall see further on how light and sight work together, first of all to point out that the focusing of the light source has the effect of sending the subject back, at the very moment of its appearance, into the opaque, the colourless, the nighttime place of its mutations:

(8) '*Night after night I had passed the house (it was vacation time)*': decomposition of the repetition night after night; night not perceived as dark but pierced by 'and studied the lighted square of the window'.

Note the violent splitting of the subject: I had passed (—) and I had studied. Cut by '*and*'; cut by (—). The parenthesis being by definition withdrawal; something introduces itself which you do not want to be introduced ('*vacation time*', vacant time), *time without work*. Sign of a movement of denial, of excuse, speech suddenly flagging, an indication of the bad conscience which is the source of the text and of . . . and of silences, and of the ambiguities which constitute the 'bad' side of the priest's discourse. Set apart, this time and this parenthesis which are isolated by the time set apart: '*it*': impersonal; '*was*': state; '*vacation*': empty; '*time*'. Impersonal, empty, state, time (+ Name = the true name of the story). Empty time between two times; time without studying after a time of study; dead time; guilty time. Presence of a double time articulated by *after, after – now, now*, and by the dyads   *passed and studied, faintly and evenly*, the movement giving the effect of immobility ('and night after night I had found it lighted in the same way'): '*in the same way*', the same and the other in the same. And by the fixation with the same which holds me and intrigues me (and I, the reader, am thus fastened in the text) the question '*why* these toings and froings?' is left out. I might read into this, if I were to stray a little, the symptom of the text's neurosis: he passed and passed again as if he could not get away from it. The entire story, like this fragment, is thus constrained, mastered by the design '*fear (– hope) longing*', by the predominance of the desire to draw near which collides with the window. Consequently, in the darkness, something is repressed whose return governs all of the subject's thought processes: I cannot see him because he is not dead, because he is going to die. If he were dead I could see him; when he is dead, I shall see him; I want him to die so that I can see him; I want him to die. That is not said.

(9) '*He had often said to me: "I am not long for this world"* ': '*He*': the unspecified subject, whose corpse lies across the fictive space, emerges at, or just after, the moment of his death through this citing of a prophecy which

is in the process of coming true, only finding the words once they are already lost:

'Idle', 'true':

Scarcely repressed, desire returns, an innocent killer, and seeks satisfaction in the words which make a cunning detour:

He had said: I am not long for this world. And I had thought his words *idle*. Now I knew they were *true*. Every night as I gazed up at the window I said softly to myself the word paralysis.

The subject simply 'said' the word, gazing at the square of light. The word and the sickness: a dangerous pair once you realize that the signified really invests the signifier, the name of the sickness effectively being the sickness: the sickness, by metonymy, being the name of Dublin, and the name of the city itself. The entire text would then constitute itself as a monstrous metaphor of saying-Dublin = saying-death. This is the track where parody slips in, for metonymy works in both directions, and if the sickness *is* Dublin, Dublin is the sickness, the work of contiguity producing to infinity the exchange which blurs the direction of causality. The reiteration of the signifier thus comes out of the play which makes the text the producer of its own reflection, the hesitation of its own letter, in any case making it impossible to set up a subject and intentionality, in that it is so difficult to extricate language as such from what language says to itself across the words of the subject. It is impossible for the narrator to constitute himself as an imaginary unity by gaining assurance from a language which escapes mastery, especially since the signifiers from a foreign tongue only make his voice echo; they cannot be used, sound objects without signification, even if they do appear in the same semantic field of the culture. With the inscription of 'Paralysis', and of what it carries in its wake ('gnomon', 'Euclid', etc.), the nascent revolution put into practice by Joyce takes effect, a revolution which shakes the foundations of 'the metaphysical enclosure' dominated both really and metaphorically by the discourse of the master (the master of God's discourse, struck down, dying, aphasic). This exile, in the ephemeral but primordial signifier which aims to 'betray' the sickness–Dublin, has as a secondary effect the betrayal of the place from which it strikes; *Ulysses*, and its task of demolishing cultural conservatism, starts here, in this text where no-one knows anything except for the text which does not know that it knows. '*Square of Window*': the lighted square speaks of the mirror; the hidden candles; the desirable (annihilation) barred. I would see the candles, says the insistent (studying) gaze: the opposition between that eye, which wishes (less) to see than to know, and '*blind*' (window blind, 'jalousie', *sightlessness*) light but also blindness; an immediate symbolic relationship with the life which is fading, the death which is coming; beyond that, with the forbidden, the gaze on death; and beyond again, with the area where blinding and castration come into play.

This mode of signification places itself from the outset beyond the limits of representation and of symbolization, in that, while rejecting psychoanalysis (the comic result of this *Vorwerfung* resounds through *Finnegans Wake*), it questions the sign about its very nature, about its production, its efficacy, as if, having admitted the idea of a textual unconscious (which Joyce had not), it had always allowed the word the possibility of having an effect here or there. But not without trepidation: that work is still regarded as sacred.

– *The disquieting work of the word*: 'Word' – 'Work' – 'World'.

– The other place, by citing foreign (Greek) words: '*Gnomon*' is, metaphorically speaking, one of the works of paralysis: the part of a parallelogram left when another parallelogram or triangle has been taken from it, the spike or pillar of a sundial, 'gnomon' revives the motif of time by opposing ritually marked time (candles) to naturally marked time (shadow cast). Its connotation is at once mathematical (Euclid), Greek and ecclesiastical; and further, the connotation of thought, interpretation: the gnomon, the one who interprets oracles, the one who tells the time, etc.

It is related paradigmatically (also perhaps by phonic attraction: '*gnomon*' – '*Simon*') to simony, which happens to be another mode of interpretation: Simon Magus wants to buy from the apostles the gift of bestowing the Holy Spirit by the laying on of hands. The simoniac trades in holy things. Confusion of the profane and the sacred. With the catechism (from the Greek *echo*, to resound, to instruct verbally). That is to say, three modes of exchange, of information, on the level of a wisdom which claims to be absolute and revealed, but which escapes the subject, who gets them back again only by listening, hence the displacement of power from the spirit to the letter. During the story '*gnomon*' – '*simony*' – '*catechism*' will be overturned at the priest's expense. But it is their names, their letters which directly mark the world: bad, cursed, '*sinful*' work. The words are not 'idle' ones. Their truth is not pure revelation but instead production of an effect; it is indeed thus that one should understand this *studious gaze* ('studied', 'gazed') and this insistence on the word '*paralysis*', which is nothing other than the functioning of death, blow by blow (the second, the third) experienced in the conscience of the narrator as sin, as transgression. The forbidden and furtive gaze upon the name '*paralysis*' is the same gesture, albeit displaced, as the gaze which seeks to see behind the window pane. Would not the relationship between the word '*paralysis*' and the mirror be the same as that between diction and interdiction, between sound and name, hearing and seeing (two kinds of prohibition)? Thus the *echo* marked in cate*ch*ism makes itself heard in unending symmetries. What is said of '*Paralysis*' goes a long way: '*It sounded to me like the name of some maleficent and sinful being.*' The common noun for the sickness is also the proper name of a maleficent and sinful being: the imagined spectacle of the soon to be dead, letter of the gaze, is repeated in the echo of the word 'paralysis', letter of the letter. This is where there is a transgression whose effect of sacred 'fear' magnetizes the text between 'hope' and 'fear', waiting–desire and delay of jouissance which the work on the word and of the word contributes in deferring: a work whose locus is first of all the word itself and by extension the text, but whose perfidious quality emanates from what it produces in the very letter of the letter, which sends its saying [*dit*] back to its own accursed [*maudit*] echo, the word [*mot*] being the name of the word, the signified serving as metaphor for its signifier without one being able to determine the part of the voice in the production of meanings. From word to being, from voice to sin, the disguises of the forbidden [*l'interdit*] are multiplied, stirring up the desire to *see*:

'*Its deadly work*': Thus it is the name which kills: the empire of the signifier which will subsequently be extended to the point of producing *Finnegans Wake*, infinitely mocking the conscientious control of the scriptor. Word, master of its grammes, inseminating itself by the introduction of the letter L into its body, which gives it the dimensions of the concrete infinite, 'word', 'world', 'work', lapsus at the source of *Ulysses*,[14] comical straying of the signified which the scriptor from the beginning, in *Dubliners*, called from the place of jouissance into the realm of the sacred. This game is still impregnated with unease because the enterprise of turning away from the beaten track is a new one, and one does not yet know what mutation of the language will be brought about in the long run by the liberation of the signifier. But how can you not delight in this inaugural audacity which burns its boats, scuttles the theological foundation of the word, reduces the master to silence, inflicts on the name-of-the-father an eclipse behind a miserable curtain, underlining in a blasphemous fashion the lettered character of the spoken word, bursting apart the ceremonial of reading and more generally of culture by rejecting from the outset any hope of a response, by taking back in the very gesture of giving ('*No*'/'*hope*'), affirming nothing except on the level of the voice by means of a repetition which magnifies the spoken, an affirmation which is supported and put at risk by a questioning of the very function of the spoken, of the lost sense, which will always remain lost afresh: there will be no end to the dream, the velvet curtains give on to that which, if there is something, is something which retreats before the name, 'something wrong', a putting to flight of the 'what he meant' of the priest, the 'what is meant by' gnomon, paralysis, simony, catechism, to the exclusion of the signified transmitted or omitted by the word, a putting into play of the word's maleficence, the forbidden's own work. Sudden appearance, during the course of the questioning, of the unattached subject, the dubious 'it',[15] which would only be perceived during the examination of what it does: I longed to be nearer to 'it' to look upon its deadly work: the 'it' is distressing because its 'being' is confused with its saying and this saying can only be heard through the annihilation of the master who guarded the Referent. Desire of the other in which organized frustration, and the starting up of the always disappointed impulse to get closer (the disembodied head in the dream, murmuring head, obliging the subject to pay attention, prescription of the ambiguous, dead man who still lives, silent word and word which silences for ever, smile of the uncertain, language of forgetfulness, story's turmoil, innocent speech of the forbidden, speech guilty of almost saying or almost guilty in slipping towards the dis-scription of *Finnegans Wake* where the gesture is Shaun's and the hand Shem's, where the same is the other is the name of the same, where *what can't be coded can be decorded if an ear aye sieze what no eye ere grieved for*, where writing invents a cause for itself *causing effects and affects occasionally recausing altereffects*, where the divided scriptor takes it upon himself-as-subject to suggest twisting *the penman's tale posterwise*, to return the story from his pen to the reader–postman, to return the signified to the signifier's address, and to do this without 'dismay'.[16](   ).[17]

(Translated by Judith Still)

Appendix

The Sisters: this story was first published, in a version quite different from that of *Dubliners*, in the magazine *Irish Homestead* on 3 August 1904, as the short story of the week. This first version, and Joyce's two rewritings, are set out with a commentary in several works, in particular: Marvin Magalaner, *Time of Apprenticeship. The Fiction of Young James Joyce* (New York: Abelard & Schuman, 1959), chapter 3 and appendix C; Hugh Kenner, *Dublin's Joyce* (Bloomington: Indiana University Press, 1956), pp. 50–3.

The story, originally ordered for a 'simple' and 'rural' magazine, was supposed to appeal to 'the common understanding and liking'. Let us note what that version did not contain: the motif of paralysis; the boy's dreams; the Persian motif; simony and confession. It was a reassuring *here*, in which the narrator–priest bond was almost non-existent in its perverse form: the insistence of guilt, of foreknowledge, of the unconscious, are not admitted. All the passages which connote 'vacancy' are late additions. Last sentence of The Irish Homestead: 'God rest his soul!' Last sentence of the third version: 'Wide-awake and laughing-like to himself . . . So then, of course, when they saw that, that made them think that there was something gone wrong with him. . . .'

Notes

1. Julia Kristeva, 'Introduction' to Mikhail Bakhtin, *La Poétique de Dostoievski* (Paris: Seuil, 1970), p. 15.
2. *A Portrait, Ulysses* and, of course, since it is a Re-Saying, the whole of *Finnegans Wake*.
3. The first paragraph of the first story of *Dubliners* (1904), Joyce's first work, published in 1914 after countless problems and disagreements to do with the censorship exercised over the entire British publishing system.
4. See the appendix for a short history of this story.
5. Freud, 'The Uncanny', in *Standard Edition* (Hogarth Press, 1953–74), vol. 17, pp. 217–56.
6. The character of the artist, substitute for the author, 'thinker' who produces one of the ideological axes of *Ulysses*, and, as it happens, master in a public school, where the relationship teacher – taught is a concrete representation of dialogue, research, reflection, a symbol of the relationships master/disciple – knowledge/ignorance, authority/submission, father/son, said/forbidden, master/servant, etc.
7. Julia Kristeva, 'Le discours sur la littérature', Colloque de Cluny, 1970.
8. We can cite, among others, the riddle of Macintosh: person? article of clothing? cover for archaisms? or the parable of Mount Pisgah . . .
9. The readerly (here translated as 'readable'), as defined by Barthes, *S/Z* (New York: Hill & Wang, 1974), p. 156.
10. *D* 357: 'When he smiled he used to uncover his big discoloured teeth and let his tongue lie upon his lower lip' (a phallus playing dead).
11. Cf. Mallarmé, 'Les mots anglais', in *Oeuvres complètes* (Paris: Pléiade, 1900) p. 947, on 's' alone and 's' in conjunction with w, h, c, l, m, n, etc.
12. *D* 356: 'I drew the blankets over my head [. . .] But the grey face still followed me. It murmured; and I understood that it desired to confess something. I felt my soul receding into some pleasant and vicious region [. . .] '
13. Wild, because let out in the text with no origin other than the absence, the ignorance of their origin; irony of the play on the antique origin of the culture which comes emptied out to the ear.
14. The allusion is to Leopold Bloom's *love affair by correspondence*, under the pseudonym 'Flower', with the lady Martha who writes to him *Poste restante*: comedy of the letter and its distribution, of the functions of language, of the transformation of the addressee and of the accidents which happen to the message, since the lady in a burst of emotion commits the following 'lapsus langways' (*Finnegans Wake* code): 'I called you naughty boy because I do not like that other world. Please tell me what is the real meaning of that word' (*U* 79/77). Listen to the mute comedy of that tumescent sonority which refrains from naming 'the other world', where the letter would become (sexual) organ.
15. 'It' occurs seven times in this text, and enjoys a disturbing potential for ambiguity; straddling the line which has difficulty in separating the body from the corpse, the living from the dead, it is the agent of a malign denaturalization. What does it really designate on its seventh appearance?
16. Quotations from *FW* 482–3.
17. These brackets open out onto the reading of a second text in which the subject named Stephen dreams himself around his proper name (5th chapter of *A Portrait*): see *Prénoms de personne* (Paris: Seuil, 1974), pp. 256ff.

3   Ambiviolences:
Notes for reading Joyce

STEPHEN HEATH*

For the Ancients the verb 'to read' had a meaning that is worth recalling and
bringing out with a view to an understanding of literary practice. 'To read'
was also 'to pick up', 'to pluck', 'to keep a watch on', 'to recognize traces',
'to take', 'to steal'. 'To read' thus denotes an aggressive participation, an
active appropriation of the other. 'To write' would be 'to read' become
production, industry: writing–reading, paragrammatic activity, would be
the aspiration towards a total aggressiveness and participation.

Julia Kristeva[1]

The prouts who will invent a writing there ultimately is the poeta, still more
learned, who discovered the raiding there originally. That's the point of
eschatology our book of kills reaches for now in soandso many counterpoint
words.

FW 482.31–4

Reading Joyce remains a problem. This can be seen easily enough from the
two rigorously complementary poles of critical reaction to *Finnegans Wake*:
the first, faced with the specific practice of writing in Joyce's text and thus
with the impossibility of converting that text into a critical object, rejects it
as 'aberration'; the second, seeking to preserve Joyce's text for criticism,
finds itself obliged to that end to 'reduce' its writing to the simple carrier of
a message (a meaning) that it will be the critic's task to 'extract from its
enigmatic envelope'. The writing of *Finnegans Wake*, however, work *in
progress* ('wordloosed over seven seas' (*FW* 219.16)), develops according to
a fundamental incompletion; the text produces a derisive hesitation of sense,
the final revelation of meaning being always for 'later'.[2] The writing opens
out onto a multiplicity of fragments of sense, of possibilities, which are traced
and retraced, colliding and breaking ceaselessly in the play of this text that

* Written at the prompting of Philippe Sollers, this piece was published as 'Ambiviolences: notes
pour la lecture de Joyce' in *Tel Quel* 50 (Summer, 1972) pp. 22–43 & 51 (Autumn, 1972) pp. 64–76.
It was intended to serve as something of an introductory approach to Joyce for the *Tel Quel* of
the time and is marked by that context throughout. No alterations or revisions have been made
here beyond a few small corrections of detail and I am grateful to Isabelle Mahieu for providing
a scrupulous English version. As far as I am concerned, the piece is thus entirely past − which
does not mean that I dissociate myself from it but only that I could not now write it in this same
way. S.H.

resists any homogenization. As 'collideorscape' (*FW* 143.28), *Finnegans Wake* is the space of a writing–reading, of an ambiviolence ('Language this allsfare for the loathe of Marses ambiviolent [. . .]' (*FW* 518.2)), disturbing the categories that claim to define and represent literary practice, leaving the latter in ruins, and criticism too. Already at the time of the composition of *Ulysses* Joyce spoke of the '*scorching*' effect of his writing: 'each successive episode, dealing with some province of artistic culture (rhetoric or music or dialectic), leaves behind it a burnt up field'.[3] In its activity, the writing scorches a path 'outside' these fields, continually destroying itself as object.

Reading *Finnegans Wake* is thus necessarily that aggressive participation described by Kristeva. What is in question is not what Beckett called 'a rapid skimming and absorption of the scant cream of sense' on the basis of 'a tertiary or quartery conditioned reflex of dribbling comprehension',[4] but entry into a world that 'is, was and will be writing its own wrunes for ever' (*FW* 19.35–6). Where criticism *ex*plicates, opening out the folds of the writing in order to arrive at the meaning, *Finnegans Wake* is offered as a permanent *inter*plication, a work of folding and unfolding in which every element becomes always the fold of another in a series that knows no point of rest. The fourth section of the book gives a whole range of discursive explications of the Letter but the latter exhausts them all (and *not* vice versa), running through them and encompassing them in the materiality of the letters of the text itself, holding them in that derisive hesitation referred to earlier. It is in relation to this activity that we should understand the description of the book as 'sentenced to be nuzzled over a full trillion times for ever and a night till his noddle sink or swim by that ideal reader suffering from an ideal insomnia' (*FW* 120.12–14). The text is never closed and the 'ideal reader' will be the one who accedes to the play of this incompletion, placed in 'a situation of writing',[5] ready no longer to master the text but now to become its actor.

I   Against continuity

The brief mention of this problem of reading allows the recognition of the limitations of this essay. Its aim is a preliminary disengagement of the possibility of reading Joyce and it is thus no more than a few notes, grouped under various headings, *towards* that reading. In which respect, there is a further aspect of the general problem of reading that should be given some consideration here and that will provide a starting point for this work of disengagement.

It was stressed above that a text such as *Finnegans Wake* is not to be read according to a process of unification. The text is not homogeneous, but ceaselessly discontinuous, a hesitation of meaning into the perpetual 'later'. It is in this context that the further aspect of the problem of reading is posed

– that of the manner in which the whole body of Joyce's work is to be read. This can, in fact, be immediately recast into the question as to whether it is possible to succeed, against the pressure of a criticism founded on continuity and identity (grasped above all in the construction of the Author-source), in reading that body of work itself according to a radical discontinuity that will allow an attention to the specificity of the practices of each text. It is hardly necessary to recall the multitude of critical studies that derive the whole of the work from 'aesthetic theories' extracted more or less opportunely from *Stephen Hero* or *A Portrait of the Artist as a Young Man*, thus offering to solve what is supposed to be 'the enigma of continuity in Joyce's work'. What is needed, against all attempts to locate some 'style' of the Author (traceable through the work as the area of some spiritual development), is the operation of a reading that, on the contrary, will remain attentive to the writing of each text in order to consider them in their totality as network of specific practices.

It is worth asking, indeed, how exactly it would be possible to speak of Joyce's style. Pound recognized the difficulty posed by Joyce's writing in this respect and expressed his irritation with *Ulysses* for this very reason: 'Also even the assing girouette of a postfuturo Gertrudo Steino protetopublic dont demand a new style per chapter. If a classic author "shows steady & uniform progress" from one oeuvre to ensanguined next, may be considered ample proof of non-stagnation of cerebral Rodano – flaming Farinatas included – .'[6] Beckett, more succinctly, in an acrostic on Joyce's name written two years before the publication of *Finnegans Wake*, spoke of Joyce's 'sweet noo style';[7] the newness, the point at which Joyce is *not* Pound's 'classic author', lying in the no-ness, the discontinuity of Joyce's writing in which no one style can be traced. It is tempting to give as a definition of the effect of the practice of writing operated in Joyce's works the fact that it is impossible to parody Joyce, to parody *Joyce* (in striking contrast to what might be done with a contemporary such as Lawrence). Parody, of course, is a mode of stylistics: the gathering together of the marks of an individuality – the style of an author – and the subsequent reproduction of that individuality. In Joyce's work, however, parody finds no simple point of attachment: where is Joyce's style? in which of the sections of *Ulysses*? what marks of individuality are to be gathered together from the conjunction of 'Ivy Day in the Committee Room' and the 'Night Studies' section of *Finnegans Wake*? In place of style we have *plagiarism*: Joyce does not express himself as the confident subject of a style; he runs through a multiplicity of styles, of orders of discourse, plagiastically open to a whole range of cultural forms that are stolen and broken in the perpetual fragmentation of the writing – a process in which the 'declamatory personality' (Flaubert's term)[8] founders in the vacillation of the play of forms, sliding through them and retraceable only in the terms of sham and forgery, terms to which we will need to return.

Joyce's works do not, therefore, form a 'portrait' of the 'Artist' to be explained or derived in univocal fashion from a supposed biography; nor is *A Portrait of the Artist as a Young Man* the source of a perennial 'Joycean aesthetic' that can account for the whole of Joyce's writing (it is significant that studies of Joyce based on this premiss are almost invariably led to reject or simply ignore *Finnegans Wake*). Joyce himself often insisted forcefully on the breaks between his various works (during the writing of *Finnegans Wake* he would ask pointedly to be told who had written *Ulysses*)[9] and that insistence deserves to be remembered. The texts should not be read as the spiritual biography of a full sourceful subject (the Author) but as a network of paragrammatic interrelations constructed in a play of reassumption and destruction, of pastiche and fragmentation. One level of this interrelation will be described here by placing the texts in conjunction with one another according to their specific practices of what will be called 'strategies of hesitation'.[10]

II   Strategies of hesitation

Jung recognized in Joyce's writing a powerful effect of negation, *Ulysses* being received by him indeed as 'bloße Negation'.[11] This recognition, usually in the form of a violent attack, was applied to each of Joyce's texts from *Dubliners*, the negativity of which led to the physical destruction of several editions, to *Finnegans Wake*, widely received as the vicious and aberrant destruction of literature, Jung having already called *Ulysses* a backside of art ('die Kunst der Rückenseite, oder die Rückseite der Kunst').[12] Literature is, indeed, a crucial focus of this force of negation: paralysis of stereotype and repetition, 'literature', a term already diminishing in value in the early writings, becomes in *Finnegans Wake*, via the passage from letter to litter, 'litterature'.[13] The early importance of Ibsen for Joyce is the degree to which his work offers the difference between a paralysed literature and a drama that seems, according to the convention of that literature, to demonstrate, scandalously, the extent of that paralysis. Hence the title of the paper on Ibsen written in 1900, 'Drama and Life'; instead of literature and stereotype, drama *and* life, the exposure of the real paralysis then received inevitably as an act of negation.

This is the context of the necessity of the strategies of hesitation of Joyce's texts. Gripped in a general paralysis, Joyce's writing is obliged to effect a constant activity of refusal of available meanings, explications, discursive forms, all the very texture of the paralysis. It is precisely the evasion and baffling of the available, the given, its hesitation, to which the writing of Joyce's early texts is devoted and which defines their negativity.

Dublin is here the wasteland, the centre of what Eliot described in his review of *Ulysses* as 'the immense panorama of futility and anarchy which is contemporary history':[14] 'that city seemed to me the centre of paralysis', 'that hemiplegia or paralysis which many consider a city'.[15] Given this paralysis, how can the writing develop its demonstration without, in so doing, itself falling into the snares of sense, fixing itself within the blanket of that paralysis, repeating its very terms? how can it baffle the expectations of reading within which the paralysis is blindly enclosed? how can it hesitate these expectations and their sense and realize that negativity noted by Jung? Joyce's writing explores various procedures in response to these problems.

One such procedure is that of epiphany, of the kind that Joyce had at one time the habit of jotting down in a notebook; the definition of a climactic moment of paralytic banality by its copying down in writing. The process of copying down is to be understood literally, since the matter copied in this kind of epiphany is as often as not a fragment of dialogue[16] – an indication of the extent to which the spread of paralysis is located in the thickening weft of sense, stifling in its all-envelopingness. (Note too how much of the writing of *Stephen Hero* and *A Portrait of the Artist as a Young Man* is made up of citations of instances of discourse, from the sermon to the brief epiphanies that reappear in the former novel.)[17] This procedure is extended in *Dubliners* in the writing of 'Ivy Day in the Committee Room', organized through the recitation of a series of commonplaces (of 'idées reçues') the stringing together of which mimes with smothering clarity the blanket of paralysis.[18]

Dubliners, in fact, extends the procedure of the epiphany into a second, more general procedure within which it can be contained. This is the development of a kind of 'colourless' writing (that zero degree of writing described by Barthes) which can be held at the same level as the repetition of fragments of discourse, framing them in an absence of any principle (of organization, of order) or, more exactly, in the signification of its purpose to remain silent, outside commentary, interpretation, *parole*. Joyce, with great precision, refers to this as 'a style of scrupulous meanness'.[19] A further procedure, that of *A Portrait*, is to rend the blanket of sense through the production of the counter-text of the fiction of the artist and his 'voluntary exile'; his para-doxical status forming a contra-position to the realm of the doxa within the interstices of which the writing can, hesitatingly, proceed.

What has to be understood is the way in which these procedures respond to the problem posed as to the position from which the writing is developed, the way in which, that is, they are operative as strategies of hesitation. How is the writing to develop without fixing itself within the whole paralysis? From the position of the Stephen of *A Portrait*? Assuredly not – Stephen has no simple reality as some liberating character. The answer lies not in any position, but precisely in the strategies, in the absence of any position, in the continual hesitation effected by the writing. It has already been said that the writing of *A Portrait* proceeds not from the position of Stephen but, as it were, in the 'between' of that position and its opposite. The strategies of hesitation place Joyce's writing not in some fixed outside (the illusion of 'Reality') but within a continual process of fragmentation, destruction, hesitation. This is the rigour of Joyce's writing; its development of a suspension of sense. Thus, in the epiphanies and the scrupulous meanness of *Dubliners*, the strategy of the copy determines precisely an absence of sense. It is this that is found so disturbing in the majority of the pieces in *Dubliners*; there is no *context*. The copy empties of reference, leaving a colourless and embarrassing platitude. 'Ivy Day in the Committee Room' *resists* meaning; flat and disruptive, the copy is self-sufficient, is itself the 'test' – the source of all the irony.[20]

The possibility of irony developed within these strategies of hesitation is crucial. Traditionally, irony is a mode of confidence and fixation, elaborated from a stable position to which it constantly refers in its critique of deviations from that position. Joyce's irony (the term is kept here for convenience and also for the kind of emphasis it finds in the writings of Nietzsche – it would perhaps be preferable to replace it by the term 'hecitency', the significance of which in Joyce's writing will be seen below) lacks any centre of this kind; it knows no fixity, and its critique is not moral, derived from some sense, but self-reflexive, a perpetual displacement of sense in a play of forms without resolution. This irresolution is the very wager of *A Portrait*; the carrying through of two fictions, that of the doxa (Dublin, the Church, the family) and that of the paradoxa (the artist), without the writing being committed to either. The writing of the book is thus a tourniquet between the two fictions and it is in this mobility that the writing hesitates irresolvably. Consider in this respect the celebrated juxtaposition at the end of the fourth and the beginning of the fifth sections of the climactic moment of the vision of the girl wading and the description of Stephen in the kitchen:

He climbed to the crest of the sandhill and gazed about him. Evening had fallen. A rim of the young moon cleft the pale waste of sky like the rim of a silver hoop embedded in grey sand; and the tide was flowing in fast to the land with a low whisper of her waves, islanding a few last figures in distant pools.

He drained his third cup of watery tea to the dregs and set to chewing the crusts of fried bread that were scattered near him, staring into the dark pool of the jar. The yellow dripping had been scooped out like a boghole, and the pool under it brought back to his memory the dark turfcoloured water of the bath in Clongowes. The box of pawntickets at his elbow had just been rifled and he took up idly one after another in his greasy fingers the blue and white dockets [. . .] (*P* 187–8)

The sudden inversion, from the distant pools created by the whispering waves to the pool under the boghole of the dripping, from the young moon cleaving the pale waste of sky to greasy fingers fondling pawntickets, in short from one writing to another, creates an expectation of irony. This expectation is baffled, however, by the absence of the sense to which the irony could be reduced; does the juxtaposition work for Stephen (showing the unbearableness of his position and the necessity for a justified exile) or against him (deflating the misty languor of the celtic twilight)? Critics continue to argue now one way, now the other, producing two versions of the book according to the tenets of classic irony. It is exactly this bafflement, this confusion (in the same way that *Dubliners* provokes a confusion in reading), that is the strategy of hesitation of *A Portrait*, that is the production of its irony of suspended sense.

The importance of Flaubert's writing for Joyce in this respect is evident (Flaubert was one of the three or four writers whose works Joyce claimed to have read in their entirety).[21] The strategy of *A Portrait*, indeed, finds a certain parallel in *Madame Bovary* with its play between the position of Emma and that of Charles, Homais and Yonville in general. Not the least of Pound's insights with regard to Joyce's work was his recognition of the possibility of this reference to Flaubert in the strategies of Joyce's writing; in *Dubliners* he found that 'English prose catches up with Flaubert'[22] and he continually insisted on a parallel between *Ulysses* and *Bouvard et Pécuchet*; 'He has done what Flaubert set out to do in *Bouvard et Pécuchet*, done it better, more succinct. An epitome.'[23] It is the reference to *Bouvard et Pécuchet* that is crucial, for the strategy of that text is again that of the copy developed as the process of a vertiginous hesitation ('in such a way that the reader does not know, yes or no, whether he is being made a fool of').[24] Hesitation, held in the strategy of style (in Flaubert's sense), stands against the stupidity of conclusiveness ('stupidity consists in wishing to conclude; we are a thread and we want to know the pattern'),[25] of fixity, of the myth of the absolute centre, the itinerary of which is that of Bouvard and Pécuchet, ever in search of the final copy, the original Truth, until they too become the compilers of the mythologies of others, lost in the play of the copy like Flaubert himself. Where is 'Flaubert' in *Bouvard et Pécuchet*? The definition of the artist as God remaining 'within or behind or beyond or above his handiwork, invisible, refined out of existence, indifferent, paring his fingernails', taken over from Flaubert in *A Portrait*,[26] is to be read, in relation to Joyce's writing, in this connection: it is not, in this relation, a question of the artist as substantial subject dominating everything from the fixity of his position, but of the absence of any position, an indifference which is here an illimitation, a perpetual movement of difference (in the very movement of hesitation) in which the subject is no longer visible, is dispersed in the writing.

In the typology of these strategies of hesitation sketched here, *Ulysses* represents at once a further extension of this irony of 'hecitency' (it is *Ulysses* that Pound likens to *Bouvard et Pécuchet*) and, in this extension, the decisive definition of a practice of writing–reading in which the subject is desubstantialized through fragmentation into the multiple processes of its inscription. (Shaw was right to talk of the negativity of *Ulysses* in relation to its treatment of the human subject.)

A mark of this new level of the activity of the writing is what Broch called the urge for totality in *Ulysses* ('Totalitätsanspruch')[27] and what Joyce described as encyclopaedism: 'It is an epic of two races (Israelite–Irish) and at the same time the cycle of the human body as well as a little story of a day (life). [. . .] It is also a sort of encyclopaedia. My intention is to transpose the myth *sub specie temporis nostri*. Each adventure (that is, every hour, every organ, every art being interconnected and interrelated in the structural scheme of the whole) should not only condition but even create its own technique. Each adventure is so to say one person although it is composed of persons – as Aquinas relates of the angelic hosts.'[28] There is scarcely need to elaborate on this description; the complexity of the development of Joyce's scheme is sufficiently well known from the indications given in the table of 'correspondences' drawn up by Joyce for Herbert Gorman and in Stuart Gilbert's book on *Ulysses* written under Joyce's supervision. What is perhaps not sufficiently recognized, indeed, is how little Gilbert's book *explains*; on the contrary, in strict accordance with Joyce's strategies of hesitation (compare in this respect the Ithaca section of *Ulysses*, Joyce's favourite) it enumerates and lists; in response to questions (interrogations of sense) it catalogues, it gives, that is, the beginnings of the series of elements that that writing of *Ulysses* perpetually unfolds. The aim of the writing of *Ulysses* is the achievement of a multiplicity of levels of narrative (of 'adventure') and inter-reference (the permutations available in the reading of the correspondences), the interplay of which will be the fragmentation of every particular one. (The grossest, and commonest, misreading of *Ulysses* is that which derives a single realist narrative of Bloom and Stephen and, with this as centre of reference, explains or abandons the writing.) It is in this multiplicity of levels that the urge for totality is to be understood. *Ulysses* is written as a *repertoire* of fictions: the writing passes across a range of fictions, of forms, juxtaposing and breaking them in a ceaseless narration. The movement from morning to night is the reality of this passage *across* of the writing in which the subject, in the hesitation, in the demonstration of fictions and the themes that demonstration invokes – birth/death, order/chaos, etc. – is lost in its ceaseless reinscription in a totality of possibilities (the writing of the interplay of Bloom and Stephen plays its part in this dissolution). Jung saw clearly in his account of the negativity of *Ulysses* how this passage across fictions was a strategy for the disengagement from sense, for a process of hesitation the self-reflexive effect of which was not the fixing of any sense in the commitment to a single fiction, but an attention to the logic of fictions and to the position of the construction of the subject within that logic: 'I sincerely hope that

Ulysses is not symbolic, for if it were it would have failed in its purpose.'[29]

III   Context/Intertext

One of the key stresses of Nietzsche's work may be summarized by the following: 'Because we have to be stable in our beliefs if we are to prosper, we have made the "real" world a world not of change and becoming, but one of being.'[30] The apparatus of a vraisemblable, the given series of beliefs defining the ' "wahre" Welt', functions as a self-perpetuating stabilization, converting the world into a realm of essence (whether theological or the fixed 'Reality' of mechanistic materialism). It is this stability that is shattered by the writing of Joyce's texts in their definition of a logic of fictions, not of truths; their attention to what is called in *Finnegans Wake* 'the fictionable world' (*FW* 345.36). *Finnegans Wake*, transforming the 'real Matter-of-Fact' of realist writing into a 'matter of fict' or 'mere matter of ficfect' (*FW* 532.29), is the negation of any vraisemblable. The writing ceaselessly violates (this is its *ambiviolent* activity) the principles of identity and non-contradiction, effecting an infinitization of fictions, of possibilities: 'we are in for a sequentiality of improbable possibles though possibly nobody after having grubbed up a lock of cwold cworn aboove his subject probably in Harrystotalies or the vivle will go out of his way to applaud him on the onboiassed back of his remark for utterly impossible as are all these events they are probably as like those which may have taken place as any others which never took person at all are ever likely to be' (*FW* 110.15–21).

Crucial to the action of a vraisemblable is the definition of a context of reference, producing, according to a process of limitation (effected in discourse by conventions of genre, style and so on), a fixed meaning. Joyce's texts, by contrast, in their unstabilization, their 'hecitency', refer not to a context – and thus not to a 'Reality' (the context defined by the vraisemblable being received precisely as *unique*, as *essence*) – but to an intertext. In these texts, that is, the context is splintered into a multiplicity of instances of discourse, fragments of sense; into a plurality, or dialogue, irreducible to the single line of a truth, as, for instance, that of realist writing naturalized, according to the context of a vraisemblable, as monologue of 'Reality'. The practice of writing–reading in Joyce's texts is the recognition of the text not as absolute origin or source (expression of 'Reality', expression of the Author, etc.) but as intertextual space, dialogue of forms which write it as it writes them. The urge for totality defined by Broch in relation to *Ulysses* is the acknowledgement of the problem of intertextuality. Writing, no longer seen as unique expression, becomes an activity of assemblage, of reading (again in the sense on which Kristeva insists), in which activity the writing subject itself is dispersed in a plurality of possible positions and functions, read within the orders of discourse. *Finnegans Wake* comments exactly on the multiplicity of 'identities in the writer complexus (for if the hand was one, the minds of active and agitated were more than so)' (*FW* 114.33–5).

Joyce declared himself 'quite content to go down to posterity as a scissors and paste man for that seems to me a harsh but not unjust description'.[31] The reference is to the literal activity of assemblage that characterizes, in part and in differing ways, the writing of *Ulysses* and of *Finnegans Wake*. The term 'litterature' might be adopted here in the precise reference it finds in Carroll's preface to 'Sylvie and Bruno', where the genesis of writing is linked to the idea of assemblage, to the possession by the subject of a 'huge unwieldy mass of litterature' in which he is lost (how can he wield it?).[32] The following are two examples of this 'litterature' in relation to Joyce's writing (the first concerns *Ulysses*, the second *Finnegans Wake*):

I have seen him collect in the space of a few hours the oddest assortment of material: a parody on the *House that Jack built*, the name and action of a poison, the method of caning boys on training ships, the wobbly cessation of a tired unfinished sentence, the nervous trick of a convive turning his glass in inward-turning circles, a Swiss music-hall joke turning on a pun in Swiss dialect, a description of the Fitzsimmons shift.[33]

the books I am using for the present fragment which include Marie Corelli, Swedenborg, St Thomas, the Sudanese War, Indian outcasts, Women under English Law, a description of St Helena, Flammarion's The End of the World, scores of children's singing games from Germany, France, England and Italy and so on. . .[34]

This heterogeneous material has no value of unity of meaning in Joyce's writing (where could this unity lie between 'Women under English Law' and 'The End of the World' or between 'the method of caning boys on training ships' and 'a Swiss music-hall joke turning on a pun in Swiss dialect'?). The value is to be found in the heterogeneity, in the very distance between these diverse elements that the writing will cross in a ceaseless play of relations and correspondences in which every element becomes the fiction of another. The unity of these elements is not, then, as is generally supposed, one of content, of meaning, but one grasped at the level of their reality as forms, as fictions. What is constructed in the play of their interrelations in the writing is a discontinuity in progress, a constant displacement from fiction to fiction. It is this discontinuity that realizes the negativity of Joyce's writing. There is no fiction, no level of narrative, that 'stops' the others (as a context 'stops' the multiple possibilities of meaning, the play of the signifier, thus avoiding the loss of the meaning). The irony of *Ulysses* is that of this perpetual displacement, that, briefly noted by Kristeva, of the capture of 'a meaning always already old, always already exceeded, as funny as it is ephemeral'.[35] It is in these terms that Joyce's irony is not, as in the case of the classic tradition of irony, contextual, but, exactly, intertextual, a strategy of hesitation opening onto 'a finally real text . . . the current letter of meaning finally formulated and played'.[36]

IV Rhetoric

What rhetoric could render account of what Eisenstein called the inimitable materiality of the effects of writing of Joyce's texts?[37] The shattering of the context in the dialogism of Joyce's writing places the texts at the same time outside the descriptive categories of rhetoric. The rupture with the classic conception of irony described above provides one instance of this. Another is given by the impossibility of the notion of metaphor in the face of Joyce's writing in so far as that writing deconstructs the fundamental (contextual) distinction between the literal and the figurative: according to what criteria are any particular elements to be identified as metaphors in a text in which every element refers to another, perpetually deferring meaning? There is, that is to say, no simple line of discourse in Joyce's writing that could provide a context for the descriptions of rhetoric. In their work on language, on forms, Joyce's texts (*Ulysses, Finnegans Wake*) pose in themselves a critical self-reflexion and it is precisely this reflexiveness on which rhetoric can have no hold and which is thus the activity of its profound and irreparable fragmentation.[38]

It is hardly surprising, therefore, that part of the work of Joyce's writing is a questioning (in the sense of an active interrogation, a dispersion, a hesitation) of rhetoric. The practice of writing, spilling out of the categories of rhetoric, permanently 'undoes' those categories. *Ulysses* and *Finnegans Wake* are perspectives on what the *Scribbledehobble* workbook nicely calls 'rhetorical scenery'.[39] The 'Aeolus' section of the former, with its 'panaroma of all flores of speech' (*FW* 143.03–04), is simply the most obvious example of this questioning, which, finally, underlies the whole activity of the writing in its shattering of the context. Thus could Joyce talk of his writing in connection with rhetoric as leaving behind it a 'burnt up field'.

V Parody – pastiche – plagiarism – forgery

A crucial strategy of Joyce's writing in the fragmentation of the context is that of parody and pastiche. It is only necessary to think of the 'Nausicaa'[40] or 'Oxen of the Sun'[41] sections of *Ulysses* or the beginnings of *Finnegans Wake* in six parodic sketches of medieval literary modes[42] to see the importance of this strategy. Parody, however, is perhaps not the correct term here. Parody, closely related in this to classic irony, constructs a context of imitation that determines a meaning, the ridiculing of the model imitated; like classic irony, it moves in one purposeful direction. It is hard to equate this activity of parody with the writing of the 'Oxen of the Sun' section or of the sketches underlying *Finnegans Wake*. What is in question in Joyce's writing is not the proclamation of irony or ridicule *against* the model imitated, but a copying that fixes no point of irony between model and imitation, that rests, in this respect, in a hesitation of meaning. This activity is that not of parody, but of pastiche, and it is worth recalling that an initial meaning of pastiche (*pasticcio*) is, according to *O.E.D.*, 'a medley of various ingredients; a hotchpotch, farrago, jumble', the term being used of an opera composed in this way. This, of course, is the very definition of *Ulysses*, 'this chaffering allincluding most farraginous chronicle' (*U* 420/423), and recalls that 'litterature' described above. The pastiches, the imitations of prose styles in the 'Oxen of the Sun' section, are part of the massive assemblage of forms, of fragments, of possibilities, of fictions, in the interrogation of which the writing is developed. The continual appropriation and fragmentation, the *purloining* that defines Joyce's writing, converts the strategy of pastiche, finally, into that of plagiarism.

In connection with the issues raised in the preceding paragraph, it may be worthwhile pausing to consider a particular technique of Joyce's writing in *Finnegans Wake* that I shall call that of the 'transforming citation'. The following have been chosen as being especially obvious examples:

1. '(plunders to night of you, blunders what's left of you, flash as flash can!)' (*FW* 188.12–13)   /   'Cannon to right of them, Cannon to left of them, Cannon in front of them, Volley'd and thunder'd.' 'Someone had blunder'd.' (Tennyson, 'The Charge of the Light Brigade')

2. 'A king off duty and a jaw for ever!' (*FW* 162.35)   /   'A thing of beauty is a joy for ever' (Keats, 'Endymion')

3. 'Walhalloo, Walhalloo, Walhalloo, mourn in plein!' (*FW* 541.22)   /   'Waterloo! Waterloo! Waterloo! morne plaine!' (Hugo, 'L'expiation' II)

4. 'When, as the buzzer brings the light brigade, keeping the home fires burning, so on the churring call themselves came at him, from the westborders of the eastmidlands, three kings of three suits and a crowner [. . .]' (*FW* 474.16–19)   /   epic simile (references to Keats, Gray, Milton, etc., together with a further reference to Tennyson ('light brigade'))

5. '(meed of anthems here we pant!)' (*FW* 41.10) 'Mades of ashens when you flirt spoil the lad but spare his shirt!' (*FW* 436.32–3)   /   'Maid of Athens, ere we part, Give, oh give me back my heart!' (Byron, 'Maid of Athens')

6. 'queth their haven evermore!' (*FW* 49.11)   /   'Quoth the Raven, "Nevermore".' (Poe, 'The Raven')

7. 'when yea, he hath no mananas' (*FW* 170.20)   /   'Yes, we have no bananas' (music-hall song)

It seems easy enough to discern an element of parody in the first of these examples, where it supports a clear effect of ridicule, working against the model imitated. In the examples following, however (and as a result of the very extent of the procedure), this becomes more and more difficult. Thus, if the second of the quotations from Byron invokes ridicule, the first seems to exhaust itself in a simple act of reference. And what of the quotation from Poe, which produces a certain wavering of sense that no element of parody can fix? The last of the examples provides the explicit manifestation of this difficulty in its frank resistance to any reading according to the expectations of parody: if the intention of parody seems evident in the transformation of 'The Charge of the Light Brigade', where, on the contrary, is the parody to be sought in that of 'Yes, we have no bananas'? On the side of the transformation or on that of the original?

The question returns us to the preference for the description of the activity of Joyce's writing as that of pastiche rather than of parody. It is a matter, always, of citation, of a continual citing of elements that will place the writing in a dialogue of forms, that will transgress the laws of the context. These transforming citations are a part of this dialogism, the transformation serving as the disorientation of the citation, its fragmentation within a shifting series of forms, the perpetual displacement of which is the activity of Joyce's writing. The examples given above were deliberately selected for their obviousness. The degree and kind of fame of 'The Charge of the Light Brigade' inevitably pulls any transformation into the realm of parody, though even this example offers resistance if read in Joyce's text in the absence of context (and not, as here, as a separate example). The process of citation in Joyce's writing, however, has a generality far beyond such examples, involving that purloining which is characteristic of its activity. Thus, to take a single instance, a longish passage of *Finnegans Wake* (545–7) is devoted to the citation and transformation of B. Seebohm Rowntree's *Poverty: A Study of Town Life*, the forms and turns of Rowntree's writing being jostled, exposed, turned back to front, devastated in that reflexivity of Joyce's writing which breaks rhetoric and its categories. In the citation of Rowntree (and the letter quoted above with details of the books Joyce was using for a single fragment of *Finnegans Wake* gives some idea of the importance of this procedure) the passage from parody to pastiche and from pastiche to plagiarism is clear. In the citation of 'The Charge of the Light Brigade' the quotation marks remain; in that of Rowntree they have disappeared. Hence the error of concluding 'from the nonpresence of inverted commas (sometimes called quotation marks) on any page that its author was always constitutionally incapable of misappropriating the spoken words of others' (*FW* 108.33–6). Joyce's writing is precisely a misappropriation; in other words, it is that writing–reading defined by Kristeva and which *Finnegans Wake* calls exactly a 'raiding'. Joyce's text might have taken as its motto Lautréamont's insistence that 'Le plagiat est nécessaire.'[43]

That insistence, indeed, is given crucially and explicitly in *Finnegans Wake* in the account of the writer as Shem — as sham ('Shem was a sham and a low sham [. . .]' (*FW* 170.25)) and forger ('What do you think Vulgariano did but study with stolen fruit how cutely to copy all their various styles of signature so as one day to utter an epical forged cheque on the public for his own private profit' (*FW* 181.14–17)):[44] 'Who can say how many pseudostylic shamiana, how few or how many of the most venerated public impostures, how very many piously forged palimpsests slipped in the first place by this morbid process from his pelagiarist pen?' (*FW* 181.36–182.03). The 'pelagiarist pen' gives the exact description of this activity of writing, uniting as it does plagiarist and pelagial, the appropriation of forms with the opening of an infinite prospect of forms traced on the ever shifting surface of the sea. Indeed, a 'shem' is the junction of two edges of lead turned the one over the other, as Joyce's writing is the junction of an interfolding of citations, 'the last word in stolentelling' (*FW* 424.35). This activity of interfolding has already been described as a strategy of hesitation, a fragmentation of context, and the term 'hecitency' that runs through *Finnegans Wake* is a direct reference to the importance of forgery, of the 'pelagiarist pen'. The 'penmarks used out in sinscript with such hesitancy' (*FW* 421.18) by Shem allude to the letters from Parnell in support of the Phoenix Park Murders forged by Richard Pigott and proved as forgeries by the misspelling of the word 'hesitancy'.[45] In the sham production of Shem ('Every dimmed letter in it is a copy' (*FW* 424.35)), the 'authordux Book of Lief' (*FW* 425.20), the original orthodox source (with the Author as *dux*, master and guide) — but how to bring it to light? — is replaced by 'Acomedy of letters!' (*FW* 425.24), the forgery of a multiplicity of forms, the dialogue of a continual 'hecitency' that knows no rest.

Mention must be briefly made, as a kind of coda to this section, of the operation in Joyce's writing of an effect of permanent parody of his own texts, that are subject to the superimposition of later writings, to transforming citation and, within the space of the single text, to a multiplication of levels of meaning — all of which places the texts in a paragrammatic network of relations of displacement and dialogue that works against ideas of context and continuity. If the term 'parody' seems appropriate here, it is in so far as, within the space of the single body of Joyce's work, the ridicule can proceed neither to nor from 'Joyce' as individuality, as source, but can only disrupt the notion of source, revaluing parody rather as the irony of *Dubliners* revalues irony. Parody here is simply a constant displacement of writings.

Two procedures may be signalled as examples in this connection. Firstly, the transforming citation which operates in the same way as described above.

Thus the opening of *A Portrait* becomes 'Eins within a space and a wearywide space it wast [. . .]' (*FW* 152.18) or 'Once upon a drunk and a fairly good drunk it was and the rest of your blatherumskite!' (*FW* 453.20–1). Similarly, the writing of *Finnegans Wake* cites itself in a process of transformations: '(Stoop) if you are abcedminded, to this claybook, what curios of signs (please stoop), in this allaphbed!' (*FW* 18.17–18) will be cited and transformed into 'Please stop if you're a B.C. minding missy, please do. But should you prefer A.D. stepplease' (*FW* 272.12–14). This citation also proceeds by the recital of titles (as, for instance, that of the stories of *Dubliners*, *FW* 186–7), more or less inserted in a derisive history ('We now romp through a period of pure lyricism of shamebred music' (*FW* 164.15–16)). Secondly, the multiplication of possible levels of meaning that blocks the reception of a meaning, that baffles the context. Joyce indicated something of the working of this effect with regard to the title of *Chamber Music*: 'The reason I dislike *Chamber Music* as a title is that it is too complacent. I should prefer a title which to a certain extent repudiated the book, without altogether disparaging it.'[46] It is the tourniquet, the indecision ('to a certain extent repudiated . . . without altogether disparaging'), that is important. *Chamber Music* actually provides a good example if the title is read according to the indication of pun given in *Ulysses* ('Chamber music. Could make a kind of pun on that. It is a kind of music I often thought when she' (*U* 281/282)). An extended example from *Finnegans Wake*, which is itself a citation of the 'chamber music' pun, is that of the motif of the flowing waters in which the lyrical flow of the river turns in and out of the flow of urine (e.g. *FW* 76.29–30, 96.14, 139.20–8, 265.15–16, 373.05–07, 462.04–06, etc.).[47]

VI   The spiral

Flaubert planned a novel to be called *La Spirale*.[48] That title might be given to the body of Joyce's work, marking the action of that discontinuity described above. Is it not precisely as a spiral that the succession of Joyce's works should be conceived? They represent not a line of development but a ceaseless work of return and disengagement, of dissemination, each text reinscribing the others to achieve a distance of parody, derision, anecdote (what is *Ulysses* for *Finnegans Wake* if not an anecdote?). The *Scribbledehobble* workbook, written round about 1924 and having a claim to be considered as one of Joyce's finest texts, is divided into sections with headings made up of titles of previous texts and, in the case of *Ulysses*, of episodes of previous texts. Each section is more or less filled with words, phrases, occasional sequences of phrases, related in various ways (via parody, commentary, extension, thematic, aleation) with the previous texts. In the explicitness of its organization, *Scribbledehobble* provides a perfect image of the Joycean spiral; a return across earlier writings but in order to open a distance, the circle not closing but disengaging a new activity of writing. The spiral of Flaubert's title referred to the narrative of one particular text. His projected novel was to be an attempt to confound in a single narrative line – that of the story of a painter – the 'real' and the 'imaginary', the events of everyday and the dreams and visions provoked by hashish, the confusion finally putting into question their habitual easy distinction. The spiral described the succession of stages undergone by the painter in the process of this confusion, culminating in a dramatic conclusion: 'The conclusion is that: happiness consists in being Mad (or what is thus so called), that is to say, in seeing the True, the whole of time, the absolute – '.[49]

Flaubert's plan finds in some sort a realization in *Ulysses* in the succession of 'streams of consciousness' that interfold and come together in an action which, in the 'nighttown' section, spills out of the limitation of any 'person' or 'Reality'. The image of the spiral is not, however, to be reduced to a single level of narrative – one amongst many others – of *Ulysses*. It is, in fact, precisely the multiplicity of levels that gives the spiral of the text, producing as it does neither the enclosing cohesion of a circular movement nor the unfolding and revelation of a meaning on a line of development but a spiral, a constant displacement of possibilities of reading. The spiral is then the realization of the urge for totality in *Ulysses*. The folly of the book is its desire to 'voir le Vrai, l'ensemble du temps, l'absolu': its absolute, however, is not the theological stasis of a fixed Absolute but the absolute of possibles, the incessant movement of forms, the spiral of returns and recommencements in which meaning is always 'later'.

The image of the spiral finds a precise reference in Joyce's writing, that of the historical theory of Vico with its conception of the spiral of *corsi* and *ricorsi*. This reference, as is well known, is basic to the writing of *Finnegans Wake*, which makes of the 'real world', the stable fixity of realist writing, the 'reel world' (*FW* 64.25–6), forming and reforming in a play of difference and repetition, the 'seim anew' (*FW* 215.23). This movement of 'vicous circles' (*FW* 134.16) – 'by a commodius vicus of recirculation' (*FW* 3.02) – is, as was Vico's work in its opposition to the unidimensional linear progress of the Enlightenment version of history, an opposition to the writing of history as the straight unfolding of a single line of development. 'The June snows was flocking in thuckflues on the hegelstomes' (*FW* 416.32–3); disorder and discontinuity ('June snows') opposes the order and continuity of Hegel's writing of the process of the realization of Geist. The characteristic of Joyce's writing is, in Beckett's words, 'the absolute absence of the Absolute'.[50] The discontinuity is the mark of this absence, an anti-synthesis: 'What a meanderthalltale to unfurl and with what an end in view of squattor and anntisquattor and postproneauntisquattor!' (*FW* 19.25–7). The synthesis is continually *postponed* in the 'meanderthalltale', meaning is deferred. 'The Vico road goes round and round to meet where terms begin' (*FW* 452.21–2).

'To meet where terms begin' may be read as an appeal not to a simple circularity[51] but to a primitive level (as 'meanderthalltale' appeals to neanderthal). This primitive level is to be understood in thinking the foundation of history eternally and contrapuntally present in the spiralling movement of *corsi* and *ricorsi* and given in language as the history of that history. For Vico the spiral is definable exactly in terms of stages of language and the historical humanities are to be included in the general science of philology. Vico's 'new science' is a passage across history in the interests of the disengagement of the logic of the movement of history; 'the ideal history of the eternal laws over which run the facts of all nations'.[52] This logic functions as a structural model which gives the intelligibility of any particular historical fact, that fact actualizing one among the multiplicity of virtualities present in the structure. The importance of this for Joyce's writing is evident. Where realist writing had made of history the fixed point of its representations, realized in narratives supported by the context of a vraisemblable that defined and ratified their typicality, their 'truth', Joyce's writing is concerned, like that of Vico, with a history of forms of intelligibility. In a very early essay Joyce had written of 'history or the denial of reality, for they are two names for the one thing';[53] the reality of Joyce's writing will be its attention to forms, no longer to 'Reality' but to the history of fictions. The history of Joyce's writing is not that produced by a context but that grasped in its realization of the intertext as scansion of fictions. It is in this sense that Joyce's writing is an interrogation of 'origins', of the 'reality' 'before' history as the very possibility of its foundation, of, in fact, the 'time' of language with which − this was Vico's central theme − history begins and which − a further Viconian theme − is perpetually present in every act of language, the horizon of its intelligibility. The spiral of Joyce's writing, finally, is the process of this interrogation.

VII   Myth

The role of myth in Joyce's writing was early defined by Eliot and, in slightly subtler fashion, by Pound in connection with *Ulysses* as that of the neutral systematization of a chaotic material: 'It is simply a way of controlling, of ordering, of giving a shape and a significance to the immense panorama of futility and anarchy which is contemporary history';[54] 'These correspondences are part of Joyce's mediaevalism and are chiefly his own affair, a scaffold, a means of construction, justified by the result, and justifiable by it only. The result is a triumph in form, in balance, a main schema, with continuous inweaving and arabesque.'[55] These definitions coincide with remarks made by Joyce, who, according to Svevo, stated that he used the Homeric reference as his 'sistema di lavoro'.[56] Similarly, Joyce described the use in *Finnegans Wake* of the mythological system derived from Vico as that of a 'trellis' over which the writing could be woven (' "Of course", Joyce told me, "I don't take Vico's speculations literally; I use his cycles as a trellis." ').[57] Beckett saw in it 'a structural convenience – or inconvenience', but went on to add in qualification, 'By structural, I do not only mean a bold outward division, a bare skeleton for the housing of material. I mean the endless substantial variations on these three beats, and interior intertwining of these three themes [i.e. the three stages of a Viconian historical cycle before the period of dissolution out of which the new cycle begins] into a decoration of arabesques – decoration and more than decoration.'[58]

In the context of these statements, one or two additional qualifications and suggestions may be made with regard to the use of myth in Joyce's work. If the myth is not the point of any commitment on the part of the writing (the myth, even as 'simply a way of controlling', being, in fact, taken up in that activity of copying and plagiarism and 'pulverized' in the writing),[59] it has, nevertheless, a crucial role for the text in that spiral of interrogation described above. Thus in *Finnegans Wake* it is a question not of a single myth, or even of a single body of myth, but of a whole diversity of mythologies, drawn from a range of cultures and using as great a number of sacred books as possible, from the Bible to the Koran.[60] This assemblage of myths in a writing which refers to them all without fixing itself in any one, leaving them perpetually in its wake, is the appeal to the play (that precisely of the wake) of death and birth, night and day, the same and the other, of difference. Broch expressed the terms of this in two remarks made on different occasions in the course of discussions of Joyce's work and the conjunction of which is illuminating: 'myth has always been mankind's closest approach to knowledge of death'[61] and 'the infinite and death are children of one mother'.[62] The passage of Joyce's writing across a multiplicity of myths opens up an endless series of traces in which death and the other are held in profile, grasped in the play of the production of fictions. Death and birth as infinity of creations, night and day as infinity of meanings, the unique actants of *Finnegans Wake* are grasped as 'Kinder einer Mutter', children, that is, of Anna Livia, of the flow of the river into the sea, finding their source, their point of 'origin' in the constant making and remaking of forms, in the patterns traced in the wake of that flow from which death and birth, night and day, give themselves in their opposition. The 'time' of the writing of *Finnegans Wake*, realized in this interrogation and fragmentation of myths, of fictions of origin, is the point of that wake of the production of fictions, of meanings, of the contexts of history and 'Reality'.

A final remark in connection with myth. In the section of *L'Origine des manières de table* entitled 'Du mythe au roman', Lévi-Strauss describes a process of degradation in myths that happens in the course of their transformations. This degradation, in which the cyclical periodicity of a myth is lost in a diversity of episodes relating to ever shorter periods of time, may be characterized as a loss of structure ('Its structural content is dissipated'),[63] a fall into seriality. This 'fall' offers for Lévi-Strauss a significant illustration of the passage from the mythical to the novelistic, the narrative of the novel being exactly a quest for structure and a repetition of the 'fall' of its loss: 'The fall of the novel plot, internal to its unfolding from the very beginning and recently become external to it – since we are now witnessing the fall *of* the plot after the fall *within* the plot – confirms that because of the novel's historical position in the evolution of literary genres, it was inevitable that it should tell a story that ends badly, and that it should now, as a genre, be itself coming to a bad end.'[64] What Lévi-Strauss also points to in that passage is the negation of the unidirectional line of narrative in process in modern writing, and Joyce's work might, of course, be taken as exemplary in this process of negation, pursued precisely in terms of the aim for another periodicity, no longer that of the novel but that of the production of fictions. The recourse to myth in Joyce's writing marks this aim clearly. The focus of that writing, as was seen in the discussion of the reference to Vico, is not the seriality of the history of realist writing, but intelligibility, structure as logic of 'origins', and the spiral of its interrogation of myths is the point of its passage outside the periodicity of that history. Is it not significant in this respect that Lévi-Strauss's own work of mythologics runs directly into the very image of the spiral ('In going tirelessly over the same myths or in incorporating new ones [. . .] structural analysis progresses in a spiral. It seems to retrace its steps, but always in order to get to deeper layers of mythical matter into the heart of which it insinuates itself and all the properties of which it gradually penetrates.')?[65]

VIII   The wake: 'le jour, la nuit'

'Mon livre [. . .] n'a rien de commun avec *Ulysse*. C'est le jour et la nuit.'[66] Thus Joyce to Louis Gillet. *Finnegans Wake* was to be, in its own phrase, a 'nightynovel' (*FW* 54.21), what Joyce's brother referred to with much irritation and more truth as 'this nightmare production'.[67] Various critics have wished to reduce this distinction between *Ulysses* and *Finnegans Wake* on which Joyce insisted by arguing, according to the criteria of realist writing, that 'at least half of *Ulysses*, and that the more important, takes place after dark, while well over a third of *Finnegans Wake* is concerned with daytime activities'.[68] It is clear that this kind of argument, whatever side one may take, is as irrelevant to the writing of *Finnegans Wake* as it is to that of *Ulysses*. What is in question in the distinction between the two books, the day and the night, is not some quantifiable amount of darkness and daylight (is it really possible still to read Joyce in this way?) but specific practices of writing. *Ulysses*, definitive end of the realist novel (that it will no longer be possible to write 'innocently', but only to repeat in the assumption of a precise ideological position), is the negation of the daylight world of the natural attitude; in its urge for totality, in its perpetual process of fragmentation and hesitation of the multiplicity of fictions it assembles, *Ulysses* begins to unlimit that world, replacing it in the intertext of the fictions of its construction. *Finnegans Wake* opens onto a further level, fixing a totality not through an encyclopaedism (which breaks the totality into a multiplicity of fictions) but through an attention to the production of meaning (which breaks the totality into the ceaseless moment of the engendering of fiction in the wake that forges the horizon against which the night and the day are grasped in their difference). Its work is on the fiction of language, its procedure that of, in Mallarmé's words, 'le langage se réfléchissant'.[69] Joyce, developing the idea of the 'nightynovel', refers in this respect to the work of the dream: *Finnegans Wake* would be written 'to suit the esthetic of the dream, when the forms prolong and multiply themselves, when the visions pass from the trivial to the apocalyptic, when the brain uses the roots of vocables to make others from them which will be capable of naming its phantasms, its allegories, its allusions'.[70] It is a question for Joyce of developing a writing able to realize what Broch calls a 'Nachtlogik',[71] for which the work of the dream provides a crucial instance. This writing is the return to the night of language, to, that is, the point of limits where the day ceases, to the point of origin where language begins. Such a return is interminable; 'language comes to us from the depths of a night perfectly clear and impossible to master', writes Foucault in his study of Roussel.[72] There is no immediate return on some 'before', there is always an irremovable 'already' (what *Nombres* calls 'cette coupure, ce recul sans cesse présents et à l'oeuvre');[73] only a constant and oblique work of questioning, a kind of perpetual 'Rückfrage' (if Husserl's term is stripped of any transcendental intention, of any possibility of coming to rest), the elaboration of a writing of fragmentation and hesitation in the detours of which, changing language in language, the area of the production of meaning, of the engendering of sense and its subject, may be grasped in its activity. Thus, for Joyce, the declaration of war on language,[74] the necessity for its putting to sleep,[75] for the refusal of 'wideawake language, cutanddry grammar and goahead plot':[76] 'In writing of the night, I really could not, I felt I could not, use words in their ordinary connections. Used that way they do not express how things are in the night, in the different stages − conscious, then semi-conscious, then unconscious. I found that it could not be done with words in their ordinary relations and connections.'[77] To describe *Finnegans Wake* as writing of the night is to describe this activity of return, the attempt to write in the moment of night into day, to *know* that process defined by Sollers precisely through the image of night and day: 'We live in the false daylight of a dead language of limited meanings: we fail to grasp the day in so far as we fail to grasp the night that we are. But we are nothing other than this nightly and daily movement of the readable and the unreadable, in us, outside us — and that we do not want to know.'[78]

IX   The wake: 'l'incompréhensible récit'

What is narrated in *Finnegans Wake*? One answer is given as follows: 'Yet is it but an old story, the tale of a Treestone with one Ysold, of a Mons held by tentpegs and his pal whatholoosed on the run, what Cadman could but Badman wouldn't, any Genoaman against any Venis, and why Kate takes charge of the waxworks' (*FW* 113.18–22). It is an old story that turns continually, in the possibilities of narrative given in that account (sort of brief actantial précis), in the endless transformations of HCE, in the references to mythologies, on the problem of origins: 'What then agentlike brought about that tragoady thundersday this municipal sin business?' (*FW* 5.13–14). The pivotal axis of *Finnegans Wake* is the myth of the fall — from 'prefall paradise peace' (*FW* 30.15), the indifference of what Beckett calls 'unrelieved immaculation',[79] into the endless movement of difference, the 'waters of babalong' (*FW* 103.11), into that wideawake language that veils the night of its production ('Let there be fight? And there was. Foght.' (*FW* 90.12–13)). The point of the fall is the tragedy of 'thundersday', the moment of language as Viconian man imitates the voice of God heard in the noise of thunder. *Finnegans Wake* speaks of 'Der Fall Adams' (*FW* 70.05), a reference, perhaps, to that account given by Hegel of the relation of language and negation: the first act of Adam ('der erste Akt') is the constitution of a mastery of things by giving them names, which, in converting them into idealities for man, nihilates them in their own existence ('sie als Seiende vernichtete').[80] The fall into language is the fall into limitation and negation.

The writing of *Finnegans Wake* is the attempt to rejoin, to *know*, that 'erste Akt', the reality of which is forgotten in the censorship of the particular language that knows itself as natural, direct expression of 'Reality', as without limits. '*We cease to think when we refuse to do so under the constraint of language*; we barely reach the doubt that sees this limitation as a limitation.'[81] Joyce's writing is the seeing of this limitation as limitation; the practice of an illimitation of language. Such an illimitation is not some refusal of language (how does one refuse language?) but a work on and in language, what Barthes calls its 'theatralization';[82] against the instrumentalization of language (that, for example, of a Wells in his protests against *Finnegans Wake*), Joyce's writing, following 'language [. . .] in its incomparable wisdom',[83] opposes a science of writing, a constant attention to language in which the limits of communication are undone in the spreading out of a play of the signifer in the passage through the ceaseless productions of which may be grasped 'the drive of meaning'.[84]

The question posed at the opening of this section may be answered as follows: *Finnegans Wake* is a narrative of language; it is this that forms its 'incompréhensible récit'. That phrase comes from a fragment by Proust in which he describes the moment between sleep and wakefulness, moment of hesitation in the brief 'betweenness' of which ('the half-day of this new concavity') is given 'the incomprehensible narrative' defined by Proust as 'the reasonable of drowsing reason'.[85] In the moment of hesitation lies the possibility of grasping *its* reason. Between night and day, silence and language, lies the possibility of opening a space in which the one and the other may be grasped in the moment of their production. Is not this the very sense of the image of writing as exile and silence common to Proust and Joyce? Joyce's 'voluntary exile'[86] is to be understood not at the level of biographical anecdote, but as a function of the conception of the activity of writing – a practice aiming to work 'before'–'beyond' the world of communication.

The focus of the writing of *Finnegans Wake* between night and day is given in the 'wake' of the title: between the wake of death and the wake of life (the wideawake language), the wake of the perpetual tracing of forms, as one speaks of the 'wake' of a ship, the disturbance, division, difference traced over the surface of the sea. This wake is that described by Derrida as *différance*, 'the movement by which language, or any other code, any system of reference in general becomes "historically" constituted as a fabric of differences'. There is no simple origin, no simple source, no immediate presence. The movement of *différance* is the horizon of the production of any so-defined presence: 'Each element that is said to be "present", appearing on the stage of presence, is related to something other than itself but retains the mark of a past element and already lets itself be hollowed out by the mark of its relation to a future element. This trace relates no less to what is called the future than to what is called the past, and it constitutes what is called the present by this very relation to what it is not.'[87] Joyce defines this movement precisely; the time of *Finnegans Wake* will be the 'pressant' (*FW* 221.17), not a simple present but a present pressing on, always already hollowed by the mark of the future; the time of the inscription of traces in the infinite movement from the ones to the others, 'at no spatial time processly' (*FW* 358.5–6). The 'world' can be conceived only from the horizon of writing as space of inscription of differences (has it been sufficiently noted to what extent the writing of *Finnegans Wake* is a continual transformation of elements into terms of language and writing?)[88] and the possibility of 'origin' lies only in the wake of the writing, in the perpetual turning of sense into form, of signified into signifier: 'The untireties of livesliving being the one substrance of a streamsbecoming. Totalled in toldteld and teldtold in tittletell tattle. Why? Because, graced be Gad and all giddy gadgets, in whose words were the beginnings, there are two signs to turn to, the yest and the ist, the wright side and the wronged side, feeling aslip and wauking up, so an, so farth.' (*FW* 597.7–12).

Water – river and sea – is the constant reality of this process; 'the constant of fluxion' (*FW* 297.28). The source of nation and notion is the movement of the ocean, 'birth of an otion' (*FW* 309.12). 'Brook of Life, backfrish' (*FW* 264.6–7): the inscription of the world given in the movement of the wake, the back-wash ('backfrish' returns also, via the slang 'Backfisch', to the youth of Anna Livia debated by the washerwomen). Anna is almighty source in the plurality given in her flow: 'In the name of Annah the Allmaziful, the Everliving, the Bringer of Plurabilities, haloed be her eve, her singtime sung, her rill be run, unhemmed as it is uneven! Her untitled mamafesta memorialising the Mosthighest has gone by many names at disjointed times' (*FW* 104.01–05). The prayer is not to the fixity of the Absolute but to the 'absolute absence of the Absolute', to the 'allmaziful' bringer of 'plurabilities', and the 'mamafesta' has no fixed title, only a multitude of titles given at disjointed times in the uneven flow. Even here the source has no reality other than in the movement of the wake, as the Letter has no reality other than in the series of letters. Anna Livia, mother and source, has no more than mythical reality; she is, finally, 'ein Alp', a spectral, fantasmatic being, a chimera. The permutations of HCE, 'eternal chimera/hunter' (*FW* 107.14), can have no end, for the writing of Joyce's text knows only that 'constant of fluxion'.[89]

As origin, *Finnegans Wake* makes continual appeal to the Letter, 'this radiooscillating epiepistle to which [...] we must ceaselessly return' (*FW* 108.24–5). This ceaseless return is the constant mulling over of versions of the fall – the host of interviews, inquisitions, trials, reports, stories, myths; the permanent explication of the world ('And so they went on, the fourbottle men, the analists, unguam and nunguam and lunguam again, their anschluss about her whosebefore and his whereafters and how [...] ' (*FW* 95.27–9)), making constant appeal to previous texts ('We are told how in the beginning [...] ' (*FW* 30.11–12); 'as the aftertale hath it' (*FW* 38.10)), all of which run back to the Letter. That Letter, however, is lost (the letter which arrives merely joins the multitude of other versions; it does not close the text but reopens it into the endless flow of the river and the permanent explication): 'Somewhere, parently, in the ginnandgo gap between antediluvious and annadominant the copyist must have fled with his scroll' (*FW* 14.16–18). The 'ginnandgo gap' separates man for ever from a simple origin, from the

Letter that will unify plurability into a definitive meaning, that will fix a final sense. 'The world, mind, is, was and will be writing its own wrunes for ever' (*FW* 19.35); what is given is writing, the inscription of traces and letters, not the Letter, but the series of letters from Alpha to Omega: 'What was it? A . . . . ! ? . . . . O!' (*FW* 94.20–2). The Letter can be grasped only as 'polyhedron of scripture' (*FW* 107.08) and *Finnegans Wake* must be a book of letters, '(Stoop) if you are abcedminded, to this claybook, what curios of signs (please stoop), in this allaphbed! Can you rede (since We and Thou had it out already) its world? It is the same told of all. Many. Miscegenations on miscegenations' (*FW* 18.17–20).

The 'hero' of the writing of *Finnegans Wake* is thus not ALP, the chimera of the Letter, but HCE, the permanent anagrammatic play of letters, the 'doomed but always ventriloquent Agitator' (*FW* 56.05–06), the 'herewaker' (*FW* 619.12), the ever present movement (agitation) of the wake of *différance*. In the context of that spreading out of a play of the signifier mentioned above, Joyce's writing recalls literature to a practice of 'letters'.[90] HCE, 'those normative letters' (*FW* 32.18), give, in their expansion and the transformations they determine, a constant insistence of the signifier in the signified, breaking the linearity of the context and opening onto the logic of the signifier.

Why HCE? Evidently because these are the letters of 'HeCitEncy' ('finally called after some his hes hecitency Hec' (*FW* 119.18)), linking forgery and strategy of hesitation in the ways defined above and reflecting the hecitency of the subject and 'his' meaning in this permutation of letters. That is one reading of HCE and it would need to be complemented by a multiplicity of others, without that complementation being considered as an attempt to find the 'real answer' to the question (it is exactly the function of the letters to deride such notions as the 'real answer').[91] There is perhaps room here, however, for one other reading of the letters in connection with the activity of Joyce's writing as it has been described so far. In the early account of the digging over of the 'allaphbed' for signs of origin, for traces of the Letter, there appears merely 'A *h*atch, a *c*elt, an *e*arshare' (*FW* 18.30–1), the signature, that is, of HCE and the introduction of Earwicker. The 'hatch' gives at once the primitive tool (hatchet, French 'hache') (it is worth bearing in mind that language and the capacity to make tools are often regarded as having made a simultaneous appearance in the development of man), but also the idea of birth (hatching from an egg), of an opening (hatch as small doorway or passageway) and of the tracing of differences (hatch in its associations with engraving). The 'celt' gives another primitive tool, together with a reference to the ancient Celtic language. Finally, the 'earshare' again refers to a tool, the 'share' of the plough being the blade for cutting and dividing, for furrowing the earth, as the verb 'to share' is the division and allocation of parts. Via a relation of substitution (earshare–earwicker), 'share' passes to 'wick' which is the old word for a primitive community, a small village or hamlet (retained in 'Berwick', for example), and is derived from Latin 'vicus', meaning a street, a way, but also being the Latin name of Vico (a fusion given in 'commodius vicus of recirculation'). 'Wicker' gives a primitive craft (wickerwork) and thus the notion of tressing together, of interweaving. It is also related to the idea of the wake (earwicker–herewaker) and is originally an East Scandinavian word (remember the Scandinavian origins of Finn and Earwicker), as in the Swedish 'vika', to bend or fold. This reading is a fiction like any other in the face of the multiplicity of *Finnegans Wake*. Its sole value lies in the connections it makes, or provokes, between origin and difference, between the opening of the 'world' and the articulation of ·divisions, between the Viconian way of history and the perpetual interfolding of meanings, the endless permutations of letters in the pliant bendings and interweavings of HCE in his agitation, in all his 'wakefulness'.

* * *

Beckett, describing the writing of *Finnegans Wake*, comments: 'This writing that you find so obscure is a quintessential extraction of language and painting and gesture, with all the inevitable clarity of the old inarticulation. Here is the savage economy of hieroglyphics.'[92] The explicit reference is to Vico's theory of the development of language, but other references are also present in such a description of Joyce's writing and, as an appendix to this section, it is worth briefly mentioning two of them, – Fenollosa and, particularly, Marcel Jousse.

'In the beginning was the gest he jousstly says [...]' (*FW* 468.05). Thus is Jousse mentioned in *Finnegans Wake* in connection with the theme of his teaching, which held the interest of Joyce and which could be connected with similar ideas, mentioned by Beckett, to be found in Vico. Joyce's interest is documented by his friends and it is known that he attended at least one lecture by Jousse. The fullest account is Mary Colum's: 'At that time the Abbé Jousse was lecturing in Paris. He was a noted propounder of a theory that Joyce gave adherence to, that language had its origin in gesture – "In the beginning was the rhythmic gesture", Joyce often said [...] If the Abbé's lecture did not interest me as much as it interested Joyce, still, it interested me a great deal, and that largely because of its original method of presentation. Around the lecturer was a group of girls, who addressed him as "Rabbi Jesus". The words spoken – one of the parables, I think – were, I gathered, in Aramaic, and what was shown was that the word was shaped by the gesture. Joyce was full of the subject [...].'[93]

For Jousse gesture was the foundation of language, the very basis of the possibility of any human communication, and the instance of gesture can be traced in the development of language. Like Vico, Jousse postulates three stages in this development which he calls *style manuel, style oral* and *style écrit*; the first is that of living gesticulation, language as depiction, the second is that of utterance miming gesture, shaped and supported by its direct reality, the third is that of alphabetism in which utterance is recorded in the medium of a language of conventional signs. This last stage is the moment of a possible loss of the reality of gesture which needs to be permanently reactivated under the envelope of language. Hence Jousse's plea for a new, active form of reading in his *Mimisme humain et psychologie de la lecture*. Something of this reactivation can be glimpsed in the description given by Colum of the form of the lecture attended by Joyce. This lecture was a demonstration of what was called 'L'Ecole de Rabbi Iéshoua', which was an attempt to recreate the gestual reality of the teaching of the word of Jesus, to refind what one of Jousse's collaborators called 'living and intact, under the Greek envelope, the living word of Rabbi Iéshoua'.[94]

In insisting on the primacy of gesture, Jousse, like Vico, insists at the same time on the primacy of 'hieroglyphic' (Vico) or 'mimographic' (Jousse) writing as directly related to the depiction of gesticulation.[95] Hence Beckett's 'inevitable clarity of the old inarticulation [. . .] the savage economy of hieroglyphics'. The loss of this clarity in alphabetic writing, and increasingly in speech, can be resolved only by an attempt to refind the basic gestuality (what Stephen calls in *Ulysses* the 'structural rhythm', (*U* 427/432)): this history is given for Jousse, as, again, for Vico, in etymology, in the return back through words to origins in gesture ('I believe that once we feel the necessity to understand better our own language we will be obliged to go back to graeco-latin sources, to the original words, to the ever concrete indo-european roots and, consequently, to the underlying mimic gestures, identical to ours').[96] The reference to Fenollosa plays its part here, in so far as 'The Chinese Written Character as a Medium for Poetry' re-emphasized for Joyce (who knew of it through his relationship with Pound) the connection between gesture, writing and poetry ('Poetry is the foundation of writing. When language consisted of gesture, the spoken and the written were identical', wrote Beckett, outlining the importance of Vico's ideas for Joyce)[97] and provided a conception of language not as realm of being and fixed identity but as process and action (rejoining Jousse's idea of language as gesture): 'for if we look at it verbally perhaps there is no true noun in active nature where every bally being – please read this mufto – is becoming in its owntown eyeballs' (*FW* 523.10–12).[98]

This brief summary has not been intended as a discussion of the work of Jousse or Fenollosa on its own terms but simply as an indication of those themes that were of interest to Joyce and that appear explicitly, as citations, in his writing.[99] Certain elements of criticism may already have been suggested by the conjunction of this summary with the preceding discussion of Joyce's writing and, in connection with the relation of these themes to that writing, the following points may be stressed. The emphasis on gesture (which opens a possible perspective against the valorization of the voice and the presence of the speaking subject, the 'logocentrism' described by Derrida) serves to think language as productivity, as production of sense and its subject, and to put in question thereby the repression of language as instrument of expression and fixed identity. Gesture, production of traces, returns language to writing as inscription of traces, institution of *différance* that gives the horizon of all expression and identity. This return is the activity of Joyce's writing, a constant theatralization of language in its productivity. Such a theatralization, contrary to the example of Jousse, is not the search for the full presence of an original living word (its practice of etymology will thus be quite different from the historical etymology of Jousse), but the development of a writing that crosses language (languages), ceaselessly pushing the *signified* back into the *signifier* in order to refind at every moment the drama of language, its production.

X   The wake: 'scribenery'

The impetus of the writing of *Finnegans Wake* is, then, the theatralization of language: the space of the text is defined as a 'scribenery' (*FW* 229.07) on which language is drawn out of the world of communication and questioned in its production; the text is the scene on which 'a vast company of actorwords'[100] agitate in a perpetual confrontation, made and remade in a 'MUTUOMORPHOMUTATION' (*FW* 281.09–10), collided together, split, fused, fragmented in the drama of the writing. The writing illimits language, breaking the accepted categories of communication in the way that was suggested earlier with regard to the categories of rhetoric; a semantic description of the kind based on the distinction 'statement' – 'presupposition' – 'implication' – 'entailment' is deprived of all possible validity by *Finnegans Wake*, which gives no context on which it could be supported. This illimitation is held in the production of an anti-language, a negation of language: 'this is nat language at any sinse of the world' (*FW* 83.12). In a sense, *Finnegans Wake* is to linguistics as Saussure's *Anagrammes* are to the *Cours de linguistique générale*, a radical contestation of the knowledge of his language constructed by the subject.[101] What Saussure is led to describe as the 'compromise' of language ('language is a compromise – the last compromise – that the mind accepts with certain symbols; otherwise there would be no language')[102] is ever threatened by the wavering of identity[103] and by the productivity of the signifier breaking the line of communication and opening onto a multiplicity beyond the mastery of the subject dependent on the compromise of context, identity and non-contradiction. *Finnegans Wake* is, as it were, the elaboration of that threat into a practice of writing; its negation is the breaking of the compromise and the accession to language as productivity; its anti-language is not an absence of language but a dramatic presence of language, *mis en scène* on that 'scribenery'.

As examples of the development of this theatralization, two effects of the writing will be considered here.

The first may be referred to as that of the 'optical listen'. Consider the phrase 'for inkstands' (*FW* 173.34). It is often said that *Finnegans Wake* is a book to be heard rather than read: nothing could be more false. Leaving aside the evident objection that no reading aloud could possibly reproduce the graphic distribution of the text (that, for example, of the 'Night Studies' section) or the play of letters, there is no reading aloud that can pass 'for inkstands' and 'for instance' together: the reading must choose; in other words, it creates a context. Similarly, however, the reading of the text on the page must integrate the vocalization of 'for instance' into 'for inkstands' in order to grasp the transformation of the former into the latter. Again, in 'greet scoot, duckings and thuggery' (*FW* 177.35) there is no possibility of a reading aloud that will pass 'scoot, duckings and thuggery' and 'Scott, Dickens and Thackeray', but, equally, the reading on the page is obliged to hold in balance the facts of vocalization. (It may be noted here how Joyce's writing can use the constraints of context in order to shatter them. 'Greet scoot' refers, in the context provided by the fixed syntagm 'Great Scot!', to the word 'Scot' but in order to make of it the basis of a quite different syntagm, 'Scott, Dickens and Thackeray', which is itself lost in the uncertain irony of 'greet scoot, duckings and thuggery'. In the wavering of this back-and-forward movement the context falls derisively apart.)[104]

This effect is what is called in *Finnegans Wake* the development of a 'soundscript' (*FW* 219.17); 'What can't be coded can be decorded if an ear aye sieze what no eye ere grieved for' (*FW* 482.35–6).[105] This 'soundscript' is not the reproduction of speech, but the ceaseless confrontation of writing and speech in which reference is involved in a tourniquet between the two, thus defining yet another strategy of hesitation. The written and the spoken are squashed together but in that very moment a distance opens between them and the reading hovers in an 'optical listen', between the one and the other, in a plurality outside any context.

The second effect is that of an 'undoing' of negation that works through the fusion of contradictories: 'every word will be bound over to carry three score and ten toptypsical readings throughout the book of Doublends Jined [. . .] till Daleth, mahomahouma, who oped it closeth thereof the. Dor.' (*FW* 20.14–18). 'Daleth' and 'Dor' provide examples in the very moment of the description of this procedure. 'Dor' fuses the order to sleep (dors) and the opening into the new cycle (door), thus reiterating the fusion in 'wake', itself a crucial instance of this procedure. 'Daleth' fuses death and multiplicity in a play of letters ('death' and Breton 'aleih', in abundance) in a way that recalls (or rather, proleptically sustains) Broch's comment on death and infinity as being the children of a single mother.[106] The following examples, taken more or less at random from the text, will help to indicate the extent and importance of this procedure in Joyce's writing (note that in these examples only the elements that participate in the fusion of oppositions are taken into consideration, the remaining multiple references not being specifically mentioned):

1. 'Sanglorians' (*FW* 4.07): Sans glory (without glory)/ Sang glory (with blood and glory)
2. 'Stay us wherefore in our search for tighteousness, O Sustainer' (*FW* 5.18–19): Support us, be our stay/ hinder us, stop us, stay us
3. 'there's leps of flam in Funnycoon's Wick' (*FW* 499.13) (= transforming citation of 'You'll have loss of fame from Wimmegame's fake' (*FW* 375.16–17)): loss of/ lots of
4. 'for the loathe of Marses' (*FW* 518.02): hate (loathe)/ love ('love of Moses!')
5. 'melovelance' (*FW* 350.13): my lance of love/ malevolence (also loveless and Lovelace, malevolent seducer of Clarissa Harlowe)
6. 'life wends' (*FW* 595.02): life goes on (wends)/ life ends
7. 'alpsulumply wroght!' (*FW* 595.19): right/ wrong
8. 'his heavenlaid twin' (*FW* 177.21): heavenly/ugly (laid) (also, of course, born–laid in heaven)
9. 'andthisishis' (*FW* 177.33): antithesis (his other)/ and-this-is-his (his same)

(Note that this effect is also produced by various other procedures; thus, for instance, the constant conjunction of mutually exclusive terms in a kind of specular parallelism: 'a few *strong* verbs *weak* oach eather' (*FW* 16.8–9); 'the *west borders* of the *east midlands*' (*FW* 474.18);'*light* and *ruft*handling' (*FW* 384.26); 'neither *bigugly* nor *smallnice*' (*FW* 384.25); 'to *post* figure out a statuesquo *ante*' (*FW* 181.34); etc.)

The force of this procedure is the hesitation of the principle of non-contradiction (not A and not-A). The law of negation, the very foundation of judgement, is constantly transgressed, broken, displaced, by a writing that suggests an other logic. The importance of the reference to the dreamwork for Joyce can be easily understood here, in so far as Freud was led to describe that work precisely in terms of an absence of any principle of negation, of a disregard for the wideawake categories of the judging subject. Indeed, Freud, in the paper 'Über den Gegensinn der Urworte' of 1911, appealed to the etymological hypotheses of Karl Abel to complement this description, hoping to find therein evidence of a primitive fusion of oppositions in language.[107] In Joyce's writing this effect of the bafflement of negation is a further part of the illimitation of language; against the compromise on which are constructed the subject and its judgement, the writing opens a constant experience of the negativity of language ('language functions as a negativity, the initial limit of the possible'),[108] experience of limits in which the subject is displaced and dispersed. The text is precisely 'that letter selfpenned to one's other' (*FW* 489.33–4).

'My hypotheses' wrote Nietzsche, and then set down as his first, 'The subject as multiplicity'.[109] It is the very hypothesis of the writing of *Finnegans Wake* in its dispersion of the subject. The Cartesian subject is a fraud ('cog it out, here goes a sum' (*FW* 304.31),[110] a shem, caught up in that interfolding of forms which leaves no return on the self but in that (mis) appropriation of the other. The Cartesian source, via the transformation of a line from Pope's 'Essay on Criticism', becomes an impenetrable darkness, 'Sink deep or touch not the Cartesian spring!' (*FW* 301.24–5). The action of Shem and Shaun ('himother' (*FW* 187.24)) is the action of this splintering of identity in the play of same and other, repetition and difference, and it is this splintering that is undertaken as the action of the writing in its strategies of hesitation, its attention to language as process in which identity and subject are produced. The two effects of the writing which have been described in this section serve towards that theatralization of language, towards the narration of the 'incompréhensible récit', the 'knowing' of that 'erste Akt' of the engendering of meaning and its world.

XI   Translation

Like Brisset in the 'Avertissement' to *La Science de Dieu*, Joyce might have prefaced *Finnegans Wake* with the remark that 'the present work cannot be entirely translated', suppressing indeed the 'entirely'. The status of non-translatability defines the totality of Joyce's text, which is already itself a multitude of translations. Crossing an immense number of languages (where Brisset worked in French alone) in order to open up the narrative of language, Joyce's writing baffles the establishment of the single equivalences between one language and another operated by translation. To translate is to establish the meaning, to isolate the signified in order to pass it through the alternative signifier of another language. Nothing is more monological than translation in its dependence on the compromise of the sign. The writing of *Finnegans Wake* is a writing against this logic in its attention to the work of the signifier. In the course of a short article, Jean Paris refers to some twenty-five languages for the reading of the single word 'venissoon' (*FW* 3.10).[111] At what point of such a reading is the operation of translation to be introduced? The only imaginable translation of *Finnegans Wake* is the development of another writing in progress, extending and disseminating Joyce's writing according to those relations of irony and parody, fragmentation and transformation, described above in connection with the passage from text to text in Joyce's work. Such a 'translation' would constitute in its relation to Joyce's text precisely an *ambiviolence*.

XII   Origin

The attempt to discover an origin common to all languages entails the reduction of the diversity of languages to a single common ground retraceable in its transformations in the babel of tongues. The writing of *Finnegans Wake* goes against this notion of origin. Running through languages, Joyce's writing poses no point of rest, no point of homogenization; it lacks what Koyré calls 'the superstition of "origins" '. Joyce's etymology is indicative in this respect: where that of a Jousse is a remounting from stage to stage, the unfolding of successive layers to reach the 'living core' of meaning, that of Joyce is an anti-etymology, the abrasive extension of words which reveals not a history but a network of fictions, the terms of which are themselves caught up in this extension, producing new fictions, and so on and on in a perpetual interfolding ('There are sordidly tales within tales, you clearly understand that?' (*FW* 522.05)). The horizon of *Finnegans Wake* is not an 'origin' but the 'world writing its own wrunes for ever', not the 'living word' but the signifier, not the Letter but the play of letters. The appeal to origin turns not into a 'prefall paradise peace but onto the void that edges the horizon of sense ('In the buginning is the woid [. . .]' (*FW* 378.29)), onto the 'ginnandgo gap' which is the loss of the Letter, onto the ceaseless displacement of the subject 'from the night we are and feel and fade with to the yesterselves we tread to turnupon' (*FW* 473.10–11). It is on this horizon that Joyce's writing attempts to work in its practice of the theatralization of language; against the mastery of the full origin, it proposes the entry into the signifier, turning all discovery of 'origin' into the development in the text ('polyhedron of scripture') of the narration, ever to be recommenced, of that 'incompréhensible récit'.

Coda

'The end? Say it with missiles then and thus arabesque the page' (*FW* 115.02–03). There is no conclusion to be reached in a reading of Joyce's text other than an ambiviolent extension of the text in a new practice of writing, arabesquing the page. Such an extension is beyond the scope of the present simple introduction to Joyce's writing and as 'conclusion' here may be simply copied a brief and little-known text by Joyce which figures among the epiphanies. It may be read as a coda to this discussion, resuming as it does, in the account of a dream, in relation to origin and language and subject, the clouding of the 'Cartesian spring':

A white mist is falling in slow flakes. The path leads me down to an obscure pool. Something is moving in the pool; it is an arctic beast with a rough yellow coat. I thrust in my stick and as he rises out of the water I see that his back slopes towards the croup and that he is very sluggish. I am not afraid but, thrusting at him often with my stick drive him before me. He moves his paws heavily and mutters words of some language which I do not understand.[112]

(Translated by Isabelle Mahieu)

Notes

1. Julia Kristeva, *Semeiotiké: recherches pour une sémanalyse* (Paris: Seuil, 1969), p. 181.
2. Lautréamont's 'plus tard', in a passage where he promises the reader revelation 'at the end of your life' and 'even perhaps at the end of this stanza' but certainly for 'later'; Lautréamont, *Oeuvres complètes*, ed. Maurice Saillet (Paris: Livre de poche, 1963), pp. 268–9.
3. Joyce, letter to Harriet Shaw Weaver, 20 July 1919; *Letters*, I, 129.
4. Samuel Beckett, 'Dante . . . Bruno. Vico . . Joyce', in *Our Exagmination Round his Factification for Incamination of Work in Progress* (Paris: Shakespeare and Co., 1929), p. 13.
5. Cf. Roland Barthes, *L'Empire des signes* (Geneva: Skira, 1970), p. 11.
6. Ezra Pound, letter to Joyce, 10 June 1919; *Pound/Joyce*, ed. Forrest Read (London: Faber & Faber, 1968), p. 157.
7. Beckett, 'Home Olga'; cit. Richard Ellmann, *James Joyce* (New York: Oxford University Press, 1959), p. 714.
8. Flaubert, letter to Louise Colet, 27 March 1852; *Correspondance*, deuxième série (Paris: Conard, 1926), p. 379.
9. Svevo records his surprise at discovering on a visit to Paris at the time of the writing of *Finnegans Wake* that 'L'*Ulisse* per Joyce non esiste più'; 'James Joyce', in Italo Svevo, *Saggi e pagine sparse* (Verona: Mondadori, 1954), p. 231.
10. It might be noted here that Vico, a key reference for Joyce's writing, argues in the third section of the *Scienza Nuova* ('Della discoverta de vero Omero') against the assumption of Homer as individual genius. Homer is to be seen rather as a poetical 'character' open to the totality of forms of his culture, which find supreme articulation in 'his' poems. Writer of the modern *Odyssey*, Joyce is likewise a 'character' in this sense, a disposition of forms.
11. C. G. Jung, '*Ulysses*. Ein Monolog', *Wirklichkeit der Seele* (Zurich: Rascher, 1934), p. 150. The reception of *Ulysses* as negation was very general: cf., for example, G. B. Shaw, 'In Ireland they try to make a cat cleanly by rubbing its nose in its own filth. Mr Joyce has tried the same treatment on the human subject', letter to Sylvia Beach, 10 October 1921; *Letters*, III, 50; E. M. Forster, 'It is a dogged attempt to cover the universe with mud, an inverted Victorianism, an attempt to make crossness and dirt succeed where sweetness and light failed, a simplification of the human character in the interests of Hell', *Aspects of the Novel* (London: E. Arnold, 1927), p. 158.
12. Jung, '*Ulysses*. Ein Monolog', p. 148.
13. 'But by writing thithaways end to end and turning, turning and end to end hithaways writing and with lines of litters slittering up and louds of latters slettering down, the old semetomyplace and jupetbackagain from tham Let Rise till Hum Lit. Sleep, where in the waste is the wisdom?' (*FW* 114.16–20).
14. T. S. Eliot, '*Ulysses*, Order and Myth' (1923), in *James Joyce: Two Decades of Criticism*, ed. Seon Givens (New York: Vanguard Press, 1948), p. 201.
15. Joyce, letter to Grant Richards, 5 May 1906; *Letters*, II, 134; letter to Constantine P. Curran, undated (1904?); *Letters*, I, 55.

16. Cf. epiphanies nos. I, II, III, IV, V, VI, VIII, IX, XI, XIII, XVIII, XXI, *Epiphanies*, ed. O. A. Silverman (Buffalo: Buffalo University Press, 1956). Reference might also be made in connection with this procedure to Swift's *A Complete Collection of Genteel and Ingenious Conversation* and, above all, to Flaubert's compilation of the *Dictionnaire des idées reçues*.

17. As is well known, *Stephen Hero* contains a longish discussion of the epiphany between Stephen and Cranly, in which it is given certain aesthetic justifications (held within the play of a perpetually vacillating irony). What is in question in the present discussion is the procedure of the epiphany as demonstrated in Joyce's recording–writing of epiphanies.

18. Remember also in this context the dizzying assemblage of fragments into a kind of staccato narrative of disrupting triviality in the 'Eumaeus' section of *Scribbledehobble*: 'chaff: stayed to tea and later proposed marriage; lady's affections went astray: under rather a cloud: wicked untruth: met a man, had a drop of port wine and remembered no more: inspired statement: ugly wound: angry boil: denied all knowledge of the matter', etc.; *Scribbledehobble: The Ur-Workbook for Finnegans Wake*, ed. T. E. Connolly (Chicago: Northwestern University Press, 1961), p. 150.

19. Joyce, letter to Grant Richards, 5 May 1906; *Letters*, II, 134.

20. 'Ivy Day in the Committee Room' was the piece in *Dubliners* that gave Joyce most satisfaction; cf. letter to Grant Richards, 20 May 1906; *Letters*, I, 62. It may be noted that Joyce proposed copying as the way to evaluate a work of art: 'the way to test a work of art is to copy out a page of it'; cit. R. Ellmann, *James Joyce*, p. 622. The valid work will be that which can support this reinscription, which *can* be copied without provoking the nausea of stereotype and repetition.

21. Stuart Gilbert, *James Joyce's Ulysses* (London: Faber & Faber, 1952), p. 92.

22. Pound, 'Past History' (1933), *Pound/Joyce*, p. 248.

23. Pound, 'Joyce' (1920), *ibid.*, p. 139 (cf. pp. 194, 200f., 250).

24. Flaubert, letter to Louis Bouillet, *Correspondance*, deuxième série, 4 September 1850, p. 238.

25. *Ibid.*, p. 239.

26. *P* 337; cf. Flaubert, *Correspondance*, troisième série (Paris: Conard, 1927), pp. 61–2.

27. Hermann Broch, letter to Dr Daniel Brody, 19 October 1934; *Briefe von 1929 bis 1951* (Zurich: Rhein-Verlag, 1957), p. 102.

28. Joyce, letter to Carlo Linati, 21 September 1920; *Letters*, I, 146–7.

29. Jung, '*Ulysses*. Ein Monolog', p. 157.

30. F. Nietzsche, *Der Wille zur Macht, Gesammelte Werke*, vol. 19 (Munich, 1926), p. 24.

31. Joyce, letter to George Antheil, 3 January 1931; *Letters*, I, 297.

32. Cf. *The Complete Works of Lewis Carroll* (London: Nonesuch, 1939), p. 257.

33. Frank Budgen, *James Joyce and the Making of 'Ulysses'* (London: Grayson, 1934), p. 176.

34. Joyce, letter to Harriet Shaw Weaver, 4 March 1931; *Letters*, I, 302.

35. Julia Kristeva, 'Comment parler à la littérature', *Tel Quel* 47 (Autumn, 1971), p. 40.

36. Philippe Sollers, *Logiques* (Paris: Seuil, 1968), p. 110. Dublin for Joyce is exactly a heterogeneity (as witness the 'Wandering Rocks' section of *Ulysses* or the organization of the pieces in *Dubliners*). Mention is often made of Joyce's letters to his Aunt Josephine requesting the verification of details relating to Dublin life – as, for example, the famous query as to whether or not it would be 'possible for an ordinary person to climb over the area railings of no 7 Eccles

street', letter to Mrs William Murray, 2 November 1921; *Letters*, I, 175. These requests – many of which, it should be noted, are for details directly relating to forms of discourse (e.g. 'please send me a bundle of other novelettes and any penny hymnbook you can find', letter to Mrs William Murray, 5 January 1920; *Letters*, I, 135) – do not identify *Ulysses* as a prime example of realist writing. What Joyce demands, in connection with the 'Totalitätsanspruch', is the maximum number of reports on 16 June 1904 in order to provide for one level of the totality of his text. Dublin, which is ceaselessly a question of identity, 'Dyoublong?' (*FW* 13.04), is at the same time 'Echoland!' (*FW* 13.05), network of fictions, of resonances in which the subject is 'listened'.

37. S. M. Eisenstein, 'Le mal voltairien', *Cahiers du cinéma* 226–7 (January–February 1971), p. 55.
38. Even a technically advanced, modern attempt to establish a general rhetoric finds Joyce's writing an indication of the limits of its endeavour and this precisely in terms of the shattering of the distinction 'degré zéro'/'degré figuré' and the impossibility of operating with the concept of isotopy; cf. Jean Dubois et al., *Rhétorique générale* (Paris: Larousse, 1970), p. 38.
39. *Scribbledehobble*, p. 139.
40. '*Nausikaa* is written in a namby-pamby jammy marmalady drawersy (alto là!) style with effects of incense, mariolatry, masturbation, stewed cockles, painter's palette, chit chat, circumlocution, etc., etc.', Joyce, letter to Frank Budgen, 3 January 1920; *Letters*, I, 135.
41. Described at length by Joyce in a letter to Frank Budgen, 13 March 1920; *Letters*, I, 138–9. It is significant though for what follows that neither Joyce in this letter nor Gilbert in *James Joyce's Ulysses* use the term 'parody' (Gilbert, in fact, argues for the term 'pastiche', p. 290).
42. Cf. *A First-Draft Version of Finnegans Wake*, ed. David Hayman (London: Faber & Faber, 1963), p. 6.
43. Lautréamont, *Oeuvres complètes*, p. 402.
44. 'Shem the Penman' alludes to 'Jim the Penman', nickname of a Victorian forger celebrated in a novel (by Dick Donovan) and a play (by Sir Charles Young), both entitled *Jim the Penman*.
45. Cf. Joyce, letter to Harriet Shaw Weaver, 7 June 1926; *Letters*, I, 241. Note that the references to forgery in *Finnegans Wake* are in no way limited to this incident. Thus, for example, in the passage quoted at the head of this piece, the word 'prouts', as well as being the anagram of the name of Proust (and many other things), refers to 'Father Prout', the *nom de plume* of F. S. Mahony, the nineteenth-century essayist (and one time master at Belvedere College) who forged Latin and Greek 'originals' for poems by his contemporaries.
46. Joyce, letter to Stanislaus Joyce, 18 October 1906; *Letters*, II, 182.
47. This example was suggested by Clive Hart, *Structure and Motif in Finnegans Wake* (London: Faber & Faber, 1962), pp. 42–3. Hart speaks exactly of 'a kind of infinite regress of self-parody in Joyce's texts' (p. 43).
48. 'La Spirale', *Carnets et projets, Oeuvres de Gustave Flaubert*, vol. 18 (Lausanne: Editions Rencontre, 1965), pp. 34–7.
49. Ibid., p. 36.
50. 'Dante . . . Bruno. Vico . . Joyce', p. 22.
51. Vico's spiral contains a conception of progress. 'His cycle, in truth, is more aptly described as a spiral, for though each cycle is repeated in the next cycle, it is repeated on a higher level'; Bruce Mazlish, *The Riddle of History* (New York: Harper and Row, 1966), p. 41. Gilbert writes that 'after each epoch of dissolution and reconstruction, a fragment of the advance gained by each spent

wave is conserved, for there is a slowly rising tide in human history' and adds
as a footnote 'I doubt if the author of *Ulysses* endorsed Vico's optimistic belief
in "progress" '; *James Joyce's Ulysses*, p. 50. Following the sense of this,
Umberto Eco states that Joyce equates Vico's theory with the 'oriental theme
of the circular character of everything [. . .] The "development" aspect is
sacrificed to circular identity, to the continual repetition of original archetypes';
L'Oeuvre ouverte (Paris: Seuil, 1965). p. 262. The debate, perhaps, needs simply
to be disrupted with Joyce's 'It's a wheel, I tell the world. *And* it's all *square*';
letter to Harriet Shaw Weaver, 16 April 1927; *Letters*, I, 251. Note also that no
more than Joyce's does Vico's movement imply the culmination of a synthesis
– *verum* is realized only *partially* in different ages – and that it too is the
manifestation of a logic, what Eco calls 'original archetypes'. More importantly,
as will be stressed below, the attention of Joyce's writing is on the side of the
signifier, the reading of a totality of historical forms through which the writing
passes and only within the movement of which, in the play of difference and
repetition, can any 'origin' be conceived.

52. G. Vico, *Principi di Scienza Nuova* (1744), *Opere*, vol. 1 (Verona: Mondadori, 1957), p. 546.
53. 'James Clarence Mangan' (1902), *The Critical Writings of James Joyce*, ed. Ellsworth Mason and Richard Ellmann (London: Faber & Faber, 1959), p. 81.
54. '*Ulysses*, Order and Myth', p. 201.
55. 'Paris Letter' (1922), *Pound/Joyce*, p. 197. In 1933 Pound wrote that 'The parallels with the *Odyssey* are mere mechanics . . .'; 'Past History', *ibid.*, p. 250.
56. 'James Joyce', p. 217.
57. Padraic and Mary Colum, *Our Friend James Joyce* (New York: Doubleday, 1958), p. 123.
58. 'Dante . . . Bruno. Vico . . Joyce', p. 7.
59. Cf. Julia Kristeva, 'A propos de l'idéologie scientifique', *Promesse* 27 (Winter, 1969), p. 58 ('the text is "mythical" in the sense of pulverizing myths: Joyce with *Ulysses* . . .')
60. This multiplicity is already present in *Ulysses* where Ulysses and Finn MacCool move side by side.
61. Broch, letter to Friedrich Torberg, 10 April 1943; *Briefe*, p. 185.
62. Broch, 'James Joyce und die Gegenwart', *Dichten und Erkennen* (Zurich: Rhein-Verlag, 1955), p. 209.
63. Claude Lévi-Strauss, *L'Origine des manières de table* (Paris: Plon, 1968), p. 105.
64. *Ibid.*, p. 106.
65. *Ibid.*, p. 388.
66. Louis Gillet, *Stèle pour James Joyce* (Paris: Sagittaire, 1941), p. 74.
67. Stanislaus Joyce, letter to Joyce, 7 August 1924; *Letters*, III, 102.
68. Hart, *Structure and Motif in Finnegans Wake*, p. 71.
69. S. Mallarmé, *Oeuvres complètes* (Paris: Gallimard, 1965), p. 851.
70. Joyce to Edmond Jaloux, cit. R. Ellmann, *James Joyce*, p. 559.
71. Broch, 'Die mythische Erbschaft der Dichtung', *Dichten und Erkennen*, pp. 243–4.
72. Michel Foucault, *Raymond Roussel* (Paris: Gallimard, 1963), p. 54.
73. Philippe Sollers, *Nombres* (Paris: Seuil, 1968), p. 15.
74. 'What the language will look like when I have finished I don't know. But having declared war I shall go on *jusqu'au bout*'; Joyce, letter to Harriet Shaw Weaver, 11 November 1925; *Letters*, I, 237.
75. 'I have put the language to sleep'; Joyce to Samuel Beckett; cit. R. Ellmann, *James Joyce*, p. 559.

76. Joyce, letter to Harriet Shaw Weaver, 24 November 1926; *Letters*, III, 146. In 1905 Joyce wrote to his brother, 'Would you be surprised if I wrote a very good English grammar some day?'; letter to Stanislaus Joyce, 15 March 1905; *Letters*, II, 86. Would there have been cause for surprise? One might remember Mallarmé and the *Mots anglais* . . .

77. Joyce to Max Eastman, cit. R. Ellmann, *James Joyce*, p. 559.

78. Philippe Sollers, *Logiques*, p. 240.

79. 'Dante . . . Bruno. Vico . . Joyce', p. 22.

80. G. Hegel, 'Philosophie des Geistes' (1803/4), *Sämtliche Werke*, ed. G. Lasson, vol. 19. I (Leipzig, 1932), p. 211.

81. Nietzsche, *Der Wille zur Macht*, p. 34.

82. Cf. Roland Barthes, *Sade, Fourier, Loyola* (Paris: Seuil, 1971), pp. 10–11.

83. S. Freud, 'Der Dichter und das Phantasieren', *Gesammelte Werke*, vol. 7 (London: Imago, 1941), pp. 218–19.

84. Sollers, *Logiques*, p. 148.

85. Marcel Proust, 'Somnolences', *Bulletin de la Société des Amis de Marcel Proust* 15 (1965), 256–7.

86. Joyce, letter to Stanislaus Joyce, 28 February 1905; *Letters*, II, 84.

87. Jacques Derrida, 'Differance', in *Speech and Phenomena, and Other Essays on Husserl's Theory of Signs*, tr. David B. Allison (Evanston: Northwestern University Press, 1973), pp. 141–2.

88. This is so widespread as to render example more or less superfluous, but consider, for instance, as an indication of this process, Shem addressing 'those present (who meanwhile, with increasing lack of interest in his semantics, allowed various subconscious smickers to drivel slowly across their fichers), unconsciously explaining, for inkstands, [. . .] ' (*FW* 173.30–4). Even names are caught up in this transformation; thus Vercingétorix becomes 'versingrhetorish' (*FW* 346.19).

89. The resonances of this image of the sea and the movement of water could be traced in different ways, but bound up with the activity of writing, in Nietzsche (the final section of *Der Wille zur Macht*), Mallarmé (think of the fourth page of 'Un coup de dés' where the word 'hésite' is placed in the midst of the troubled ocean), Lautréamont (the 'strophe de l'océan'), Proust (water provides the greatest number of images in *A la recherche du temps perdu*) . . . For Joyce, one would need to look also at the account of Bloom's admiration for water and sea (*U* 592–3/671–2), as at a brief image such as Stephen's 'These heavy sands are language tide and wind have silted here' (*U* 50/44), which is very close to Saussure's image of the junction of sea and air developed in order to characterize language as play of articulations. It is not without interest either that Joyce's earliest surviving piece of writing begins with a description of the calm of the sea broken – *waked* – by the violence of a storm: 'the scene when the wild anger of the elements has waked again the discord of confusion'. 'Trust not appearances' (1896), *The Critical Writings of James Joyce*, p. 15.

90. 'With its twenty-four signs, this Literature exactly called Letters . . . ', Mallarmé, *Oeuvres complètes*, p. 850.

91. H. M. Robinson poses the question as demanding a 'real answer' and suggests the 'Hoc est enim corpus meum' of the Mass; 'Hardest Crux Ever', in *A James Joyce Miscellany*, ed. M. Magalaner (Carbondale: Southern Illinois University Press, 1959), pp. 195–208. This does not, in fact, give HCE but HEEC, but it is undoubtedly one of the multiplicity of references (and no more than that). HCE is already a more ('Ecce Homo. Crown of thorns and cross' (*U* 81/80)) or

less ('A hocuspocus of conflicting evidence' (*U* 564/643)) explicit signature in *Ulysses*.

92. 'Dante . . . Bruno. Vico . . Joyce', p. 15.
93. Colum, *Our Friend James Joyce*, pp. 130–1. Cf. M. Colum, *Life and the Dream* (London: Macmillan, 1947), p. 394, and R. Ellmann, *James Joyce*, p. 647. The date of this lecture is placed by Colum as early 1931 but the recorded dates for the 'Rabbi Iéshoua' demonstrations are 1928/9 (Théâtre des Champs-Elysées, Sorbonne) and then 1933–5 (Société de Géographie, Faculté de théologie protestante). It is not impossible that Colum has confused the date. The only public lecture I have been able to trace in early 1931 was on 'Méthodologie de la psychologie du geste', given in the first half of May (cf. *Revue des cours et des conférences*, 15 May 1931, pp. 201–18); this lecture seems to have borne no formal relation to the 'Rabbi Iéshoua' demonstrations.
94. Gabrielle Baron, *Marcel Jousse: introduction à sa vie et à son oeuvre* (Tournai: Casterman, 1965), p. 104.
95. Jousse influenced the thesis by Tchang Tcheng Ming, 'L'Ecriture chinoise et le geste humain' (Sorbonne, 1937).
96. Marcel Jousse, *Mimisme humain et psychologie de la lecture* (Paris: Librairie orientaliste Geuthner, 1935), p. 4.
97. 'Dante . . . Bruno. Vico . . Joyce', p. 11.
98. 'a true noun does not exist in nature (Fenollosa) any pronouns?: phonetic theory is unsound', *Scribbledehobble*, p. 96.
99. Apart from works already mentioned, reference was also made for the writing of this summary to the following (all of which could have been available to Joyce at the time of the writing of *Finnegans Wake*): M. Jousse, *Etudes de psychologie linguistique: le style oral et rythmique chez les verbo-moteurs* (Paris: Beauchesne, 1925); 'Les lois psycho-physiologiques du style oral vivant et leur utilisation philologique', *L'Ethnographie*, Bulletin semestriel, 15 April 1931; 'Le mimisme humain et l'anthropologie du langage', *Revue anthropologique* (July–September 1936), 201–15; Abbé R. Jacquin, *Notions sur le langage d'après les travaux du P. Marcel Jousse* (Paris, 1929). It is interesting to note that the first of these works is placed explicitly within the domain of a semiology (Saussure's *Cours* providing the motto at the opening of the book) and it is possible that Joyce employs the word 'semiological' (*FW* 465.12) with Jousse in mind – the word occurs only a few pages before the main reference to Jousse (*FW* 468.05). It is also interesting to note that the argument of this work is conducted almost entirely through a juxtaposition of quotations from a multitude of sources, the 'thesis' being developed in the resulting mosaic – a process not without some resemblance to Joyce's 'assemblage'. It also needs remembering, however, that Joyce's *writing* is, finally, quite distinct from Jousse's return to the *living word*. Jousse comments at the close of *Mimisme humain et psychologie de la lecture*: 'Contrairement à ce qu'affirmait Mallarmé, le monde n'existe pas pour aboutir à un livre, mais pour se transformer par le livre ou mieux sans le livre, en une pensée vivante et créatrice' (p.18). For Joyce's writing there is no break between world and book, for the world is always already writing ('is, was and will be writing its own wrunes for ever'); words and things move together in the ceaseless production of 'the world'.
100. Victor Llona, 'I don't know what to call it but it's mighty unlike prose', in *Our Exagmination Round his Factification for Work in Progress*, p. 95.
101. Cf. Julia Kristeva, 'Du sujet en linguistique', *Langages* 24 (December 1971), 115.

102. F. de Saussure, *Les Sources manuscrites du Cours de linguistique générale* (Geneva: Droz, 1957), p. 45.

103. 'Any symbol, once it is launched into circulation — and no symbol exists other than *because it is* launched into circulation — is at that very moment totally incapable of saying in what its identity will consist in the following moment'; Saussure, cit. Jean Starobinski, *Les Mots sous les mots* (Paris: Gallimard, 1971), p. 16.

104. Note also in connection with this example the operation of what is a constant derision of the name in Joyce's writing, and a prime focus of which is Joyce's own name, endlessly permutated in the text but never fixed as 'Joyce', the name of the subject remaining irretrievable in its identity in the practice of the writing.

105. Cf. 'For instance Shaun, after a long absurd and rather incestuous Lenten lecture to Izzy, his sister, takes leave of her "with half a glance of Irish frisky from under the shag of his aparallel brows"'. These are the words the reader will see but not those he will hear'; Joyce, letter to Harriet Shaw Weaver, 27 June 1924; *Letters*, I, 216. 'It is not to be read — or rather it is not only to be read. It is to be looked at and listened to'; Beckett, 'Dante . . . Bruno. Vico . . Joyce', p. 14.

106. Should this appear improbable (but according to what criteria of probability is Joyce's text then being read?), it may be worth remembering that 'aleih' is, or was, used in Breton to mean 'wide open' in the phrase 'to open wide a door'. This meaning is held in the fusion of the oppositions into 'Daleth' with its reference to Hebrew, and is taken up again immediately in the appearance of 'Dor', through which it relates to the whole complex of meanings centred on the term 'wake'.

107. S. Freud, 'Uber den Gegensinn der Urworte', *Gesammelte Werke*, vol. 8, pp. 214–21. The contrast with Hegel might be made again here in connection with Hegel's use of words fusing contradictories and on the basis of A. Koyré, 'Note sur la langue et la terminologie hégéliennes', *Revue philosophique*, 112 (1931), 409–39. Hegel values German for its possession of a number of words uniting opposite meanings, a fact which demonstrates for him 'ein speculativer Geist der Sprache' (cit. Koyré, p. 422n). The term 'aufheben' gives at once the classic example of this in its union of the ideas of both suppression and preservation and, in its reference to the Hegelian dialectic, the point of divergence between the use of oppositions in Hegel and their use in Joyce's writing. Joyce's writing resists the movement of Hegelian idealism and the sublimation of oppositions; its force is the 'inhabiting' of oppositions that opens not onto a sublimation but, demonstrating limits, onto, as it were, an *excess* that is the unmasterable foundation of the movement of oppositions, their 'wake'. It is a question here not of the fusion of a new identity but of an illimitation, of a reference to multiplicity. For a theoretical treatment of this reference, see Gilles Deleuze, *Différence et répétition* (Paris: P.U.F., 1968).

108. Roland Barthes, *Le Degré zéro de l'écriture* (Paris: Seuil, 1953), p. 23.

109. Nietzsche, *Der Wille zur Macht*, p. 17.

110. Remember that 'to cog' is to 'cheat', 'deceive', 'employ fraud'. The *O.E.D.* gives a late nineteenth-century example (near to Joyce, b. 1882) of the verb as meaning to 'crib', i.e. to copy fraudulently, to *plagiarize*.

111. Jean Paris, 'Finnegan, Wake!', *Tel Quel* 30 (Summer, 1967), 61.

112. Joyce, *Epiphanies*, p. 7 (no. VII).

4   riverrun

JACQUES AUBERT

This essay proposes, for the further purposes it may serve, a reading of the opening lines of *Finnegans Wake*, or, to be more precise, of the opening word.[1] Needless to say, such an enterprise immediately comes up against an observation which we must always remember to underline: *Finnegans Wake* is unreadable − and André du Bouchet deserves credit for singling out just this as its distinctive characteristic.[2] Yet, in our view, this unreadability is not associated with a blunt refusal, with the suspended activity represented by an abandoned reading (as he maintains), but rather with an initial state of suspense. From the very first word *Finnegans Wake* sets out to be impenetrable:

riverrun

for this word is not to be found in any dictionary. And we cannot even obtain a purchase on it, for something else is missing, something which ought to precede it: either the subject if this is a verb, or the article if a noun. Or, on the other hand, if no preceding element is in fact lacking, then a capital letter has been omitted, that is, a form of differentiation within the word itself, and it is perhaps doubly lacking if 'riverrun' happens to be a proper noun. One could, of course, object that the word is almost readable: 'river' followed by 'run'; but we are denied an analytical reading of precisely this sort: the 'almost' remains rigorously irreducible. And it is also to be noted that 'riverrun' is unhearable (or is all but so, and we shall come back to this): it does not correspond to any vocable which the ear can honestly claim to recognize. We could of course construe it as: 'River, run!'. But in this case a pause, a silence, is missing which would confer a sense on the words, and also, by virtue of this, on what would become a sentence − and it is ironic to note that it is to a silence, but an absent silence, that we would owe this threefold sense.

So, our first conclusion is: if 'riverrun' remains unreadable, it is because it remains *undifferentiated*. Reading is obstructed by lack of difference. And, curiously, this difference would consist of: either a + (the article, or the subject, or the mark which would transform 'r' into 'R'), or a − (a silence), or indeed a + ('R') followed by a − (the separation of 'river' and 'run') followed by a + (a comma). In short, in order to read 'riverrun', to wrest it from the undifferentiated, we need to bring differences in potential into operation. What we have just seen is merely the beginning of *more than one possible series*; we still must establish the motion of the system, only one static element of which we know at present, we must work out the gearing, the axes and so on, of a wheel only a few of whose cogs we can now distinguish. But the lesson to be learnt from this instance of unreadability is already clear: that we must continue with our reading.

It will be observed that these metaphors, as used mechanically here (literally so), fail to cohere, for some are borrowed from mechanics, some from electricity or from cybernetics (where differences in potential function as signals). 'riverrun' seems to evoke the humming of a motor which is momentarily stuck or is building up tension; in order to free our reading, to transform this humming into an articulated sound, we must help the motor to get under way, and give it a throw; we will then be better able to see whether in fact something was locking, or whether there was only an excess of friction or a simple jamming of the cogs or components. We will then have to work out whether and how these images and others work coherently together, and what kind of mechanism this is.

Let us read the sentence quickly then, without stopping:

riverrun, past Eve and Adam's, from swerve of shore to bend of bay, brings us by a commodius vicus of recirculation back to Howth Castle and Environs.

The motor has started to run. We can say at least that something resembling a system has become manifest: 'riverrun' figures as the subject of 'brings', it functions as a *noun*, more specifically as *subject*. This places a more familiar system before us, a grammatical one, whose rules may provisionally be accepted. This being the case, we can, for example, eliminate the series based on the question of the presence or the absence of a capital letter; we can discern a coherent set, and we know that what is lacking is a grammatical element: what is missing before 'riverrun' is an article, the means of articulation of the noun. But which article? Its degree of definition remains to be analysed.

Our second conclusion: the process of differentiation of purely discrete elements leads us to isolate a double articulation: noun–verb, noun–article. But reference to a grammatical norm is in itself insufficient, and moreover still does not reveal the precise nature of the articulation. In particular, it does not enable us to describe how the reading process we have had to use works. What matters is the *mechanism* of this articulation: what comes 'after' allows us to define what went 'before', 'brings' enabled us to read 'riverrun', and now 'riverrun'. . . . In brief, we cannot separate normal mode of operation from reverse mode; it is as if articulation functioned by means of a closely integrated system of forward and reverse motion.

However, the apparent reversibility of the mechanism need not, for the moment, be our chief concern. We must try to find out as much as we can about its nature, before focusing on theoretical models (mechanics? or thermodynamics? or cybernetics?) and their interactions. And the way to learn more is to study the system at the moment it comes to a stop: its final state ought to help us to define its operation as a whole and to assess the respective roles of differences in potential and of the various articulations, and the relationship between them. And moreover, it being possible, as we shall see, to conceive of the process of articulation as a kind of play, the extent to which this tactic which we are forced to use can in fact be described as cheating, in the sense of skipping ahead of the slow linking together of the various series to arrive at the 'right' solution, will reveal whether the system is authentically ludic.

This is the final state:

A way a lone a last a loved a long the

The first task is to discover a possible connection between the two states. There is at least a degree of complementarity: an article was missing, and the book ends with an article. And there is more: this closing fragment provides us not only with a definite article, and several indefinite articles, but also reveals how indefinite articulation comes about and what motivates its connection with definite articulation.

The series of indefinite articles is indeed remarkable. The first one, in 'A way', seems commonplace at first: an article followed by a noun. But the ones which follow − 'a lone a last a loved a long' − seem strangely out of plumb, each being followed by a mere adjective, without the slightest trace of a substantive. Rather, 'a lone' and 'a long' seem to result from the dismemberment of an adverb and of a preposition: the article arises as if from a gap, from some play between these two categories. And in retrospect, we are tempted to say the same of 'A way' with reference to the adverb 'away', if we allow that a trace of our reading of this word does linger in our minds. So, in retrospective hesitation, we are led to call into question the validity of our reading of 'A way' as an article + a noun. Because of the absence of a substantive where one was to be expected, we tend subsequently to contest its presence, though it had seemed indubitable; we tend to regard it simply as a possibility, a sort of mental echo which it would be difficult to identify. Finally, it would be worth noting that, once more, in order to be rigorous and comprehensive, our reading has had to work in both directions, moving both with and against the flow of words.

All this leads us to conclude: we are witnesses to the *actualization of a noun* as it emerges from an echo, by means of the dismemberment and differential analysis of a set of adverbs and of a preposition; and this actualization coincides with another process, that of articulation, or the *actualization of the article* (in this case, the indefinite article). It would appear that what we see here in action is the process defined by Gustave Guillaume in particular: 'The article is [. . .] the act of nomination devoid of any semantic content [. . .]. It is an actualizer, and is used to bring about the transition from latent to actual noun (that is from a virtual value of the language to an element within the sentence).'[3] It is all the more remarkable to note that in the case of Joyce, the article and the shade of the noun emerge from adverbs and prepositions, and so stand as particular instances of the well attested phenomenon of second-degree formalization (occurring often in the Indo-European languages), by virtue of which 'values originally *assigned* to a word through inflexion become values *designated* by a separate word'.[4] To sum up, we could say that the two-way process described above reveals the true *genealogy of the noun.*

We began with the observation that 'riverrun' was unreadable. We next saw that it was not articulated, and verified this by referring to the text. But what must be noted is that a sort of magnetic effect irresistibly draws the two processes together: that is, the potential nominalization described above, and the potential articulation contained within 'riverrun'. A potential articulation within 'riverrun'? This is certainly the case, and not only because having reached the end of *Finnegans Wake* we discover the justificatory article which was missing at the outset, but also because the word contains within itself the principle of articulation. For here, as in anatomy, articulation consists of the *interplay of volume and of void*, the reciprocal exchange of full and empty.[5] Now, 'riverrun' is indeed characterized, as a noun, both by an excess and by a lack; we immediately recognized that its unreadability derived from its not seeming to belong to human language (it was perceived as noise, as *in*articulate sound), but also from its being over-articulated, from the lack of play between 'river' and 'run'; on the one hand, 'river' engages with nothing, and on the other, engages too tightly with 'run'. In the final analysis, the point is this: *the interplay is out of place*, that is, it does not occur between 'river' and 'run', but in front of the first of these two words. In the beginning, there was play on play, and there lies the real impertinence of the text. And within this initial play the potential for articulation and for nominalization alike is contained: they will spring out of the space between the two poles represented by 'the' and 'riverrun'.

Joyce, let it be noted, is not overdemanding, the mechanism he has created is economical: the initial interplay is constituted by the smallest gap possible. Later on, play on a letter or on the gap between letters will very often suffice to engage the mechanism, will suffice, for example, to pass from one language to another, that is, in effect, *from one series to another*. We might simply point to the particular emphasis placed on the letter *n* from the opening of the book onwards, as for instance in this dialogue:

You tollerday donsk? N. You tolkatiff scowegian? Nn. You spigotty anglease? Nnn. You phonio saxo? Nnnn.

(16.05–07)

This conversation between the representatives of the two races invading the British Isles follows the guided tour of the Wellington Museum. As a result, the 'N' of the first reply is usually read not merely as the suggestion of a negation, but also as Napoleon's initial. Once more, the mode of operation is striking: we would normally expect, after the question, a complete negative; as it is, it is merely outlined, and the outline itself is atypical: 'N.' and not 'N . . .'. As in fact we shall see, the space belonging to these missing dots will gradually be filled (but this space only) by several *n*'s, as if the letter was somehow unable to forego its own company completely. So, an unusual, skeletal negative brings the memory of Napoleon to mind; curiously, it is second-order memory (the memory of the highly comical visit which stands in place of memory) that recalls the Memory in its monogrammatic purity. 'N' is thus read as the suggestion of a negation and as the *inscription* of the great man, of the conqueror, that is as an affirmation *par excellence*; even, one might say, as a *self-inscription*.

The second question, which is identical in its orientation but differs in its sense, elicits 'Nn' as an answer, that is, a new signal introducing several new series:

(1)   As an answer, 'Nn' comprises:
    (a)   *the repetition of the trace of a negation*, and we could spend some time trying to assess the logical value of such a repetition;
    (b)   a stutter, or, in psychological terms, hesitation before a negation;
    (c)   represented in this stutter, in Viconian terms, the emergence of language through an attempted imitation of thunder[6] perceived as the voice of God.
    In the case of each of these, we are left with an 'almost', on the threshold of a *n*eutral state, in which an abrupt transition from yes to no is no longer quite possible.

(2)   But if we limit ourselves to the minimal difference in the answer itself, without making prior reference to the context, the last case above no longer seems as simple:
    (a)   'Nn': a capital followed by a small letter, man following God, human language having lost the original potency of the Logos. In its function as differential element, ' – n' signals the process of *degradation* of the Logos and the process of *assumption* of human language alike. In this perspective, *Series (1)* articulates with *Series (2)*: the great man is succeeded by a lesser man, Napoleon by 'Napoléon le petit'[7], and as a matter of fact the remainder of

Finnegans Wake will serve to confirm the thematic importance of the Second Empire.

(b) The ' – n' of 'Nn' also represents the linking together of the Great Man and the unknown man (cf. the use of the letter *n* in liturgical texts to reserve a place for a new name), of the (too well?) Known and the Unknown Soldiers (cf. *FW* 27.13, 227.27) – a linking together which can be read simply as an antithesis, but which from the point of view of history carries with it the threat of decline.

(c) This same ' – n' contains one last inversion, which is in fact fundamentally subversive: it is also the *sign for a raising to an in(de)finite power*. All that precedes is directly encompassed and modified by this power: the Great Man, his Inscription, etc. 'N' as the capital of 'n' becomes *a force of infinite power to the highest power* (!) within language ('N' as proper noun indicated by an initial). And moreover, this power inscribed in the initial letter, *power as* (because it is the?) *initial*, but placed within this system where everything operates and is articulated in both directions, will also appear at the ends of words, *on the horizon*, as it were: 'N for greeneriN' (226.31). Thus Napoleon, etc., is inscribed in, springs from, resurfaces in and from within 'Green EriN': vertiginous.[8]

And, more vertiginous yet, this power does not function through identities, or clearly assigned values (Napoleon, God, Language, History . . .), but by means of the tension created by the gaps between them. For this reason, each of the replies to the questions which follow in the passage quoted above, by virtue of a logic carried to the point of madness, is accorded an extra – *n*. . . This commentary could be pursued at far greater length, until we come across, a page and a half before the end of *Finnegans Wake*, this dubious leavetaking: 'And can it be it's nnow forvell?' (626.33), in which *n* as power seems almost to function in reverse.

*   *

*

In the beginning, we said, there was play on play; a form of play which we have had to set up and adjust ourselves, both in opposition to reading, since we had to rely on the unreadable, and with the help of reading, since some form of priming was necessary. 'riverrun' was found to be unreadable, and we have ended by reading it. But this reading remains incomplete and imprecise; this imprecision will now be accounted for.

We were able to make a connection between the two sentence fragments and reconstitute the full sentence only by first of all connecting the noun 'riverrun' with the verb 'brings', according to the most economical interpretation. In so doing, we imply that 'riverrun' is the subject. But, while it does confirm the general mode of functioning of the discourse, our forwards/backwards reference to 'A way a lone a last a loved a long the', the half-sentence with which the book closes and which links up, as we know, with the opening one, once more calls into the question this attribution of the function of subject to 'riverrun'. Such an assignation is precarious; it does not belong to 'riverrun' by right, but nor is it necessarily an imposture; it depends on the series of earlier assignations, themselves based on the work done by the space between the primordial letter *A* and the elements with which it connects: one of these series, for example, would posit a gap between 'A' and 'way', and so would tend to make 'way' the true subject of 'brings', and, in parallel, to transform the articulation of 'a lone' into 'alone', of 'a long' into 'along', through the elimination of gaps. But if on the other hand we reduce these gaps right from the start, if we read 'Away' instead of 'A way', an adverbial function of sorts comes into play, as a result of which we would read 'alone' instead of 'a lone', but this jams, stalls immediately, because 'last' and 'loved' can only be adjectives; according to this hypothesis, the noun is present only in its virtuality, and will be actualized only by the articulation eventually introduced by 'the'.

But there is no way out; any choice between these two eventualities remains quite impossible: they must necessarily co-exist, since in the final analysis, indeed as we know from the beginning, 'last' and 'loved' can function only as adjectives. . . Let me sum up. Both means of articulation, the definite and the indefinite articles, 'the' and 'a', provisionally designate two nouns as possible and actual subjects: 'riverrun' and 'way'. But while our analysis allowed us to make these functional assignations, it also points to gaps, spaces for two nouns, following 'loved' and 'last', which themselves become possible subjects of 'brings'. So, gaps, empty spaces, in front of 'riverrun', between 'A' and 'way', determine functions which in turn determine spaces which determine other modes of functioning. . . And it must now be said that precisely where our analysis is false, in casting 'riverrun' as subject, it is itself *functional*: in this game, error and deception are as indispensable as cheating.

Our reading of 'riverrun' was not only erroneous, it was also incomplete. For if the printed word was unreadable, being voice-borne it is not altogether impossible for the ear to hear it; it awakens echoes which must now be discussed. And these echoes, moreover, belong to distinct language domains. They can be transcribed, it would seem, in either of the following ways: 'river ran' and '*riveraine*'.[9] With reference to my own experience, let me point out an initial paradox to which it would no doubt be inappropriate to attach critical importance but which is more than a mere anecdote: it is almost always an English speaker who hears '*riveraine*', whereas a German-speaking Swiss (Fritz Senn) was the first to hear 'river ran'. We must now examine the space which sustains these echoes, the volume in which they are born, subsist, insist, since it is evidently because of a closure, a wall (the one built by Tim Finnegan the mason?) that they become manifest.

'river ran' echoes a line from Coleridge's *Kubla Khan*: 'Where Alph, the sacred river, ran [. . .] '. But it would be too easy to fall back here on the space of culture: to do so would be to see this reminiscence merely as decorative effect, if not as an audible wink. There are two points to be underlined. In the first place, Joyce has joined together the essential and the primordial: Alpha first of all, then the Article, and Articulation, and finally the Sacred; and in such a way that Coleridge's line can also no doubt initiate other series: the mountain (Alp) as source of every river, and nightmare (German *Alp*), the source of . . . To put it briefly, Joyce here includes, but in a tracing, all possible mythical dimensions: he leaves us with the echo of the mythical, and not the Mythical itself. This brings us to our second point: what concerns us here is a true *echo*, and not what is too often understood by the term, that is, a reverberation, a reflection or a simple association. What we have here is indeed the *truncated repetition* of an expression, not a complete expression which sets the imagination wandering. The echo signals both a precise *text* and its *absence*, its total non-presence. It is not possible to reconstitute the original expression directly and irrefutably from the echo: identification remains fundamentally problematic, but at the same time a sound perceived as an echo never fails to recall some expression to mind. Once more, the reader is invited, or rather obliged, to work his way up through the text – just as one works one's way up-river, against the current[10] – and once more we are faced with the question: what are the operational limits of this reversibility?

The second echo, '*riveraine*', despite its apparent simplicity, is quite complex: it has meaning as such in only one frame of reference, that is, the French language; but it has the auditive value of a French word pronounced by an English speaker. Here the echo marks a tension, the gap between two series, English and French, and the connections between them (cf. Napoleon–Wellington in *Finnegans Wake*). This is one of its modes of operation. But '*riveraine*' presents a third characteristic, a further value which this time is related to the text itself: as I. 8, 'Anna Livia Plurabelle', in particular, informs us, the '*riveraines*' in the book are the washerwomen positioned on the banks of the river, a symmetrical pair of witnesses and commentators on events, on the *flow* of events. If this value remains scarcely perceptible on a first reading, by the second one this fact is known and is automatically registered in the mechanism, thus causing a further calling into question of each of the various series. This reactivation is based on the interplay between 'river' and '*riveraine*', the interplay of stable and fluid, of witness and event; there are several options: witness viewing event, for example, *and* event viewing the witness, and so on – without omitting to mention that all this interacts and combines with the initial English–French interplay. So, yet again, in the case of the second of the two echoes, now internal rather than external, we have differences in tension, reversals of function, interactions of several types. Further series can be envisaged, especially with the 'reverend' addressee of the Letter as starting point. I should say, without the slightest irony, that the following passage seems to me to be of critical importance: 'Dear. And we go on to Dirtdump. Reverend. May we add majesty? Well, we have frankly enjoyed more than anything these secret workings of natures [. . .] (615.12–14).

We can come to no absolute conclusion. My sole purpose was to show how *Finnegans Wake* is read, how it can be read, and to point out the theoretical problems which, from the outset, the act of reading implies. I should simply like to say that in the case of this text, a text which constantly calls representation into question, not only by playing with perspective but also by inverting categories, which runs counter to the mechanisms of language and of myth while also obtaining from them a prodigiously high output, we still must define as rigorously as possible the interconnections between the various systems it uses, linguistic, mechanical, cybernetic and so on, and the modes of articulation of one with another.

(Translated by Patrick O'Donovan)

Notes

1. These 'Preliminary notes on the mode of functioning of *Finnegans Wake*' date from 1969, and are not intended to be definitive, but rather as an exploration; it is hoped to extend and develop them with the help of further studies now in progress and which derive from the same methods.
2. 'Lire *Finnegans Wake*?', in James Joyce, *Finnegans Wake*, Fragments adaptés par André du Bouchet (Paris: Gallimard, 1962), pp. 29–31.
3. 'Le problème de l'article dans la langue française' (1919); see Edmond Ortigues, *Le Discours et le symbole* (Paris: Aubier, 1962), 2, ch. 4.
4. Ibid.
5. In this connection, consider the innumerable telescopings together of expression and the sexual act in *Finnegans Wake*.
6. The two *n*'s of the French word are emphasized: 'to*nn*erre' [Tr.].
7. Victor Hugo wrote a satire on Napoleon III with this title [Tr.].
8. In the French, 'Verte EriN'; hence 'vertiginous' [Tr.].
9. As will be seen, *riveraine* is a French word, meaning 'dweller on the river-bank (or side of the street)' [Tr.].
10. The verb in the text is *rebrousser*, and the author quotes Littré to justify its use in this context [Tr.].

5 Lapsus ex machina

JEAN-MICHEL RABATÉ

Writing has no sooner begun than it inseminates itself with another reading. The *Wake, fin negans*, begets only beginnings but invalidates all origins, in a system which can be described as a word-machine, or a complex machination of meanings, probing and programming the seamy sides of meaning. This perverse semic machine has the peculiar ability to distort the classical semiological relation between 'production' and 'information', by disarticulating the sequence of encoding and decoding:

> The prouts who will invent a writing there ultimately is the poeta, still more learned, who discovered the raiding there originally. That's the point of eschatology our book of kills reaches for now in soandso many counterpoint words. What can't be coded can be decorded if an ear aye sieze what no eye ere grieved for. Now, the doctrine obtains, we have occasioning cause causing effects and affects occasionally recausing altereffects.   (*FW* 482.31–483.01)

The text is not just 'coded', since the writing of the 'prouts' − combining Proust, and Father Francis Mahony disguised as 'Father Prout', in short the professionals and the forgers of literature − receives meaning from the readings discovered by a *poeta*, an agent of creative *poiesis* whose gender is ambiguous. If it is not coded, it can be decoded, de-corded, unwoven, line by line, across the polyphonic obliques which intersect in 'counterpoint words'; thus the feedback of 'altereffects' already scrambles the metonymic chain of causes and effects, since a reading–writing of affects, on the alert, supposes the beginning and the begetting of an 'eareye', constantly lured by the text into believing it has only to *beg* the question of sense. Thus, too, can the quest of sense go on: the fact that the hearing glance implied by this paradoxical reading functions as a lapsus gives a hint and points to the way one could attempt to fill the blank space of desire left hollow by − or in − the machine. We shall see that perhaps it will be necessary to defer its problematic in order to orientate ourselves in the dedalapsus of *Finnegans Wake*, that labyrinth of chained lapsus. First we shall tie ourselves to the question of the codes in the machine and their relation to the seriality of the chains; then we shall try to analyse the site where the lapsus occurs: what does the text perform (or rather: what does it really cause) when the lapse recurs?

I   'Finnegans Wake': Series-machine

Joyce, to Suter, on *Work in Progress*: 'I feel like an engineer boring into a mountain from two sides. If my calculations are correct, we shall meet in the middle. If not . . .'.[1] Adorno, on Schönberg: 'Twelve-tone rationality approaches *superstition per se* in that it is a closed system – one which is opaque even unto itself – in which the configuration of means is directly hypostatized as goal and as law. The legitimacy of the procedure in which the technique fulfils itself is at the same time merely something imposed upon the material, by which the legitimacy is determined. This determination itself does not actually serve a purpose. Accuracy or correctness, as a mathematical hypothesis, takes the place of that element called "the idea" in traditional art. This "idea", to be sure, degenerated to an ideology in late Romantic art . . .'.[2]

Following Joyce's description of himself and of his work very precisely, one might posit that *Finnegans Wake* is a sort of machine; let us reconsider the famous passage in the letter to Miss Weaver: 'I am glad you liked my punctuality as an engine driver. I have taken this up because I am really one of the greatest engineers, if not the greatest, in the world besides being a musicmaker, philosophist and heaps of other things. All the engines I know are wrong. Simplicity. I am making an engine with only one wheel. No spokes of course. The wheel is a perfect square.'[3] This 'punctuality' refers to his regular delivery of drafts and written fragments. Joyce, musician, philosopher, and engineer: we must preserve his triple profession. And the combinator, the co-ordinator (engineer) seems to cap the other two. The simplicity of the paradox is that the squaring of the circle eliminates, disqualifies the other engines which are governed by a proper function. This machine has no other aim than that which it accomplishes itself in running. But for all that it is not necessary to admit that Joyce resolves this paradox: his machine is a circle and a square; he does not reduce either figure to the other, their incompatibility is a driving motor in the progress of the text.

The fourfold division of history according to a Vico revisited by Joyce, who added a fourth moment of dissolution to the division between the ages of the gods, heroes and men, rolls squarely on the great circle of language which turns on itself. The weird word-machine therefore seems to have been built by a crankyhandy-man who potters about in the repair shop of culture, halfway between an inventor's dream of finding the absolute formula and the Lévi-Straussian concept of '*bricolage*' as an imaginative individual recreation of cosmogonic parameters. But let us note that *bricolage* refers us back to military hardware and poliorcetics, since a bricole is a kind of catapult, whereas the 'engineer' devises weapons and instruments of destruction. With such a brick-hole, a hole in the brick-wall erected by the hubristic builders of a tower, the tower of Babel perhaps, we reach a motif which recurs with insistent familiarity in *Finnegans Wake*, and can graft onto it the French overtones of *coller* [to stick together] the broken de*bris* and fragments of a culture which others might be intent on shoring away from chaos.

The metaphor of the machine describes not only the book's theoretical functioning, but also the labour which has constructed it: 'I am also trying to conclude section I of Part II but such an amount of reading seems to be necessary before my old flying machine grumbles up into the air.'[4] Joyce as engine driver or pilot is clearly aware that thus he builds an autonomous, almost automatic machine; this is why he can envisage entrusting it to James Stephens.[5] It is indeed a question of threads, stitches and weave, of a braid which we the readers cannot finish. But we can, perhaps, broach the heart which the book gives itself when it glosses itself as: 'our wholemole millwheeling vicociclometer' (614.27). This 'vicociclometer' is an internal combustion engine which uses the decompositions and recombinations of elements of the past: everything returns and leaves in the anastomosis (systole and diastole) of a notched wheel which distributes the male and female roles: to man, catastrophes, and to woman, the transmission of the tradition. The letters ('letter from litter' (615.01)) always ultimately reveal 'the sameold gamebold adomic structure of our Finnius the old One, as highly charged with electrons as hophazards can effective it' (615.06–08).

Joyce means to capture in his machine all the fluxes he diverts, the flux of language and the flux of history. At this point, when daybreak brings elucidation, chasing away the night which rounds all that is angular, an invariant is revealed, a structure which carries four 'homely codes' (614.32), the codes of the Family. These codes are like the four holes left by the professor's fork on Anna Livia's letter. Beckett identified Viconian structure and rhythm (beat),[6] and this punctuation of history emerges more or less clearly from one moment to another: 'the [. . .] quadrifoil jab was more recurrent wherever the script was clear and the term terse' (124.21–2). It is true that one does not find this Adamic structure in the most dense and confused passages of the dream. However, the fact that there is recurrence and invariants seems to draw us towards a 'structuralist' point of view. Just as Lévi-Strauss superposes his myths in order to disengage a structure from them, so Joyce superposes his quite different stories on this atomic structure, this simple schema of oppositions, tensions, desires within the Family. Every position within the figure is overdetermined, is a superposition: 'And a superpbosition! Quoint a quincidence! O.K. *Omnius Kollidimus*'[7] (299.08–09, with the sigla of the Family given in a note). Or to summarize still further, 'O.K. Oh Kosmos!' (456.07). But the 'O.K.' can also be reversed as 'K.O.' or 'chaos'; this is because the verb 'collide' (cf. the 'collideorscape' constituted by the book (143.28)) implies the collision, violence, and war of contraries and of tongues. One feels the effect of this violent accident, of the contingency which makes electrons jump all over the place: the anti-etymological movement leads to 'the abnihilisation of the etym' (353.22). No return to an Adamic or a natural origin; the fiction of the nuclear Family permits only the nuclear fission of the text.

At this point we should like as a commentary on reading itself to return to the tension − that one always risks neutralizing − between square and circle, in order to read it as a tension between *structural* and *serial*. This would be the squaring of the circle of *Finnegans Wake*, founding a serial practice of language on a structural theory of universal history as the history of the Family.

Here Lévi-Strauss himself, who in the Overture of *The Raw and the Cooked* opposes the two systems of thought, will help us. His fundamental reproach is that 'abstract' painting, like serial music, forgets the first (natural) level of articulation of language. He criticizes contemporary painting, which he compares to Chinese calligraphy, in these terms: 'the forms used by the artist have no prior existence on a different level with their own systematic organization. It is therefore impossible to identify them as elementary forms: they can be more accurately described as creations of whim, fictitious units, which are put together in parodic combinations'.[8] In recalling Beckett's remark about the concept of structure in *Finnegans Wake* ('This social and historical classification is clearly adapted by Mr Joyce as a structural convenience − or inconvenience. His position is in no way a philosophical one'),[9] I should like to demonstrate the reasons which suggest that Lévi-Strauss's words can define *Finnegans Wake*, this play with creations of whim, through which one gives oneself up to a parodic combination − or a combinatory parody − with units which are not units.

In order to state the differences more clearly and to link them to the notion of 'code' as it is replayed in *Finnegans Wake*, I shall summarize here Umberto Eco's theses opposing the theory of structural communication to that of 'serial thought', which he defends against Lévi-Stauss's arguments.[10] The structural method recognizes three fundamental points: every message can be decoded thanks to a pre-established code, common to the interlocutors; there is an axis of selection and an axis of combination; every code relies on more elementary codes. Serial thought, on the contrary, posits that every message tends to call into question the code, that the 'notion of polyvalence undermines the foundations of the Cartesian axes' of selection and combination, and lastly, that what is essential is to characterize the historicity of the codes, 'to open them up to debate, so as to generate new modalities of communication'. 'In other words, whereas structural thought aims to discover, serial thought aims to produce.'

Finnegans Wake uses the schemas of communication and code several times the better to challenge them. A whole part of the book is presented as a listening in to 'communicators', voices, or minds like those which inspired

Yeats's *A Vision*: 'Hallo, Commudicate! How's the buttes? Everscepistic! He does not believe in our psychous of the Real Absence [. . .]' (536.04–06). Here 'scepticism' shortcircuits 'communicator'. The 'lessonless missage' of the radio in II. 3 is 'For the greeter glossary of code [. . .] Am. Dg.' (324.21–3). The Jesuit motto 'Ad majorem Dei gloriam' is inverted into 'Am Dog'. As early as *Scribbledehobble*[11] one can find: 'Everyword for oneself but Code for us all.'

Joyce seizes on the theological nature of the affirmation of the Code.[12] *Finnegans Wake* crosses the theories, and shakes them up in order to return to the here and now of reading–listening: 'Now gode. Let us leave theories there and return to here's here. Now hear. 'Tis gode again' (76.10–11). We return to listening to series which proliferate and transform themselves into musical tropes which are always *de trop*, in order to play the variables against the entropy of structural identity: 'Scant hope theirs or ours to escape life's high carnage of semperidentity by subsisting peasemeal upon variables' (582.14–16). The fragmentary peace of the 'litters' gathered by Anna Livia will therefore play the *iter* off against the *sempiter* thanks to these serial stories by the 'elucidatorials of sempiterserials'.[13] The serialized novel gives a specific periodicity to *Finnegans Wake*: this is because in the play of letters/litters, 'structure deteriorates into seriality'.[14] For the single site of the text generates the serial time of readings which are always implied in the page: 'there you are somewhere and finished in a certain time,' his time can always 'turn out to be a serial number of goodness gracious alone knows how many days or years' (118.8–11). The 'chaosmos' of the letter, for example, is 'moving and changing every part of the time' (118.22–3); the inflexions, pronunciations, letter, and 'changeably meaning vocable scriptsigns' (118.27) lose all fixity and introduce a historicity into the copresence of multiple contradictory codes.

Joyce's point of view with regard to plurality, his polytheistic and parodic bias, imply multiplication ('multiplied words')[15] and therefore the generation of stories. The series arise from these 'multiplicables' (4.32); for instance, the twelve questions of chapter I.6 are prefigured by the numbers twelve, three and four (Shaun has misunderstood three of the questions and left four of them in disorder (cf.126.7–9, also 513.29–36)). The structures play on triangles (the triangle of the basic family relationships) which double over to form lozenge, square (the square of (hi)story carried by the four old annalists), and circle. Numerical multiplication on the one hand; unfolding, translation, addition of point or line on the other.

All the stories finally compose a figure, a geometrical schema; but whereas the latter is only the place of intersection of a number of series, the former continue mutually to generate. The story of Burrous and Caseous may well lead to the triangle A-B-C (167), but it is hastily brought in to 'cut a figure', to put an end to the story, and above all, it fails to tie up all the loose ends of the story: it will give way to the direct enunciation 'No!' (167.18), in reply to the question. And the series will continue to proliferate, to resound in the other chapters. What of these series? From the beginning of I.6, for example, one hears a series of foods (butter and cheese) interweave with a series of names from Roman history (Brutus and Cassius), which seems to imply a series of 'theoretical' or metaphysical oppositions (Time/Space, Sight/Hearing . . .). The simple fact that food is mentioned entails further references to all the possible foods which summon all the members of the Family (161.25–31). The rival twins draw all the rivals of history and literature towards food: 'like shakespill and eggs' (161.31) covers, with 'bacon and eggs', the Lord Bacon who was claimed to be the author of Shakespeare's plays. In order to analyse the seriality of *Finnegans Wake*, analysis of recurrence is not enough, as it would be in the case of motifs.[16] Two allusions trigger off a series, and its reading is necessarily reversible: as Dunne, the inventor of the concept of the 'serial universe'[17] puts it, the first term is still outside the series, which comes into effect only with the second term, which implies a regressive analysis. 'Down-to-the-ground benches' (161.34), the school benches, are only integrated into the political series on page 167 when we read allusions to democracy, and into the sexual series, when we read 'When she is not sitting on all the free benches' (166.11). Each series generates a sub-series: 'Sellius Volatilis', false Roman name, is salt, one of the ingredients of the family meal, and it gives rise to the economic series (to sell) and prefigures the chemical series (salts, acids, and bases). A single element is enough to trigger off a chain-reaction, and to magnetize the other elements of a latent group.[18]

How the hierarchies of the stories within stories ('tales within tales' (522.05), 'tales within wheels' (247.03)) make the circle of language roll, accomplishing this closure/opening of the book (the mention of the 'to be continued tale' at the end of Anna Livia's monologue (626.18) is taken up again on 28.25–7: 'serial story', with the same allusions to a Norwegian saga), but also dislodge, dislocate, force all the triangles, must be clearly understood. Whereas *Scribbledehobble* held to the principle of embedded stories: 'desperate story telling, one caps another to reproduce a rambling mock-heroic tale' and 'begin a story of A & B, then B & C, C & D' (pp. 25 and 27), *Finnegans Wake* is not content infinitely to permutate coupled terms which can only make their triangle rotate; it simultaneously affirms the necessity of the triangle and its impossibility. When Joyce glosses the passage on religious dogmas in the story of the Mookse and the Gripes (I.6), he writes: 'when he gets A and B onto his lap, C slips off and when he has C and A he loses hold of B'.[19] That series are generated by the impossibility of there being figures of resolution – which are nonetheless structurally necessary – is, we shall see, what functions more dynamically in the lapsus.

How in this 'combinatory of parodies' are the series produced? In this respect the chapter of twelve questions (I.6) is strategic, for it is the first recapitulation of all the narrative elements, characters and places in the book. For brevity's sake, one might simply suggest that it is here that one grasps the genesis of the series in the list: the Rabelaisian list, frequent in *Finnegans Wake*, furnishes a matrix of undeveloped narratives, through its privileged relation to the enunciation (in this chapter, through the play of questions and answers). The principal difference between the first, predominantly masculine part of book I (chapters 1–4) and the second, more feminine (chapters 5–8), is that the first part presents a sequence of anticipations in an ever more nebulous trial, whereas the second offers answers to the question: 'who is?' — it is the 'quiz'. In chapter 5 we read apropos of the letter: 'Who [. . .] wrote the durn thing' (107.36); chapter 6 begins with 'Who do you no' (126.02), and the leitmotiv of chapter 8 is 'Tell me all about Anna Livia' (196.02). This question sets flowing all the lists (lists of rivers and of presents in this chapter). The list is the ruse (*List*, in German) of listening ('They list. And in the porches of their ears I pour.' (*Ulysses*, 197/196)) which enumerates the series of names, titles, insults. We have already found the list of names of HCE (pp.71–2), and that of the titles of the letter (pp. 104–7), and question 1 of chapter 6 recalls the lists of HCE: 'hidal, in carucates he is enumerated' (128.05), 'variously catalogued, regularly regrouped' (129.12), 'assembled and asundered' (136.06). Each list engenders or summarizes stories, for each title is a potential tale. A whole interpretation of Earwicker's sin is readable in a seven-line title (107.01–07). The hierarchy of sequences begins with the letters of the alphabet, extends to the lists, and is organized in each of the six stories (the tales of the Prankquean, of the Mookse and the Gripes, of Burrous and Caseous, of the Norwegian Captain, of Buckley and the General, and of the Ondt and the Gracehoper), deployed and redoubled.

These dozen stories ('another doesend end once tale of a tublin' (335.27–8)) constitute the basis of the 'infernal machinery' of *Finnegans Wake*. 'Infernal machinery (serial number: Bullysacre, dig care a dig) having thus passed the buck to billy back from jack [. . .] as the baffling yarn sailed in circles' (320.33–35). Tradition is this passage from story to story, as the turn to speak passes to the next player, or as the baton changes hands in a relay race: 'tradition stick-pass-on' (474.04) (the passage of the witness of tradition). The four old Irish annalists narrate a fixed (Hi)story while spreading [*disséminant*] Family gossip with their endless chatter. Their sexual ambiguity is linked to the feminine 'pass the key', taking up the story of Arrah-na-pogue, who saved her brother MacCoul by passing him the key in a kiss. Every historical event can be redistributed in this matrix of series in which the functioning of language is unveiled. (Hi)story fabricates, and fabricates itself, as an echo-chamber, reflection of past echolalias. The echonomy of *Finnegans Wake*, its amalgamative alchemy, and the permutations of the letters of the alphabet (cf. 284.11–14), are at once combinatory, and principles of dispersion and enunciation: 'Economy of movement, axe why *said*' (i.e. 'x', 'y', 'z') (432.35; cf. 167.7). The 'caravan series' (285.21) of numbers which give the figures of the family refer in the margin to the exclamation '*Nom de nombres!*'. This struggle for the narrative, to tell or to steal the story, governs the division between the sexes — for curiously, it is not the same thing to have the story and to tell it: 'Let young wimman run away with the story and let young min talk smooth behind the butteler's back' (12.02–04).

It is not just fortuitous that one also perceives in this 'butler' the butter that unites all the Family characters in the same sauce. Butter appears in all the lists ('*Buttbutterbust*' (106.33) to designate the Mamafesta, '*Grease with the butter*' (71.13) for HCE, 'on the bier through the burre' (130.12) for Finn), and it plays a strangely privileged role in *Finnegans Wake*. Therefore what link between butter and soul underwrites their combination in 'soul butter' (230.23), and why for example do we read in Budgen's biographical notes: 'For about half the time it took to compose *Ulysses* Joyce lived in Zurich, at that time the second capital of psychoanalysis. Joyce preferred butter as a subject of conversation'?[20] Two passages will perhaps supply an answer, by linking this 'subject of conversation' on the one hand to enunciation, and on the other, to the publication of the book. One should really gloss page 561 in entirety, but to simplify, the two critical sentences may be cited: one sees the daughter of the family, who is called 'Buttercup': 'Her bare name will *tellt it*' (561.12), and: 'as they too what two dare not *utter*' (561.30). 'Butter' appears here, obviously, as the stammered or repressed form of *Utter* (enunciate, pronounce). Elsewhere we read: 'a (suppressed) book [. . .] the paper [. . .] has scarsely been *buttered* in works of previous publicity [. . .] for pastureuration' (356.20–24). Here butter alludes to the paper in which it is wrapped and to the pasteurization of publication.

Butter is a derivative of milk, and occupies a position parallel to the eggs in maternal production. The eggs are the belligerent twins and the final omelette (union of the sons forming a little man — *homme*-let — of the father): milk is a substance which divides into butter and cheese. The quasi-identity of milk and eggs is underlined by the fact that '*Nex quovis* burro *num fit mercaseus?*' (163.15) — which echoes the Latin phrase 'ex quo ligno fit Mercurius?' — is replaced by '*Eggs squawfish lean yoe nun feed marecurious*' (484.36). The second — culinary — Latin expression is denounced as a trope or sequence and also as a degenerate imitation ('fakesimilar'): 'Ho look at my jailbrand *Exquovis* and *sequencias* High marked on me fakesimilar in the foreign by Pappagallus and Pumpusmugnus' (484.33–5). We shall see how the tropes and parodic series are played and outplayed by the enunciation — the utterance — that conveys them and how the enunciatory process implies the lapsus.[21] For in this passage, for example, Shaun has just opposed his actions to the distortion of his education in the memory of the tradition (excellent analyst who hears a lapsus in any statement): 'I brought you from the loups of lazary and you have remembered my lapsus langways' (484.24–5).

II   The performative utopia of 'Finnegans Wake'

Finnegans Wake is not so much written polyphony as experience of patterns of prosodic polyphones: it is woven, braided, loomed with voices. Accents, rhythms, verbal intensities. Note the transformation of the *First Draft*: 'if there is a third person being spoken about it all proceeds from a first person speaking to a second person who is being spoken to'[22] into *Finnegans Wake*: 'if there is a third person, mascarine, phelinine or nuder, being spoken abad it *moods prosodes* from a person speaking to her second which is the direct object that has spoken to, with and at' (268.16–22). To prosodize the *Gradus ad Parnassum*: one would have to scan these inflexions of speech in order to link the enounced with the act of enunciation.

Now the concept of musical 'voices' brought into play by *Finnegans Wake* amounts to involving, in a very complex relationship, one or more subjects (I) speaking in their discourse. For example, in Professor Jones's demonstration the expression 'if we please (I am speaking to us in the second person)' (161.05–06) has no other function than to draw attention to him speaking in front of his class, with all the ambiguities of his role and theirs ('and you too and me three' (161.30)), within the context of the underlying family tensions: 'I have completed the following arrangement for the coarse use of stools and if I don't make away with you I'm beyond Caesar outnullused' (161.34–6). The course of menstrual blood is doubtless latent in the 'course' of 'coarse use', and 'stools' signifies faeces. The enounced which follows (the tale) is related to the situation of the enunciation, the narrative of the assassination of the Father complicating the power relations between audience and narrator. To convince is to get rid of. The role of narrative is to annul the other in order not to be annulled. This can only be done so long as one is speaking.

If every narrative is conveyed by first-person voices, it must be understood how the voices are not reducible to psychological instances, how they are inserted into a mobilization of the potential energies of language itself, in so far as it permits the accomplishment of acts and gestures. Joyce often calls this phenomenon 'mood'. We shall analyse it in accordance with the theory of performatives. Here is how Joyce conceived of the aim of modern writing: 'In writing one must create an endlessly changing surface, dictated by the mood and current impulse in contrast to the fixed mood of the classical style. This is *Work in Progress*. [. . .] In other words we must write dangerously:

everything is inclined to flux and change nowadays and modern literature, to be valid, must express that flux.'[23] This new mood is therefore opposed to the 'emotional limitations' of classical literature. The 'endlessly changing surface' of the new literature is formed by the interweaving of series and voices. Rigid themes give way to a mixture of genres where rhythms and intonations play the part of rhetorical topoi.

The performative[24] is defined as the present action of the speaker when his enunciation has as its aim the accomplishment of the action enounced (I declare the meeting open). The description of the language of *Finnegans Wake* given by Beckett takes on a slightly different meaning when one re-reads it in the light of the theory of performatives: 'His writing is not *about* something; *it is that something itself*. [. . .] When the sense is sleep, the words go to sleep.'[25] To see this as the desire to create a microcosm in *Finnegans Wake*, a substitute for the divine macrocosm, is perhaps to jump too hastily to metaphysical conclusions:[26] if Joyce does have this aim, analysis of the examples cited by Beckett proves that it is first of all a question of showing what the language of *Finnegans Wake* itself realizes, what it transforms and what it produces. Beckett seems to oppose in some sense the constative (about something) and the gesture of the sentence which produces the sense. In any case, it seems to be a theory of this type, close to the Austinian theory of illocution, a generalization of the performative, but without positing a psychological subject, which permits Joyce to reconcile the linguistic conceptions of Vico with those of Jousse, the Jesuit and linguist whose lectures on the anthropology of gesture Joyce avidly attended in the thirties; for Jousse puts gesture first, then rhythmic speech. Vico, on the contrary, writes: 'for all nations began to speak by writing, since all were originally mute'.[27] Beckett's words make it possible to begin to understand how *Finnegans Wake* does not describe the dream, does not inform about it, but generates it, is this dream in gesture *and* in gestation. In this sense, *Finnegans Wake* is not about something, but is about the fact that it is this thing.

The performative verb (to ask, to promise, to order, to congratulate, to reprimand) is necessarily self-referential: it accomplishes something in speaking, and in speaking, it speaks of itself. Illocutionary force generalizes the action accomplished by the simple performative without being auto-referential. The best example of this is the imperative, like those turns of interrogation, those particular intonations which transform an indicative into an order or a promise. Joyce goes further, applying the status of active verb to language as a whole: 'a true noun does not exist in nature',[28] he noted, following Fenollosa; he articulates the whole range of these language-games in *Finnegans Wake*. Let us take a simple example, in which the imperative arises between Shem and Shaun. Shaun (as Justius) says: 'no longer will I follow you obliquelike through the inspired form of the third person singular and the moods and hesitensies of the deponent but address myself to you, with the empirative of my vendettative' (187.28–31). The deponent to which Justius alludes is, firstly, his deposition (to depone), his testimony against Shem, in the third person. But in the grammatical sense, the deponent is a passive form with an active meaning (cf. 523.07–09: 'the deponent [. . .] may have been (one is reluctant to use the passive *voiced*)'). Shaun's gesture amounts to a denunciation of his whole deposition as having been carried by a *mood* (tone, humour, pathos) which here is revealed to be brutally imperative: 'stand forth'. Hesitation is the key to this tortuous strategy: it is up to us to read the tones and voices between the lines; we must learn to identify not so much the subjectivity which is speaking as the true subject of the enunciation and its context, its musical and grammatical game. The range of voices (active, middle, passive) linking the subject to the action of the verb, and of modes[29] (in the musical sense, major or minor; otherwise indicative, subjunctive, imperative, expressing fact or desire, possibility or command), forces us to decipher everything given as fact in terms of wanting, of power; in short, in terms of verbal action and of the relations between the subjects of enunciation.

The facts are not independent of an enunciation: the 'ipsofacts' (156.09) are promulgated by the Mookse: a whole aspect of *Finnegans Wake* is intended precisely to constitute a hypothetical fact (fact/fict) with 'unfacts' (57.16). Austin remarked that often the same sentence is used both as performative and as constative.[30] He gives a list of 'roles' which can be filled by explicit performatives: heading it, one finds mood, tones of voice, rhythms and accents which mark insistence, adverbs and relative particles, then the gestures accompanying the enunciation and the circumstances that surround it. The performative is rarely pure; its analysis bears on regressive series (this is verified in Austin's successive aporias), but it is necessarily an illocutionary horizon of *Finnegans Wake* – even if it is always shifted, replayed, again mislaid. This would be the utopia of a discourse with magic power (when Joyce said, 'I can do all I want with language', he meant mastery of style *and* prophecy), where the act would be identified with its utterance in a perpetual self-reference in the present. Just such a temptation, of a perpetual presence of performative self-commentary, is marked in Shaun's deposition on Shem's language (which simultaneously deposes and dismisses that language, forces its decline): 'one continuous present tense integument slowly unfolded all marry*voising mood*moulded cyclewheeling history' (185.36–186.02). The voices and modes make the universal history the present of a writing right on the skin, right on the body of the subject speaking or acting his 'dividual chaos'.

Let us see in a specific example of performative utterance how the voices are, however, inscribed in the story which they even cause to advance. To say that the story is a *fatum* is to say that 'it was written' and that 'it must be done'. At the end of I.6, allusions to legislators abound (Solon, Roman law), and the law returns in the game of questions with question 12: '*Sacer esto?*'(168.13).[31] The Latin future imperative is the formula which places outside the law, excludes by its very enunciation. Earlier we read similar formulae in Professor Jones's discourse: '*Ubi lingua nuncupassit, ibi fas! Adversus hostem semper sac!*' (167.31–2).[32] These are quasi-literal quotations from the Law of the XII tables. Joyce did not have to look far in order to find them, for they appear in Vico's *New Science*: '*Adversus hostem aeterna auctoritas esto*' – according to Vico, the enemy in question would be the plebeian, exposed to the hatred of the noble Patres – and '*Uti lingua nuncupassit, ita jus esto*'[33] – the purchase is valid even when it is only verbally agreed: to speak is already to bind oneself through a pact. Vico, like Austin, cites Euripides' *Hippolytus*, 1.612: 'I swore with my tongue but my mind I kept unsworn',[34] and he glosses it by noting that this line had shocked the Romans, accustomed by the Law of the XII tables to commit themselves by their word, to their word (*ita jus esto*).[35] Austin opposes duplicity to the 'seriousness' required of the performative. What matters here as regards the specific operation of performatives in *Finnegans Wake* is the way in which the citations have been deformed: *jus* is replaced by *fas* ('speech') which plays against *sac*, which already pre-dicts *sacer*.

Fas and Sac(er) have a performative role that Jus would not have. For here we witness the passage from religious to heroic law, and then to human law (the origin of these laws is the plebeians' demand that they be *written*, so that the Patres would not have the monopoly and so that the plebeians would have the right to marry and to buy: '*acta legitima plebeia*',[36] says *Finnegans Wake* (85.13)). Vico, talking of 'ordinary judgements',[37] writes that they involve the same respect as divine judgements: the *religio verborum* still exists. These juridical acts are governed by consecrated formulae, of which not a single letter can be changed (*qui cadit virgula, caussa cadit*).[38] Praetorian *Fari* (speech) is a language which cannot be changed and which compels action. It implies the Fatum, the inexorable order of things: 'whence later the name *fatum* was given to the ineluctable order of causes: producing the institutions of nature, as being the utterance of God. This may also account for the Italian verb *ordinare*, as applied especially to laws, in the sense of giving commands which must necessarily be carried out' (Vico, p. 356). This recurs in *Finnegans Wake*: 'Are those their fata which we read in sibylline between the *fas* and the *nefas*?'(31.36). The speakable/unspeakable is also to be deciphered between the licit and the illicit. Reading plays between enunciation and denunciation, said and gainsaid [*le dit et le dédit du texte*]: textual hesitation of 'heresistance'.[39] The divine Providence of the fatum gives way to the 'farce of dustiny' (162.02), and 'the establisher of the world by law' (55.08–09) is also the author whose rights are not assured: '*Filius nullius per fas et nefas*' (443.12). Earwicker's saga is 'antilibellous and nonactionable, and this applies to its whole wholume' (48.18–19). One is always between the conceded enunciation (*fas*) and the interdict (*nefas*) which commits to Sacer, to condemnation to death. Therefore *Finnegans Wake* plays more on the 'failures', the 'infelicities' which annul the performative and which Austin attempts to list.[40] *Finnegans Wake* is the collection of vitiated acts, snags, self-sabotage, inappropriate uses of performatives which do not perform; this is one of the aspects of the theme of 'felix culpa' become 'foenix culprit' (23.16). It is no chance that the two principal Austinian categories of 'infelicities' – *misfires* and *abuses* – play to the utmost in the text. One need only cite Finnegan's first fall: 'it may half been a *missfired brick*, as some say, or it mought have been due to a *collupsus of his back promises*, as others looked at it' (5.26–8). The mis-fired, flawed brick is equivalent to a failure to keep one's word, a breach of promise: the collapse is therefore also lapsus. The lists concerning HCE are lists of 'abuses': insults, it is true, but also abuses of confidence and dishonesties on his part. Besides, the series of 'abusive names he was called' (71.05) is compiled by HCE himself, and his aggressor leaves him silent, revealing his inability to speak: 'telling how by his selfdenying ordnance he had left Hyland on the dissenting table' (73.01–03). Infelicity is the lapsus revealed on the performative level; the same structure is repeated in the sexual act which cannot be accomplished, the failure of which is pronounced in typical performatives: 'Withdraw your member! Closure. This chamber stands abjourned' (585.26–7). *Finnegans Wake* never stops burlesquely reaffirming the seriousness of its meaning: 'This is seriously meant. Here is a homelet, not a hothel' (586.18). We shall see how the failure applies more specifically to the masculine serious/serial 'omelette' outplayed by the transformations of language.

In every case the true/false opposition is eliminated. In order to suggest a parallel between Chomsky's grammatical theory and Austin's illocutionary theory, one would have to show how *Finnegans Wake* functions as performance, defined by acceptability/non-acceptability (as opposed to competence, defined by grammaticality/non-grammaticality), and the performative, defined by success or failure (as opposed to the constative, which is governed by the true and the false). The problem of acceptability concerns the whole reading, for it cannot arrest the series or locate them on tropological levels of meaning, and the perpetual failure of the performative leads us to see that everything enounced comes under an enunciating voice or a subject of enunciation, but that it is, in its very movement, *denounced*: the thing enounced which cannot be grasped independent of its enunciation comes to invalidate its enunciation in return. It is a perpetual antiphrasis, each expression a dramatic irony: 'while I am not out now to be taken up as unintentionally recommending' (163.29). In ambiguous expressions like 'to understand this as well as you can [. . .] I have completed the following arrangement' (161.33–5) one sees that the second person is only a pretext for the performative status of a demonstration, the sole aim of which is to convince the speaker: indeed one can read this as either (1) to let you understand, or (2) to be able to understand: I understand only when I speak, when I enounce. Once again, the historical situation of the Law of the XII tables can serve as a point of reference here, since they are laws (like so many questions) decreed *for* the plebeians *against* the Patres and *by* the Patres: and this reproduces the schema of the enunciation. This play of annulment governs the sentences and the dialogues. When the eleventh question put to Shaun asks if he would give alms to the *beggar* Shem, Shaun replies that the very fact of putting the question about a beggar is 'begging the question' (149.15): it is a *petitio principii*. The answer calls into question the question, confuses the roles of enunciation ('it would be far fitter for you, if you dare!'). For in order to speak, the responding subject must put himself in the place of the Father (which will also make him trip, stumble over his words, get it wrong, contradict himself); the second stage is therefore the *petitio paternitatis*: to claim the right of succession, against everyone else, by implicitly recognizing 'Qualis pater, talis filius'. The third stage is the undermining play of self-parodic references, which finally *apostils this petition* (both the *petitio principii* and the *petitio paternitatis*) by taking it up again, modifying it, adjourning it, through a system of marginal references.[41]

III   Relapsed t(r)opology

1   Enuncitation

Finnegans Wake operates on the rhythms of spoken language, a multiplicity of voices relay each other on every page: the procedures of enunciation lead to these illocutory effects which we have attempted to analyse. But the book also glosses its own reading, refers to itself as the book of all books. Within performative language, self-referentiality repels and dislocates the act of enunciation, and works to create a citational network. The transforming mechanism of citations and self-citations reinjects these fragments of culture or intertextuality into a series of moods and voices, rhythms or verbal modalities, which cannot be identified with any precise character. The iterability of every enounced, caught in a play of deformed echo-references, undermines 'evenementiality' [*événementialité*] by revealing linguistic conflicts, the fabrication of ideology in discourses, and the general transformation of language effected by the text.[42] Therefore the performative aspect of *Finnegans Wake* may perhaps stem less from strong, locatable subjects of enunciation than from the constant self-referentiality of the book.[43]

This self-referentiality is attested by the dominant form of the performative in *Finnegans Wake*, the promise, which is always the promise of meaning, of a clarification to come: 'I shall explex what you ought to mean by this [. . .] in the subsequent sentence' (149.30–2): of course, the subsequent sentence brings no clarification. 'Hoping against hope all the while that, by the light of philosophy, (and may she never folsage us!) things will begin to clear up a bit' (119.04–06): 'We shall perhaps not so soon see' (32.02). It is a series of prolepses and adjournments, procrastinations, tergiversations and hesitations which defer meaning: 'I'll take your reactions in another place after themes' (159.21–2), 'Read next answer. [. . .] See previous reply' (167.26–8). From the moment one reads what a voice proffers there is no centre, there is no origin independent of the Hole/Whole of the book: 'turn wheel again to the whole of the wall. [. . .] There was once upon a wall and a hooghoogwall a was and such a wallhole did exist' (69.05–08). By condensing the two English terms for 'whole': ALL and WHOLE in WALLHOLE, Joyce makes the hole (HOLE) arise from the whole. The reader is always between the hole of reading, between two references which disperse meanings and times (before, after, not yet, and already), and the whole of the whole book taken as a closed system − which is however opened again onto intertextuality and universal history. The usual schema of the 'Incipit Parodia' of this process would be:

(1)   I incite (the performative)
(2)   I anticipate (the promise/*différance*)
(3)   I anti-cite (the citation coming to affirm the transformation of the expression and its intertextual dispersion). The performative voice, situated by its aggressions and questions, finally enounces the power of the cultural codes which crumble the family codes. The tropal fugue advances, but backwards: 'proceeded with a Hubbleforth slouch in his *slips backwords*' (73.18–19).

Meaning is always promised and repulsed: '(I am purposely refraining from expounding the obvious fallacy as to [. . .] the *lapses lequou* asousiated with the royal gorge)' (151.26–9). The lapsus cuts speech short and reduces the efficacy of promise to difference of meaning. Shaun claims to be capable of enouncing the works of Shem the writer but refuses to do so: 'And one of these fine days, man dear, when the *mood* is on me, that I may willhap *cut my throat with my tongue* tonight but I will be ormuzd moved' (425.25–8). This states the relation between the enounced and the enunciation: to cut one's own throat or lips (lips, lisp, lapse), one's vocal cords, with one's speaking tongue. The self-invalidation of the performative indeed functions as dissemination; in the same passage, Shaun claims to be 'innocent of disseminating the foul emanation' (425.10–11): but the 'muttermelk' (425.09) − 'mutter' connects mother and mumbling − of his blood has just betrayed him by making an emulsion, curdling and revealing his guilt ('the muttermelk of his blood donor beginning to work' (425.09–10)): he too is a party to this 'Acomedy of letters' (425.24).

The play of Whole and Hole reappears in a different sense: the tongue comes to castrate the voice or the head: 'About that and the other. If he was not alluding to the whole in the wall? That he was when he was not eluding from the whole of the woman' (90.21–3). The wall is the wall of the city built by Finn the mason, the citation of the culture founded by HCE: a Babel which oscillates betwen intertextuality and totality. The *hole* is the sex of the woman, which is only mentioned in order to bury her in it.[44] The text and its voices allude to cultural holes–wholes, but elide the feminine hole – not whole. For there the logos 'comes to nullum' (298.19–21). The Viconian circle – now vitiated/vicious – is no longer closed, passing from the erection of the city to the dissemination of the citations, then to the eluded castration; it is a camshaft without any point of origin.

The story narrated is an expenditure, a provisional discharge, which eludes the expectation of meaning ('— You are alluding to the picking pockets in Lower O'Connell Street? — I am illuding to the Pekin packet but I am eluding from Laura Connor's treat' (507.26–9)). The function of the parable is to mask the lack by giving the appearance of an answer which is in fact only a variation on universal (hi)story which even so it cannot stop itself from narrating. When one rounds another lap, the *ricorso* leads not to a gain in information but to a dissolution which modifies the initial order; it is a leap, a *faux-pas* which precipitates a new cycle: 'The letter! The litter! [. . .] Borrowing a word and begging the question and stealing tinder and slipping like soap' (93.24–7); here the cycle is resumed – from the intertextual plagiarism (borrowing) to the false dialogue (begging the question), the parody of divine effects (steal thunder), and finally the lapsus which prevents the capture and identification of fixed meanings. The printed paper is made of such traps: 'For that (the rapt one warns) is what papyr is meed of, made of, hides and hints and misses in prints' (20.10–11);[45] the misprints make 'misses' of print: once again, woman is present in the writing.

Lapsus holds the key to the dream just as woman holds the key to the Book in her letter. These lapsus are the key to the moments of convergence when all the series overlap, where all the recurrences explode abruptly. There meaning is made, at least for the affect of the reader/listener. Sleep is a gigantic lapsus: the etymology of *sleep* is from *slœpan*, that is, 'labi', to slip: as in *Finnegans Wake*: 'O foetal sleep! Ah, fatal slip!' (563.10). Sleep is a *lapsus linguae* and a *lapsus calami* which reappears in the nightmare (*Alp*, in German) of the flow of the story: *Lapse* of time, flow (laps) of the river, bearing off all the heresies, lapses and relapses. One slips on the reading: 'To be slipped on, to be slept by, to be conned to, to be kept up. And when you're done push the chain' (278.n.5). The lavatory chain joins the chain of generations: and let no more be said about it, but already it's beginning again, one is drawn along at the other end of the chain.

One of the most illuminating proverbs used by *Finnegans Wake* is 'There's

many a slip 'twixt the cup and the lip' − it is one of the links between
enunciation (lip), lapsus (slip), and sleep, making possible the great dream
of the book. 'There is many asleeps between someathome's first and
moreinausland's last' (116.20) brings into play the *between* of home and exile
(*Ausland*). The thousand and one nights of *Finnegans Wake* are presented
thus: 'It is the Thousand to One Guinea-Gooseberry's *Lip*perfull *Slip*ver
Cup' (342.15−16): it becomes a horse-racing cup, a *Prix lapsus*: the cup of
female courses overflows whilst lips never cease to murmur that they will pass
us the key in a kiss. 'But there's many a split pretext bowl and jowl'
(161.21−2). *Split* marks the scission of the two brothers (cheek by jowl): rival
riversides. The lapsus links Earwicker's sexual sin (sinse): 'rarely heard now
save when falling from the unfashionable lipsus of some hetarosexual'
(120.34−5) to this flux of memory and letter: 'the vocative *lapse* from which
it begins and the accusative *hole* in which it ends itself; the aphasia [. . .]
leading *slip by slipper* to a general amnesia of misnomering one's own'
(122.03−06).

2   Geomastery

Woman would therefore be the place of the lapsus (its inverted signifier ALP
− lap) and man its provoker, producing it by his serial and serious fall.[46] It
is in woman's lap that the dream of the contradictory (hi)stories performed
by man in periodic times occurs and recurs. 'Father Times and Mother
Spacies' (600.02). The Father loses, stammers, sins, fails: he is killed by the
Son. The mother perpetuates and recuperates, she does not produce
(hi)stories (like the Father) but matter: she spreads signifier. Woman must
fit into the machine of which Vico is the 'producer' (255.27), whereas the
Father is the 'god of all machineries' (253.33); the mother, 'parody's bird'
(11.09), can only function once defined by means of figures (numbers and
diagrams). Therefore the whole problem will henceforth be to geometrize
her, master her, by making her a sex, a triangle, or her pure function, that
is, to be THE mother. 'Gran Geamatron' (257.05)!

The same movement occurs in II.1 and II.2: the mother is measured in
order to be reduced to her sex: 'She's her sex, for certain' (250.01). When she
comes to call her children in after their games, she is described in all her
mensurations (bust, hips, thighs, weight . . .) by the Producer who introduces
her (rather like Marge, in 164.07): 'brought on the scene the cutlet*sized*
consort' (255.29). In the children's homework, once Anna Livia has been
drawn in the two circles and the triangles of the first problem in Euclid, the
two brothers see the 'it' of their mother: ' [. . .] apl lpa! This it is an her. You
see her it. Which it whom you see it is her. [. . .] I've read your tunc's
dimissage' (298.01−07). They dimension her: 'I'm glad you dimentioned it!'

(299.05–6). They prove that her sex must be greater or less than one, that it has a 'magnetude', for if not, all logos/logarithms would fall back into the hole which would make their whole scene disappear (cf. 'And quite as patenly there is a hole in the ballet trough which the rest fell out' (253.20–1)), and they could reproduce themselves, which is said to be impossible. They must limit the expansion of the mother: 'since her redtangles are all abscissan for limitsing this tendency of our Frivulteeny Sexuagesima to expense herselfs as sphere as possible, paradismic perimutter, in all directions' (298.25–9). The frivole vulva must not twirl about freely, nor spread or spend itself in an indescribably spherical space. The lozenge, two diamonds combined, makes her visible, permutable. Issy's note reads: 'are we soddy we missiled her?' (299.n.1). Now become missive or missile, she is ready for the missal of the book.

The margin is turned back on itself by the hand that traces the lines of the text. The 'leaping lasso' of the 'feminine libido' (123.06 and 08) is 'sternly controlled and easily repersuaded by the uniform matteroffactness of a meandering male fist' (123.09–10). The hand of the unknown author of the letter imposes the line on the volutes and unpredictable arabesques of woman. The victory of day at the end of the book demands a little clarity: 'Stand up to hard ware and step into style. [. . .] For newmanmaun set a *marge* to the *merge* of unnotions' (614.15–17). The two margins of Shem and Shaun (II.2) are opposed to the 'footnotes' of Issy (who writes: 'words all in one soluble' (299.n.3)), in order to draw a line, to demarcate a limit (119.08, 292.31), to cut into the amalgam and the confusion of the dream.

It is not enough that woman be a triangle: she must double over to form a lozenge or a square if possible, so that her flux can sustain the rhythmic course of the universal (Hi)story. On the masculine side it is the subject that is constantly divided and multiplied. One divides into two (contraries) and, to totalize the sum ('summone'), two must become three: the 'Totumvir' (585.24) is constituted by a Triumvirate ('How their duel makes their triel' (238.31)). Man is additive, a massproduct ('I, huddled til summone be the massproduct of teamwork, three surtouts wripped up in itchother's' (546.14–16)); he allows the feminine circumference ('perimutter') a marginal liberty (it is $\pi = 3.14$): 'and enfranchised her to liberties of fringes' (548.19). Woman can only choose between the *mater*, her tamer, who gives her a role by giving her children ('who can her mater be?' (225.32)), and *matter*, flowing, undifferentiated matter: 'We're all found of our anmal matter' (294.n.5). This tension will govern the whole problematic of writing as mastery and loss, bodily flux and work on structural figures.

But in her privileged relation to writing, woman as *Hen* is 'like' a woman, but plays a man's part: 'she is ladylike in everything she does and plays the gentleman's part every time' (112.16–17). As hidden mother of the Book, 'transmaried' to Earwicker (50.11), she allows its trace to be kept, she links the serial stories, without any concern for meaning ('If you only were there to explain the meaning, best of men' 28.10–11)). She stitches up and patches the story ('sewing a dream together' (28.07)) in an ambiguous, parodic gesture; for we have already read: 'ere were sewers' (4.14). 'Sewer', she who sews, binds books and backs them, is also the sewer, collector of ordure (litters, offal/offwall), the ever more polluted river which carries the dirty linen of Dublin. The Mother, woman having acceded to the signifier, is an endless flow in which all the voices merge; she is on the side of listening (lsp/lst). Finally, it is she who gives body to the male *utter*, which she makes *butter* or above all *better*. One must imagine Anna happily buttering . . .

Conclusion

In *S/Z* Roland Barthes talks of the idleness in which we are held by classical writing which has programmed everything and leaves us, the readers, passive.[47] Joyce points in this direction in several statements made to Power when he declares himself to be anti-classical and anti-Romantic.[48] Conversely, modern writing would tend to make the reader not a consumer but a producer of text, of the text conceived as being 'writable', not just 'readable'. *Finnegans Wake* would be the 'writable' text par excellence, constituted by the reader in his reading, since the performative is displaced from the subject of the enunciation of the novel to the subject reading/listening to the book, the circularity of which moves between whole and hole. 'His producers are they not his consumers? Your exagmination round his factification for incamination of a warping process' (497.1–3).

The very form of this rhetorical question clearly shows that Joyce privileges neither producer nor consumer in a process which warps, falsifies, batters types and meanings. For his text hesitates between the *writable/unreadable* which the reader must rediscover at the cost of an excessive investment or an 'ideal insomnia' (120.14), and the *readable/risible* – that 'readable' which attacks us brutally in the laughter that takes us unawares when we are faced with a sentence or a word. As Freud well said, the more one looks for the meaning of the joke, the less one laughs, for laughter comes from an economy – in *Finnegans Wake*, an impossible economy. The paradoxical economy of *Finnegans Wake* carries along a perpetual mobilization and a cumulative discharge which is liberated in fits and starts in the laughter which surges up now and then, is triggered off by the sense of a suddenly significant nonsense, without a place consecrated by the wit and prepared in advance for the reader, without the author having foreseen the points of intersection of the crazily entwined series. The whole 'risicide' (161.17) strategy of the 'risible universe' (419.03) doubtless converges towards this unstable mixture, the *writable–risible*, the pure *jouissance* of the signifier outside meaning, the eye listening to its *wrisible* with that parodic laughter which in *Ulysses* would unite Stephen *and* the schoolboys around his riddle,[49] in a single vocal emission, that latent laughter which shakes us in the face of the 'jolting series of prearranged disappointments' (107.33) of the *Wake*: 'jolting', that is, bumping and jumping, as unforeseen as the accidents of speech, these lapsus; 'prearranged', being marked in the very texture of the text, inscribed in its structure.

The work accomplished by *Finnegans Wake* after *Ulysses*, in its wake, is in part the will to resume it, exhibiting its seams. *Finnegans Wake* would be the total book, putting an end to the dichotomy between reader/critic and writer: 'carefully digesting the very wholesome criticism' (163.36). Criticism is resumed, cited, consummated, and consumed in *Finnegans Wake*: it is a perpetual self-commentary which says more about itself in advance and in prolepsis than one can say about it. Criticism is exhausted in a perverse play of references (true or false), in which it must completely dissolve. Perhaps by enlarging the sense of the word 'criticism' one might apply to *Finnegans Wake* these sentences from Freud:

Nor have we any need to enter further into the question of how pleasure could arise from the alternation between 'thinking it senseless' and 'recognizing it as sensible'. The psychogenesis of jokes taught us that the pleasure in a joke is derived from play with words or from the liberation of nonsense, and that the meaning of the joke is merely intended to protect that pleasure from being done away with by criticism.[50]

But criticism is, nonetheless, indeed affirmed to be 'wholesome' by the professor: it is 'wholesome' because it produces the 'whole' − it totalizes. No author has been more concerned than Joyce as to what criticism would say about his work − he projected four more essays on *Finnegans Wake* to follow *Our Exagmination*. He must have been aware that the performance realized by his text made it necessary to have ministers to perform his perpetual mass. The critics would perhaps only be the butter to nourish the enzymes of *Finnegans Wake*. The text takes us for a ride, makes us 'butter'.[51] The *cantus firmus* of such a *missa parodia* could well be destined to arise in the cultural imagination of the reader become 'critic' despite himself. It is perhaps the reader who reconsecrates and recharges the book. '*Tout est sacré pour un sacreur, femme à barbe ou homme-nourrice*' (81.28–29). The consecrator combines the profane (swear-words: *Nom de nombres*!) and the sacred; the bearded lady and the nursing father are two sexually ambiguous roles (like the *poeta*): this French expression is cited as an example of a prayer. Is it not a prayer, a 'patrecknockster' (81.28) to the great book that we make through our most fundamental performative (criticism), which says: you are The Book, sacring or consecrating, or again, summing (simultaneously assigning and citing) the *Summa* of *sonner* (to ring):

> *Les sommes nocturnes révèlent*
> *la somme des mystères des hommes.*
> *Je vous somme, sommeils,*
> *de m'étonner*
> *et de tonner*[52]

And in *Finnegans Wake*: 'cog it out, here goes a sum. So read we in must book. It tells. He prophets most who bilks the best' (304.31–305.02).

(Translated by Elizabeth Guild)

Notes

1. Frank Budgen, *James Joyce and the Making of 'Ulysses'* (Oxford: Oxford University Press, pbk ed, 1972), p. 356.
2. T. W. Adorno, *Philosophy of Modern Music*, tr. A. G. Mitchell and W. V. Bloomster (London: Sheed & Ward, 1973), p. 66 (my emphasis).
3. 16 April 1942; *Letters*, I, 251.
4. 16 February 1931; *Letters*, I, 300.
5. 20 May 1927; *Letters*, I, 253.
6. Samuel Beckett, 'Dante. . . Bruno. Vico. . Joyce', in *Our Exagmination Round his Factification for Incamination of Work in Progress* (London: Faber & Faber, 1929), p. 7.
7. To quoin: to raise or secure with a wedge; quoin: corner-stone; corner; wedge; key-stone; angle; angular object (*S.O.E.D.*).
8. C. Lévi-Strauss, *The Raw and the Cooked: Introduction to a Science of Mythology*, 1, tr. J. and D. Weightman (London: Cape, 1970), p. 21.
9. 'Dante . . . Bruno. Vico. . Joyce', p. 7.
10. Umberto Eco, 'Pensée structurale et pensée sérielle' (1968), *Musique en jeu*, 5 (November 1971), 45–56 (47–8).
11. *James Joyce's Scribbledehobble, the Ur-workbook for Finnegans Wake*, ed. T. E. Connolly (Evanston: Northwestern University Press, 1961), p. 138 (Circe).
12. See Lévi-Strauss, *The Raw and the Cooked*: 'However, by virtue of its theoretical presuppositions, the serialist school is at the opposite pole from structuralism and stands in a relation to it comparable to that which used to exist between free thought and religion' (p. 27).
13. *Scribbledehobble*, p. 139.
14. Lévi-Strauss compares certain myths to the serial *roman-feuilleton*: 'In the myths as in the roman-feuilleton creation proceeds by imitations which gradually distort the nature of the source' (*The Origin of Table Manners: Introduction to a Science of Mythology*, 3, tr. J. and D. Weightman (London: Cape, 1978), 'From Myth to Novel, 2: The Daily Round', p. 130). Don't we have here all the parodic play of *Finnegans Wake*?
15. *Scribbledehobble*, p. 27.
16. It is not possible to equate this process with the stylistic colouring given by clusters of images hinged around a motif which predominates in *Ulysses*. A comparison with the saturation of the chapter 'Lestrygonians' by food-items would be necessary at this point.

17. J. W. Dunne, *An Experiment with Time* and *The Serial Universe* (London and Boston: Faber & Faber, 1927 and 1934). In many respects, the story of Professor Jones can be read as the story of the conflict between Dunne's theories and those of Wyndham Lewis. Dunne often takes a certain 'Jones' as a fictitious character (see, for instance, *The Serial Universe*, p. 72): there may be an echo of this habit in the passage.
18. Pierre Boulez defines the series as: 'a hierarchical function engendering permutations and manifested through a distribution of intervals independent of horizontal or vertical functions' (*Notes of an Apprenticeship*, ed. P. Thevenin, tr. H. Weinstock (New York: Knopf, 1968), p. 202). Seriality passes from trope to stories and to all the elements of the text.
19. 3 September 1933; *Letters*, III, 285.
20. Budgen, *James Joyce and the Making of 'Ulysses'*, p. 323.
21. Throughout the article, *l'énonciation* is translated as '(the) enunciation', and *l'énoncé*, as '(the) enounced' [Tr.].
22. *A First-Draft Version of Finnegans Wake*, ed. David Hayman (London: Faber & Faber, 1963).
23. A. Power, *Conversations with James Joyce*, ed. Clive Hart (London: Millington, 1974), p. 75.
24. See J. L. Austin, *How To Do Things with Words* (Oxford: Oxford University Press, 1962), and E. Benveniste, *Problems in General Linguistics*, tr. M. E. Meek, Miami Linguistics Series, 8 (Coral Gables, Florida: University of Miami Press, 1971).
25. 'Dante. . . Bruno. Vico. . Joyce', p. 14.
26. J. S. Atherton, *The Books at the Wake* (London and Boston: Faber & Faber, 1959), Introduction, p. 16.
27. G. Vico, *The New Science*, 3rd edn (1744), tr. T. G. Bergin and M. H. Fisch (Ithaca, N.Y.: Cornell University Press, 1968), § 429 (p. 138). For a detailed analysis of this confrontation between Vico and Jousse, see Stephen Heath, 'Ambiviolences', above, pp. 55–7.
28. *Scribbledehobble*, p. 96 (where Fenollosa is mentioned), and *Finnegans Wake*, 523.10–11.
29. *Mode*: mode and/or mood; it is impossible to maintain this ambiguity in English [Tr.].
30. J. L. Austin, *How To Do Things*, 'Lecture VI', pp. 73–6.
31. 'Let him be accu(r)sed'.
32. Roughly: 'As he has declared with his tongue, let it be the law! Against the enemy, eternal curse!'.
33. 'Against an alien the right in property shall be everlasting', *The New Science*, § 638 (p. 240); 'As the tongue has declared, so shall it be binding', *The New Science*, § 968 (p. 358).
34. J. L. Austin, *How To Do Things*, 'Lecture I', p. 9. Vico gives the translation of Cicero: 'Juravi lingua, mentem injuratam habui' (*De Officiis*, 3.29.108), *The New Science*, § 968 (p. 358).
35. *Jus* and *fas* are roughly synonymous.
36. Record of the lawful actions among the plebeians.
37. Vico, *The New Science,* IV, ch. III, 'Of Ordinary Judgements', p. 356.
38. 'He who drops a comma loses his case', *The New Science*, IV, ch. VI, § 965 (p. 356).
39. See Hélène Cixous, *Prénoms de personne* (Paris: Seuil, 1974), pp. 237–86. 'My jointspoiler' (*FW* 201.10) has been translated by 'mon briseur à plat de ma

jointerésistance' by Beckett, Perron, Jolas and others (James Joyce, *'Finnegans Wake', fragments adaptés suivis de 'Anna Livia Plurabelle'* (Paris: Gallimard, 1962), p. 100).

40. See J. L. Austin, *How To Do Things*, 'Lecture II', p. 18.

41. To apostil: to write marginal notes (*S.O.E.D.*).

42. On this subject see Jacques Derrida, 'Signature Event Context', in *Margins of Philosophy*, tr. A. Bass (Chicago: Chicago University Press, 1983), pp. 309–30.

43. This self-referentiality is very strongly affirmed by Joyce himself, for instance in relation to the 'Patrick and the Druid' passage (*FW* 611–12), which he says is a defence of, and attack on, the book itself (see the letter of 20 August 1939; *Letters*, I, 406).

44. This should be developed by a close study of Lacan's approach to women as being 'not-whole', *'pas toutes'*, in *Le Séminaire XX, Encore* (Paris: Seuil, 1975): any speaking subject can posit himself as 'VXOX', outside the imaginary completude of the phallic position (see pp. 68–71).

45. Between fabrication (made) and recompense (meed) one sees the play of the young girl (maid); *FW* constantly replays this hesitation concerning the prefix mis- and Miss.

46. 'I am speaking of the serious real. What is serious . . . can only be serial'(Lacan, *Le Séminaire XX, Encore*, p. 23).

47. See *S/Z*, tr. Richard Miller (London: Cape, 1975), 1, pp. 4–5.

48. A. Power, *Conversations*, pp. 74–5 and passim.

49. 'He stood up and gave a shout of nervous laughter to which their cries echoed dismay' (*U* 33/27).

50. Sigmund Freud, *Jokes and their Relation to the Unconscious*, tr. J. Strachey and A. Richards, Penguin Freud Library, 6 (Harmondsworth: Penguin Books, 1976), p. 181.

51. In the slang of the *Ecole Militaire* where I taught last year, 'to butter' meant 'to take someone for a ride until they get angry'.

52. R. Desnos, 'L'Aumonyme' (1923), *Corps et biens* (Paris: Gallimard, 1968), p. 58. 'Nocturnal sleep reveals/the sum of the mysteries of men./ I summon you, sleeps,/to thunderstrike me.'

6 The matrix and the echo: Intertextuality in *Ulysses*

ANDRÉ TOPIA

I The status of the quotation: the two networks

Since the end of the nineteenth century, the status of the quotation has been one of the most crucial and problematic aspects of writing. Indeed the literary text is situated more and more in relation to the multitude of other texts which circulate within it. Having become the moving receptacle, the geometric locus of an *hors-texte* which traverses and informs it, it ceases to be a block closed in by stable boundaries and clear origins of utterance. It then appears as an open configuration, strewn with landmarks and furrowed by networks of references, reminiscences, connotations, echoes, quotations, pseudo-quotations, parallels, reactivations. Linear reading gives way to transversal and correlative reading, where the printed page becomes no more than the point of intersection for strata issuing from myriad horizons. For the contemporary reader, their projected shadows cannot be avoided. Witness the perplexity in response to such works as T. S. Eliot's *The Waste Land*, Joyce's *Ulysses*, or Pound's *Cantos*. One could apply to these works the words of Michel Foucault in regard to Flaubert: 'It is a work which from the outset takes shape in the realm of learning: it exists in a certain fundamental relation to books [...]. It pertains to that literature which exists only in and by the network of what has already been written: a book whose substance is the fiction of the book [...]. Flaubert is to the library what Manet is to the museum [...]. Their art arises with the birth of archives.'[1]

Of course there is nothing new in the idea of a literary past that can be constantly used as an aesthetic model or for moral instruction: imitation and quotation are its two principal modes. All the literature produced prior to a given work is thus conceived of as a vast reservoir of examples (and even of *exempla*, in the rhetorical sense of the term), an open public repertory, broken up into a group of already prepared compartments, a mine from which the author has only to extract the piece suitable for illustrating his own text. But the term 'illustrating' accurately indicates the ancillary status of the quotation. Indeed the whole system of classical quotation rests on two prohibitions: the prohibition against modifying the borrowed fragment and the prohibition against reversing the hierarchy which puts the borrowed text in an auxiliary status (aesthetic, didactic, moral) to the bracket text. No true interaction is established. There is simply the juxtaposition of two texts where only contents come into play, and their contiguity does not lead to contamination. As for imitation, it neutralizes all real relationship in favour of a one-way filiation. The secondary text does not act on the primary text, which remains inaccessible and impregnable. Thus in each case we are confronted with rupture and separation behind an apparent union.

In the evolution towards a literature of the intertextual, Flaubert occupies a strategic position: he is among the first to have deliberately blurred the hierarchy between the original text and the secondary text.[2] The disappearance of quotation marks and the systematic use of indirect free speech (*style indirect libre*) were decisive in the exchange between levels of discourse. Indeed, indirect free speech establishes an unstable intermediary zone allowing the narrator to operate on two levels of discourse at the same time. He thus seems to take responsibility for all the discourse foreign to the text, while not actually doing so, and leaves a margin of hesitation as to its origin. This technique, which prevails in *Bouvard et Pécuchet*, will later be used extensively by Joyce: in the interior monologue, the text splits and disintegrates, becoming vulnerable to a multitude of other texts which it receives without entirely maintaining control over them.

The consequence of this is, first, the possibility of manipulation of the borrowed text and, secondly, a return effect from the new version to the original version which it contaminates and puts in perspective. Hence an increasing instability in the notion of origin: discourses weave through the text in such a way that one cannot really distinguish the original from its more or less distorted version. The element of parody is injected into the texture of the writing in such a manner that the reader is confronted with variations which he is tempted to take for the norm, which in its turn is inevitably subverted by that hesitation between origins. The text − which one then hesitates to call original, parody or quotation − becomes a place where the author pits discourses against one another, always distorting them slightly.

We have thus a whole process ranging from simply copying to rewriting, and passing through the different degrees of parody and reactivation. There is a radical departure from the classical conception of parody, which maintains a scrupulous parallel between the primary text and the secondary text, and where the analogy with the original matrix is preserved to the smallest detail, according to a scale of rigid correspondences and conversion laws demanding perfect mastery of the genre. The relation between the primary text and the secondary text is no longer a dichotomy/transposition between two components differently arranged, according to fixed rhetorical and thematic rules, but implies a devaluation of the very structures of writing.

We end up with a system of distortion and contamination by which the parody subverts the text from within.

We are then quite close to the idea of writing as loss, as analysed by Jacques Derrida in Plato's *Phaedrus*. Just as writing opens the way to an infinite series of inferior duplicates, re-writing by distortion opens a breach in the integrity of the 'original' work, exposing it to a series of imperfect copies. The whole problem lies in the relation between the original and the series of copies. Either the original is radically removed from the copies, ontologically separate from them (and then a one-way motion occurs: the original engenders the series of copies, but is never threatened by them), or the copies become substitutes for the original and pass for it. In this second case the hierarchy is reversed. The main question is that of the gap, of the supplement, and this question arises as well in the intertextual conflict as in writing in general. Derrida has shown the danger involved in this *supplément*. 'As soon as the supplementary outside is opened, its structure implies that the supplement itself can be "typed", replaced by its double, and that a supplement to the supplement, a surrogate for the surrogate, is possible and necessary.'[3] The danger arises when the duplicate ceases to be a simple copy, identifiable as such, and becomes so similar to the original text that it is no longer possible to tell them apart. The devaluation then works in both directions. This problem is at the centre of what we could call the 'vertical' analysis of the intertextual network: the essential moment is in fact when the borrowed text, extracted from its original context, begins to deny its origin and filiation.

Thus, once the three elements that come into play are postulated – the borrowing text (or bracket text), the borrowed text, and the original corpus from which the borrowed text is extracted – the intertextual problem can be envisaged in two different ways. One might examine the relationship between the original corpus of the borrowed text and the version of the borrowed text as it appears, remodelled, in the heart of its new context (echo is not repetition, re-utilization is not restitution). Or one may prefer to stress the relationship between the bracket text and the re-utilized fragment in the midst of the new aggregate formed by their co-existence, working from the hypothesis that this co-existence is more than mere juxtaposition and that the encounter of two texts inevitably engenders a new textual configuration qualitatively different from the simple sum of two units. The quotation then becomes a graft which 'takes', that is, which takes root in its new environment and weaves organic connections within it. From the encyclopedic corpus of examples one passes to an organic corpus with links to both the original network and the final network. The quoted fragment preserves its ties with its original space, but is not inserted into a new environment with impunity, that is, without significant alterations taking place within both the fragment and the new environment.

In both cases we are dealing with the question of paternity, of filiation. In the first (or vertical) perspective, it is a matter of analysing the relationship of filiation and analogy (similar to that between a matrix and its offspring which resembles it more or less faithfully) which a slightly re-modelled and distorted text continues to entertain with its origin, and of determining to what extent it survives the re-modelling. In the second (or horizontal) perspective, the central question is the homogeneity of the montage: what is the status of the new configuration formed by bringing together two texts (fusion, separation, or intertextuality)? How much responsibility does the origin of utterance in the bracket text take for the material coming from elsewhere?

In the following pages we place ourselves at the crossroads of the horizontal and vertical networks to analyse, first, intertextual polyphony ('Lotus-Eaters' chapter) and then the conflict between levels of discourse ('Cyclops' chapter) in *Ulysses*.

II   The subversive variation

In *Ulysses* the paragraph of Bloomian interior monologue is the privileged place of the intertextual play. Its hallmark is its aspect of discontinuous conglomerate. Instead of a linear continuum, the reader is presented with an aggregate of short sentences, most often fragmentary, at times reduced to mere scraps. Two apparently opposed characteristics co-exist in the same text; on the one hand an external monolithism: the textual block gives the impression of a typographic mass impossible to order according to obvious articulations – on the other, a texture of composite aggregation: the arbitrary assembling on the space of the page of a heterogeneous material whose units are merely gathered side by side, welded to one another. Thus the block is externally massive and compact: each of the units appearing at the same level as the others, there seems to be neither progression nor hierarchy among them. But on the other hand, within the block, each unit, as it is not linked to the others by a compelling logical structure, tends to become autonomous and form an independent island. So that the model of narrative sequence does not apply to the Bloomian interior monologue. Each assembled unit is both different from and similar to the others: the apparently irreducible difference between them renders them all alike in relation to the law presiding over the totality of the block.

There have been frequent attempts to discern in the Bloomian sentence a kind of order by 'association' – called 'stream -of-consciousness technique', or 'associative logic', or even 'sub-language' – prior to the emergence of speech. But these approaches are insufficient to convey the implacable architecture of Joycean writing. We are dealing with a text that is highly organized, firmly coded and programmed down to its most minute units, but whose organizational law has been carefully camouflaged by systematic fragmentation and even pulverization. While in novels such as those of Virginia Woolf the aim is to dissolve the boundaries between sentences, to string them into one long musical phrase blurring and effacing the discordances only to reintegrate them in a larger unit, Joyce does exactly the opposite. He carefully places insidious discordances at strategic spots, gathers them together in a montage by juxtaposition and makes this the privileged vehicle of meaning. These discordances can involve a text not present on the page as well as textual units actually present and contrasted with each other. Woolf's text starts from the discontinuity and multiplicity of the real and attempts to impose on it if not an order, at least an ordered surface. On the contrary the Joycean text takes as its point of departure an extremely strict and organized law which it then proceeds to actualize in a fragmented text. Thus the true origin of the text is in a law exterior to it, and not in a unifying subject. With Woolf, everything constantly comes back to a unifying subject which supplies linkages, imperceptible connections in the form of associations of ideas. With Joyce on the other hand we are constantly witnessing the disappearance of the psychological subject Bloom. And despite all this, something is speaking, something which structures the discourse more profoundly and implacably than a psychological 'I'. Ceaselessly at work in the Bloomian text are matrices of discourse, compelling patterns which the language of the subject Bloom is forced to enter. And the whole impact of the text is in the tension, the apparent contradiction between these matrices, on the one hand, which only appear in a fragmentary and degraded form, and on the other hand the polymorphic texture of the typographic continuum which is at the same time their geometric locus and their medium.

Each unit embraced in the montage is thus in fact the actualization of a paradigm, the projection onto the space of the page of one or several codes exterior to the text. Hence the relationship of equivalence and opposition, rather than of continuity and complementarity, between the different units. The textual mosaic can be read as easily in the mode of extreme differentiation as in the mode of total equivalence. Everything depends on whether or not the initial paradigm is taken into account at the moment of reading. The Bloomian text may be read as a locked text, a rigid partitioned conglomerate − or, on the contrary, as a mobile, open text where everything ceaselessly circulates, each of the fragments maintaining the same relationship with the paradigm. The linear horizontal order becomes secondary to a vertical order, which is a relation between the code and its actualization. Horizontally, the text begins to move because the montage technique constantly creates a multitude of mobile configurations. Vertically, the text is informed and vivified from the exterior by an 'other text', from which it draws its origin and of which it is a more or less adequate copy. And a purely horizontal analysis, which would merely assemble the textual units that are under the jurisdiction of the same code, would result only in a thematic grouping of 'leitmotivs' thereby ignoring the specifically intertextual dimension. On the contrary, to traverse the Bloomian configuration one must follow at the same time the vertical circulation (recalls, pseudo-quotations, reactivations) and the horizontal circulation (montage). Each word maintains a relationship of tension with both the network from which it draws its origin (implicit corpus of existing texts or rhetorical matrices) and with the network in which it is included without being altogether integrated (the actual typographical block of the page in *Ulysses*). The Joycean intertext is founded on this dual relationship.

Let us take as an example the long reverie stirred up by an advertisement for a brand of tea near the start of the 'Lotus-Eaters' chapter (73/71–2). At the beginning we find the following words: 'choice blend, made of the finest Ceylon brands'. This sentence, which at first reading does not differentiate itself from the rest of Bloom's disconnected thoughts, is in fact the fragmentary reprise of an advertising message read from a box of tea packets glimpsed a few moments earlier. But thus enveloped in the Bloomian reverie it does not appear in quotation marks. This disappearance of quotation marks is crucial: it eliminates all typographic indicators permitting the distinction of the different levels of discourse. Nothing permits us to know *a priori* if the sentence 'belongs' to Bloom or not. With no responsible origin of utterance assigned to these words, we integrate them into Bloom's discourse – until we remember that they are the reprise of a quotation, this time presented clearly as quotation, in the preceding paragraph. This hesitation, this faint vibration of the text to which no clear and immediate paternity is attributed, is often found in the Bloomian monologue. Bloom takes over and reactivates discourses formed outside him, for which he takes responsibility – up to a point. The result is an incessant feedback effect between the discourse reactivated by Bloom and the words of Bloom himself, to such a point that the difference between the two often becomes indiscernible. In taking up these coded discourses in his own manner, Bloom appropriates them all, distorting and perverting them to greater and lesser degrees. But conversely the Bloomian utterances, even when they are of his own 'creation', take on an aspect of collective crystallization, of cliché. The properly Bloomian discourses and the exterior discourses are finally all equivalent in a sort of unstable equilibrium, a mobile milieu which partakes of both the 'psychology of the character' and the most highly institutionalized codes. The most personal utterance may take on an aspect of cliché, and the most shopworn stereotype often finds itself promoted to the rank of an original formulation.

Thus the text becomes a configuration within which both orphaned and hypercoded discourses circulate. The reactivated text, having lost a large part of its original denotative function (the context on which its functional legitimacy was based), finds itself in a sort of nomadism. The reader is thus confronted with what one might call a surplus of code, a supplement of code. Far from offering a preconscious reverie, the Bloomian interior monologue provides us with the code pure and simple, but a code without an immediate end, one might almost say an aimless code, ready for every adventure and vulnerable to every distortion. This surplus code is one of the most fascinating aspects of Bloomian language: it is partially neutralized by the breakages caused by the discontinuous arrangement of the paragraph, but the *hors-texte* is no less obstinately present in the background as the immense corpus of texts and repertory of codes of which *Ulysses* is the transient and degraded point of crystallization.

Next sentences: 'The far east. Lovely spot it must be: the garden of the world, big lazy leaves to float about on, cactuses, flowery meads, snaky lianas they call them.' We find here the same problem of attribution: of the five expressions used, only one ('cactuses') is not a cliché. What could be taken at first reading for an imaginary description is in fact nothing less then discourse pure and simple. The very structure of the sentence shows that we are at no point dealing with a *mise en scène*, an imaginary decor, a topography, but that on the contrary the composition of place never goes beyond a series of more or less reactivated clichés. What is given us here is nothing but *topic*, topic which does not hide behind an appearance of realistic elaboration but which on the contrary shows itself for what it is: exploratory probing and sampling. The clear designation of the theme at the beginning of the development ('Far East') in fact plays here the role of a kind of title, a chapter-head which automatically summons, elicits, and reels off the whole series of generic expressions which fit it and belong to its 'compartment'. Rather than a space of reverie we are dealing with a linguistic, a rhetorical, an encyclopedic space. Rather than playing out the unbroken continuum of a description, the text scatters indices each of which corresponds to a subclass, a subgroup of a dictionary grouping, a vast repertory of clichés on the 'Far East'. As for the words 'Far East', they are in the end nothing more than a cybernetic key regrouping the whole series of expressions/indices/examples accumulated in Bloom's mind under this heading. Thus rather than an 'evocation' of the Far East, we are dealing with a recomposition of one of the multiple layers of Bloomian knowledge, with the projection onto the text of a certain state of knowledge and language which is articulated around the 'character' Bloom.

This serial order will be systematically used in the 'Ithaca' chapter in the form of a question/answer catechism, a development of the compartmentalization peculiar to the topic. Each question, each chapter-head then has the function of limiting more or less arbitrarily the field of the text by delimiting a precise compartment, a *quaestio* in the scholastic sense of the term. The function of the answers (as well as, here, the 'picturesque' borrowings which nourish Bloom's adulterated exoticism) is then to cover the delimited compartment as thoroughly as possible, all the while remaining strictly inside it. Hence the curious impression of padding, of catch-all produced by the text. Once the point of departure is supplied, it is as though the material were ready to spring out fully formed. The Bloomian text has this distinctive feature: that its clichés are extraordinarily reactivated by the manipulations carried out on them, by the architecture of the text, which is the specific place of Joycean art.

Thus the Bloomian text may sometimes appear as a vast tautology. It seems to be no more than a succession of examples brought from elsewhere and projected onto the space of the book. The whole movement of the text is then in the greater or lesser compatibility between the delimited field and the examples which come in to fill it. It is poles apart from a literature whose aim is to bring the real into existence. When reading *Ulysses* one has the impression that all the material in the book is already contained potentially in the great manuals and dictionaries of language, of the sciences, of popular wisdom.

This does not mean that Bloom is merely a machine: the material is forever being disarticulated and rearticulated. The entire process of the text is in the series of variations possible between perfect adequacy and radical inadequacy. Between the two one finds an infinity of minute displacements and distortions which are the very flesh of the Joycean text. We get the impression that beginning from a stimulus (analogous to an item from a nomenclature, a key of a computer, a section-heading from a catalogue, the call-word of an index) Bloom tries on (and tries himself at) a succession of actualizations falling within the range of the existing discourses. And what makes this process fascinating is that it is always problematic, and that there is never perfect congruence between the initial program and its fulfilment (we see this aspect again in the novels of Beckett). It is as though Bloom were groping, pressing different keys in succession, exploring different networks and, rather than actualizing and developing only one, were content with juxtaposing variations. So that there is always a slight but crucial gap between topic and discourse.

Thus the whole produces a sort of unstable compromise. And one of the difficulties in reading *Ulysses* comes from the contrast between on the one hand the extreme elaboration of the code for each of the expressions at work (the cliché is indeed the fixed result of a long sedimentation, it is a 'finished product'), and on the other hand their inability to communicate an ensemble of viable meaning. The Joycean text is not 'viable', is not 'transformable' into the real. The whole artifice (and the whole success, as well) of the great works of realist literature is in the fact that this transformation appears so self-evident that it is obliterated. In *Ulysses*, on the other hand, the two elements are dissociated; the matrix is set apart from its various imperfect products. Thus the text appears encumbered with the debris of its own imperfect productions, a little like a machine that leaves in its wake a series of aborted products all bearing the stamp of their origin and designating it, but unable to form a coherent whole. This dissociation radically interferes with any realist reading of *Ulysses*, preventing the real and the discourse from folding over on each other. The text never builds a simulacrum of the real but sets out '*en creux*' a deeper process, that of writing itself. The imperfect product, rather than masking its origin and passing as an autonomous object, self-sufficient in its perfection, undertakes the archaeology of its own production.

However, though constantly inadequate to its purpose, the Bloomian discourse is always in quest of explanations and interpretations in the fields it explores. It never stops at simple nomenclature but quickly goes on to reasons and causes. But we soon perceive that its reasoning belongs rather to scientism than to science: the explanation, too, is spun out in the mode of stereotype.

For example, in the reverie on the Orient, it goes from more or less botanical considerations on Oriental vegetation to pseudo-ethnological, pseudo-anthropological remarks on the causes of apathy in Orientals. We then find successive evocations (each time in a degraded mode) of climatology, chemistry, medicine, the physics of liquids, and the mechanics of solids. None of these explanations is developed. What Bloom is aiming for is a relentless interrogation of the most inhabitual aspects of reality. But he refrains from seeking its laws, synthesizing it, or subsuming its data in generalizations with universal value. What counts is not so much each explanation (itself a cliché) as the juxtaposition of simultaneous, concurrent and often contradictory explanations. While coherent explanation implies the choice of one level from which the others proceed, it is precisely this hierarchy which Bloom dissolves. Instead of a reasoning, strictly speaking, we have a sprinkling of concurrent levels which are at times apparently scientific (chemistry, physics), at times akin to metaphor (comparison of the lethargy of Orientals with hothouse plants, comparison of the water lilies with the swimmer in the Dead Sea, image of the man walking on rose petals), both levels mutually devaluing and relativizing each other in their alternating counterpoint.

But Bloom is far from being a mere machine, by turns receptor and emitter of clichés. Between reception and emission comes distortion. There is an example, in this same paragraph, in the image of the man floating in the Dead Sea ('Where was the chap I saw in that picture somewhere? Ah, in the dead sea, floating on his back, reading a book with a parasol open. Couldn't sink if you tried: so thick with salt.') The miracle of Christ walking on the waters is implicitly suggested behind this reminiscence of a magazine photo which is its parodic double. The bather floating while reading a book is the image of the twentieth-century man who, having accepted the disappearance of religious values (the Dead Sea has been struck by lightning from the sky), absorbs himself in an introverted hedonism. While Christ walking on the waters effected a movement of ascension and victory over the weight of matter by the miracle of divine faith, the bather can sink no farther because he has already become one with the amorphous liquid element. For the image of a superhuman miracle we find substituted the image of a tourist absorbed in vegetative pleasure.

Now in the whole 'Lotus-Eaters' chapter we find an extraordinary sampling of 'other texts' circulating, ranging from pure retranscription to total rewriting. It is fascinating to examine to what point the progress of the Bloomian monologue is capable of aggregating a whole mass of material injected from other textual spaces without its integrity threatening to shatter: fragments of popular songs, folk ballads, operatic arias or religious hymns; scraps of quotations from poems, novels, plays, nursery rhymes; bits of magazine and newspaper articles; proverbial phrases, maxims of popular wisdom. Furthermore, one can notice a proliferation of specific types of discourse within which Bloomian speech flows by a sort of mimicry and contagion. Formulae from theories of physics (73/72), journalistic eloquence (74/73), the style of military commands (74/73), the style of an opera libretto (78/76), simperings of prudish coquettishness (80/79, 82/81), the familiar language of a child going to fetch his father at the pub (72/71), cries of roving ice cream vendors (82/81), confessional phrases (84/83), the effusive public confessions of repentant prostitutes (84/83), phrases from wills bequeathing money to the church (84/83), expressions of politeness mingled with vulgarity (85/83), abridged pharmaceutical formulae (85/84), the discourse of solicitation aimed at attracting bettors (87/86), the language of cricket (87/86). One has the impression that the diversity of the real is conveyed primarily through the diversity of discourse. Whatever the specificity of the real, it is as if one could always find a discourse precise enough to render it. The discourses become the royal road to the restitution of the real. Thus Joyce distances himself from the method of the realist author who seeks to model his style on the contours of reality. The Joycean postulate is that in the tiniest fragment of discourse, a complete cross-section of the real is unveiled.

Advertising is the privileged mediation of these anonymous discourses. Bloom's consciousness is somewhat like a radio band constantly swept by all types of signals, much like a magnetic field or an electronic network crisscrossed by multiple circuits. And in this criss-cross pattern advertising occupies an eminent place because it is, *par excellence*, both an anonymous and an omnipresent text, the debased contemporary version of the *texte pluriel*, in the form of triumphant stereotype turned privileged message. Capable of entering any stylistic code with extreme facility, it is for Bloom the quintessence of twentieth-century discourse. It is the perverted but perfectly elaborated use of the rules of classical discourse, the latest avatar of ancient rhetoric, which was originally the art of persuasion. Moreover, it is a coded discourse which is substituted for the sacred discourses of the past and, just like these sacred discourses, it conveys an injunction, a parodic and degraded version of religious commandments. But whereas the religious code had to be deciphered, advertising deciphers itself on its own and is instantly transformed into consumption. While the discourse of the priest appears in the church as an opaque idiom severed from its original aim, advertising triumphs in its functional transparence. Throughout the chapter one must read the two discourses in counterpoint and contrast.

For it is perhaps in the work performed on the discourse of Catholicism that the most subversive dimension of intertextuality appears in 'Lotus-Eaters'. Pervaded with anecdotes, conventional formulae, stereotyped pious imagery, the Catholic text appears here as the antithesis of what it is supposed to be. The great ritual discourse omnipresent in the lives of the Dubliners, it appears eminently vulnerable to the milieu in which it is used, whereas it should be the standard invulnerable to any distortion. The fragmentation and dissemination of the liturgical language of the priest during the mass are in themselves evidence of the profound debasement suffered by the sacred Word. The great Christian body (sacred corpus of the Church and corpus of sacred texts), the indivisible and unfragmentable totality of the teachings of Christ, is no more than a powder of isolated words, a sprinkling of short sentences and scraps of sentences separated from the living spiritual continuity which gave them all their incantatory and sacred power, cut off from the great text of the divine Logos, and therefore vulnerable to all blasphemous manipulations and distortions.

One of the most effective devices is the counterpoint between religious discourse and para-religious discourse. In the mosaic of the Bloomian reverie, we find at the same time quotations belonging to the 'orthodox' corpus of religious discourse (quotations from hymns, fragments of prayers, passages from the Bible) and elements that could be called para-religious: these are all the discourses arising from the social code surrounding religion and issuing from the confusion of these two levels, discourses where social appearances and the routine of devoutness override true faith. Thus the sacred speech falls prey to parasitic voices which are merely its corrupted avatars: confession ('Penance. Punish me, please [. . .]. And I schschschschschsch. And did you chachachachacha? And why did you?'), donations to the church ('Bequests also: to the P.P. for the time being in his absolute discretion.'), theological discourse employed to impress a judge during a trial ('He had his answer pat for everything. Liberty and exaltation of our holy mother the church.') (84/83). These frozen, empty ritual codes are nothing more than an endless succession of degraded reverberations re-echoed by believers anaesthetized by a paralysing religion. And contamination by the style of advertising is in itself the sign of deeper deterioration. We see successively a missionary's sermon announced by a poster analogous to the advertising signs scattered through the chapter ('Same notice on the door. Sermon by the very reverend John Conmee S.J. on saint Peter Claver and the African mission. Save China's millions.') (81/80); the notice, again in the style of advertising, of a public meeting of the Salvation Army ('Salvation Army blatant imitation. Reformed prostitute will address the meeting.') (84/83); a gaudy sample of the above mentioned prostitute's style ('How I found the Lord.') (84/83).

The whole blasphemous dimension is thus in the encounter of the religious text and the profane text. The device of juxtaposition and counterpoint leads imperceptibly from one discourse to another by a truly devastating levelling effect. One never knows if one is in the orthodox sacred text or in one of its corrupt variations. Little by little the idea becomes clear that Catholicism, by its very essence as code and ritualized institution, itself secretes these parasitic practices — to a point where it could be said that in this constant oscillation, there is no longer a true Christianity to distinguish from its worldly distortions. The corruptions are not mere avatars of the sacred text, but are the text itself. We have a perfect example in the page where the whispering hypocritical confessions of the Dublin devout appear in the same paragraph as the self-accusatory protestations of repentant prostitutes in the Salvation Army. The two passages are placed practically one after the other, before a backdrop (and thus, symbolically, a common source and origin) of the sacred discourse of the priest saying Mass, whose fragmented speech appears just before and just after this paragraph (84/82–3). The sacred word is thus a background noise, over which the profane and blasphemous variations created by Bloom's thoughts emerge. A complete parodic polyphony is set up little by little. The strictly sacred text is no longer there except as a reference point which reappears here and there to allow us to measure both its distance from and its proximity to the degraded variations descended from it, which make up the very substance of Dublin Catholic discourse.

But the intertextual polyphony is not found solely in the alternated montage. It may also find its way into one passage taken in isolation. In the most orthodox of religious texts, parasite texts may insinuate themselves to distort its initial meaning, and vice versa. Bloom has an extraordinary gift for debunking the most institutionalized codes.

'Who is my neighbour?' (82/80). These apparently innocent words pronounced by Bloom on entering the church are also the question asked to Christ in the Bible by the lawyer in answer to the injunction 'Thou shalt love thy neighbour as thyself' (Luke 10.29), to which Christ replies with the parable of the Good Samaritan.[4] But these words, borrowed out of context, take on a completely different orientation here as they are placed after the phrase: 'Nice discreet place to be next some girl.' The Biblical meaning does not completely disappear but remains there as a vague reminiscence, the passive servant of this usurpation.

There is the same devaluing encounter in the words 'Hokypoky penny a lump' (82/81), by which Bloom punctuates the absorption of the Host by the faithful at church. They are in fact the words shouted by wandering ice-cream vendors ('Hokey, pokey, a penny a lump'), as well as the reprise of a child's nursery rhyme ('Hokey pokey winkey wum') (whose protagonist, we may note in passing, is the king of the Cannibal Islands, another symbolic detail in the context of the absorption of the Host). Thus the telescoping of these cliché formulae shows us a host turned ice-cream cone and a priest become wandering vendor. Religion dallies in the sickening sugariness of sweets and in babbling regression to infantile submission.

Finally, the most concentrated and subversive example of intertextual writing is perhaps found in the treatment of the word 'corpus', a word central to the Eucharist (which is being performed before Bloom in the church) since it designates the body of Christ brought to life in the sacrament. Here the word 'corpus' intoned by the preacher is immediately punctuated by Bloom with the word 'corpse' (*'Corpus*. Body. Corpse.') (82/80). The phonic proximity of the two words corpus/corpse produces a contamination effect: they become interchangeable. This equivalence is all the more tempting as 'corpse' actually does refer to a body, but a dead body. Bloom here surreptitiously obliterates the radical difference between life and death: stripped of their sacramental significance, the body of Christ is no more than a cadaver, the Host no more than a cake, as it was previously a 'lollipop' (82/81), or elsewhere, a gherkin picked from a jar ('He stopped at each, took out a communion, shook a drop or two (are they in water?) off it and put it neatly into her mouth.') (82/80). This deliberate myopia is all the more devastating in that here the body of Christ is also Life, recreated by the sacrament of communion. Once this Life is eliminated from the ceremony, all that is left is a ritual, a succession of mere gestures, an empty form ready for every perversion. Hence the ease with which the discourses of the grocery (the analogy to the gherkin), or medicine ('Shut your eyes and open your mouth.') (82/80), are adapted to the ceremonial.

But if such conflicts are brought into play by these isolated encounters, it is because these conflicts are constantly triggered and reactivated by a compelling all-inclusive network which permeates the chapter all the way through. One example demonstrates this. When Bloom, in the beginning of the chapter, has just suffered a bitter frustration of his voyeuristic pleasure because a passing tram has blocked his view of the silk-sheathed leg of a woman entering a taxi, he remarks on the event in the following words: 'Paradise and the peri.' (76/74). The immediate recollection is of the title of the second section of a poem by Thomas Moore, *Lalla Rookh*. But it goes further: in Persian mythology the *peri* are creatures issued from fallen angels expelled from Paradise until their penance is fulfilled. The encounter between these two contexts calls up an image of Bloom brutally wrenched from his paradise, a woman's legs. And the chapter is strewn with these surrogate Edens devoid of all spirituality and where a paralysing inertia takes the place of bliss: the gelded horses whose supreme Eldorado is a peck of oats (78/77), the Chinese who find bliss more readily in an ounce of opium than in the missionaries' sermons (81/80), the natives fascinated not by the words of Father Farley, but by the lenses of his spectacles, which give off blue-tinged glintings (81/80), the faithful reaching ecstasy by swallowing the Host as one eats a piece of candy (82/81), the beggar who sleeps like the blessed during communion (82/81), the Italian eunuchs for whom castration has brought bliss (84/82). If we link together all these examples we eventually lay out a symbolic network covering the whole surface of the text. As soon as a discourse obviously external to Bloom is inserted into his monologue, it is at once caught up in this architecture which is far more compelling than it appears at first reading and which runs through the chapter like another text. Each time a distortion takes place, it is because the textual fragment becomes part of the network.

What makes the distortion so immediate is the fact that the text is saturated by two parallel and superimposed networks: on the one hand the realm of dogma, of Christian institution, of Catholic discourse; on the other the symbolic network of lethargy, inertia and surrogate paradises, equally omnipresent. The nodal points in the text, the strategic intertextual nexuses, are the moments of interference between these two spaces. A phenomenon of crystallization, of catalysis, then occurs, somewhat like a saturated liquid which suddenly precipitates. This is why one must not be deceived by the disordered and fragmentary appearance of the text: each fragment has behind it all the space it stems from, and the polysemous crystallization at the core of a single passage is in fact the point of juncture of two inclusive spaces. And the intertextual nebula appears as a highly organized configuration.

III   The matrix and the echo

The 'Cyclops' chapter expands the intertextual mechanisms already noted in 'Lotus-Eaters': dissociation into heterogeneous and antagonistic levels of discourse. Here the conflict appears at its height: it seems that the discourses at work have reached such a state of differentiation and autonomy that they split apart. One passes from tension to dissociation. The chapter breaks up into two alternating utterances: the linear and chronological progress of the first person narrative (the Nameless One) and heterogeneous textual blocks which are constantly cutting into this narrative flux. We have thus a text that is fundamentally bifid: on the one hand a narrative texture unified around a speaking subject, with reality as its underlying substratum (the account of the events in the pub) and obeying all the conventional laws of a dramatized oral tale: unity of place (the pub), of characters, of time, of action (with even an element of suspense: how is Bloom going to get out of it?) − on the other hand foreign bodies quite obviously proceeding from a textual space completely different from that of the Nameless One, giving the impression of being fragments of a vaster text from which they have come unfastened, like erratic blocks circulating without origin and without aim. Even while included in the same typographic continuum, the two texts seem to unfurl in two parallel spaces without either of them ever encroaching upon the other. One has, as it were, the impression of watching a film into which someone has spliced, at regular intervals, fragments of reels belonging to other films, or a collage where the description of a figurative scene is juxtaposed with fragments of newspapers or posters.

Each insertion is apparently motivated: indeed, each one has its starting point in a theme or a character or sometimes a mere detail briefly mentioned in the narration, and which the insertion seems to develop and rewrite. The existence of these links, however tenuous, has prompted many critics to read each insertion as the rewriting, in another style, of what has just been said by the Nameless One. But such a reading confronts serious obstacles. In fact, the trigger theme which makes the junction between the narration and each insertion is so reworked by the insertions that it fails to provide a real transition between the two texts. What is there in common between Alf Bergan saying that he thought he saw Dignam a few moments before, while the latter is actually dead, and the long account given of a spiritist seance Dubliner-style (299–300/300–2)? or again between the evocation by the Nameless One of a judge who sides with the poor against the rich, and the extensive fresco depicting Sir Frederick the Falconer dispensing justice before the Gaelic tribes (320–1/322–3)? or finally between the Citizen shouting 'Sinn Fein' and the lengthy flamboyant journalistic account of the execution of a young Irish nationalist (304–8/306–10)? In fact, each insertion displays a stylistic and rhetorical elaboration which largely transcends the narrative starting point and creates another reading space. One cannot perceive the specifically intertextual relation between narration and insertions if the latter are seen merely as another version of the former.

Let us first analyse the two discourses separately. The nameless One's shapeless and meandering account is both unable to structure itself according to 'stylistic' turns of phrase, and to structure its object: the episode in the pub. One is dealing with repetitive and obsessive speech, each moment modelling itself on the contour of the event, unable to resist any possible opportunity for a pure retranscription of overheard dialogues or the pleasure of long calumnious digressions. It is incapable of building a scene, setting a stage, using rhetorical turns of phrase or repeating anything other than the judgements of the mysterious acolyte Pisser Burke, the crystallization of a collective speech and ultimate guarantor of truth. In fact it is devoid of all that makes for the specificity of the insertions.

In comparison with the preceding chapters, we witness a deliberate impoverishment. The technique of the interior monologue gives way to an oral narrative which is *not* interior monologue, but a narration by a person whose identity is never known, addressed to an equally anonymous interlocutor. This imperialism, this terrorism of the first person narrative serves to radically alter the relation between the discourse and the real. It means the end of the subtle narrative architecture set in place since 'Telemachus', where meaning proceeded less from a content transmitted by a narrator than from a textual network where everything was conveyed through the contrasts between the different zones of the chapter on the one hand, between the text and the underlying intertext on the other. A break occurs between the event accomplished once and for all, definitively cast into the past (the episode in the pub) and the voice of the narrator, which is the sole mediation at our disposal to grasp this event. The real retracts into the hypothetical and is completely masked by a sort of screen constituted by the voice of the narrator. The whole narration appears as a supplement to the event, a cumbersome supplement whose only effect on the supposed truth it possesses and never doubts for a moment is to cause it to retract still further. Whereas with Bloom an insidiously subversive seesaw effect took place between the different codes playing against each other, we have here a speech that is fundamentally nonsubversive because the slight gap, the faultline which permitted the emergence of meaning, has disappeared. Speech has become a slave to what it tries to communicate, and is condemned to replay it till the end of time.

Compared to this mudslide the insertions read like fireworks. Their variety makes all attempts to classify them seem illusory. However, if we take for our point of departure writing techniques rather than themes, groupings can quite easily be achieved.

1   Journalistic discourse

— sentimental clichés and epic amplification in the style of the yellow press (304–8/306–10)
— the literary page (309–10/311–12)

— the account of the nationalist gathering (315–16/316–18)
— the jargon of sports journalism (316–17/318–19)
— society news
. the elegant wedding (325–6/327)
. the visit of a distinguished personage (323–3/334)
. the ceremony of farewell to a royal visitor (341/342–3)
— the pseudo-scientific chronicle in journalistic style
. the account of a spiritist seance and the apparition of a spirit (299–300/301–2)
. the report of a natural cataclysm (342–3/344–5)

2   Forms of specific discourses

— legal jargon (291/292–3)
— medical jargon (303/304–5)
— the style of wall graffiti (331–2/333)
— the clichés of condolence (312/313–14)
— the style of children's literature (313/315)
— the style of parliamentary debates (314/315–16)
— the eloquence of a nationalist diatribe (324–5/326)
— religious discourse
. the Book of Common Prayer (327–8/329)
. the liturgical style (337–9/338–40)
. biblical poetry (343/345)

3   Literary discourses

— the style of the epic
. epic amplification in the manner of the archaic Celtic saga (294–5/296–7)
. geographic and encyclopedic panorama in the vein of epic description (292–3/293–5)
. allegory (298/300)
. portrait of the epic heroine (318/319)
. the archaic Celtic chronicle (321/322–3, 323/324)
. the epic vignette (330–1/331–2)
. the medieval romance (334–5/336–7)

One sees now why critics have often understood the chapter's parodic value to lie in a purely thematic contrast between narration and insertions, between the sensational, theatrical and hyperbolic aspect of the insertions and the prosaic and even sordid dimension of the goings-on in the pub. But this devaluing juxtaposition of the legendary universe of the epic (and the magazine) and the sordid world of Dublin is the least interesting aspect of the chapter. Rather than starting from a contrast between two universes, we must begin from the conflict between two levels of discourse.

But it would also be a mistake to assimilate this conflict to an apparent pluralism in writing, often practised in literature since the end of the nineteenth century, which consists in presenting the reader with a succession of discourses of various characters, each relating in their own voice events which are often identical. This is the case, for example, with Browning (*The Ring and the Book*), Faulkner (*As I Lay Dying, The Sound and The Fury*), and Virginia Woolf (*Mrs Dalloway*). Intertextuality in the true sense of the word is absent from these writings. For the different testimonies are in fact 'styles', each modelled on the psychology of a character, the collection of these distortions being unified in the end by an author controlling the whole process. This is not the case in 'Cyclops', where on the one hand the narration, although in the first person, continually refers back to the collective and anonymous, and on the other hand the insertions are anonymous pieces which never draw their stylistic specificity from the idiosyncrasies of a 'character' or the partiality of a 'point of view', but are much more a nearly mechanical, however brilliant, display of writing devices.

The whole difference between alternation of points of view and conflict of discourses can be summarized by the distinction made by Mikhail Bakhtin between 'stylization' and parody. In what he calls 'stylization' there is no real conflict between the different voices: 'This is not a collision of two ultimate semantic authorities, but rather an objectivized (thematic) collision of two represented positions which is wholly subordinate to the author's ultimate authority.' On the other hand, in what Bakhtin calls 'parody' ('dialogism' as opposed to 'monologism'), we have to do with utterances which are at the same level, not taken over by an author, and thus in conflict. 'The weakening or destruction of the monological context occurs only when two equally and directly object-oriented utterances come together. [. . .] Two embodied thoughts cannot lie side by side like two objects − they must come into inner contact, i.e. must enter into a semantic bond.'[5]

We find in this quotation two ideas that can be applied to 'Cyclops'. First, the distinction between 'style' and 'ultimate semantic authority' (the equivalent of the French term *énonciation*): no author is there in fact to include and neutralize the oppositions in the chapter. Next, the basis of the theory of montage (of which 'Cyclops' is a perfect example, coming just at the time when the technique was beginning to develop with Griffith and Eisenstein): the combination formed by juxtaposing several sufficiently contrasted units is qualitatively different from the simple sum of these units, and necessarily produces a crystallization of meaning which goes beyond their respective differences.

Let us now try to define the two writing techniques brought into play. The speech of the Nameless One is a good example of literally alienated discourse through which circulates a whole collection of imported stereotypes. His obsession is the ceaseless search for origins and guarantees outside himself. And in this, his discourse is pure echo, and even the echo of an echo. He is the prototype of Dublin speech, which is only an infinite series of reverberations. And he is profoundly Dublinesque inasmuch as he is merely a resonating chamber within which reverberates something which has already been spoken, itself an echo which will in turn produce other echoes, and so on to infinity. He is nothing more than a fleeting stage in the infinite series of repetitions.

And what is fascinating in this speech is that although it is a succession of repetitions and echoes, it appears as original, as being an origin. It takes over its imported material as though this material were arising for the first time, as though suddenly uttering a truth which did not exist a few moments before. The Nameless One identifies himself totally with an already-spoken which is his flesh and blood. And, in this, we glimpse through his discourse the essential difference between oral intertextuality and written intertextuality. The voice, even when content to re-deliver words already delivered by others, cannot prevent itself from taking them over. Contrary to the written text, the voice is more than a simple mediation. Even if it repeats, this repetition is not performed with impunity. The written, printed, typographic text possesses a neutrality and an inertia which are far removed from the spoken word, which is always identified, to a greater or lesser extent, with the voice which utters it. Hence this phenomenon of near possession which makes the Nameless One, though re-saying the already-said, seem to be bringing it into existence for the first time. He becomes its origin and its founder.

There is a fetishistic dimension to the Nameless One's attitude towards the anecdotes he reproduces, the speech he repeats, the voices he mimics, the scenes he almost replays for his audience. Repetition becomes magical rite, echo becomes incantatory ceremony, restitution becomes conjuration. Whereas the written text is immediately contaminated by all the possibilities of mass reproduction which loom up behind it (journalism, mass media, etc., as is the case with the insertions), for a fleeting moment the voice gives back to its utterance the appearance of an original creation. This ceremony recurs constantly in Joyce: in the dialogues of *Dubliners* (in particular 'Ivy Day in the Committee Room' and 'Grace'), in the words of M'Coy at the beginning of 'Lotus-Eaters', in the interminable discussions among the journalists of the *Irish Freeman* in 'Aeolus'. In the magic of pub conversation, the immense corpse of the Dublin already-spoken continually returns to life vicariously for a few brief moments.

Moreover, this repetition has an essential function in participation: it is through its mediation that the Nameless One becomes an integral part of the Dublin community and, thus, exists. In this respect one could compare Molly Bloom's monologue in 'Penelope' and that of the Nameless One in 'Cyclops'. In both cases we find a speech which is fundamentally oral, meandering, relatively unstructured, using familiar language. But the formulae Molly uses are never frozen clichés. They are on the contrary extraordinarily original and individualized. As distinct from that of men, the language of women does not necessarily pass through that collective voice and that participation in a global entity of which the pub is the crucible and the microcosm.

Let us return to the insertions. What they have in common is that each is a highly coded and organized picture. Each of them offers the systematic and quasi-mechanical unfurling of a discourse that is wholly constituted, completely prepared, fully armed, which then 'covers' the real like a rhetorical grid, like a sort of formal matrix whose existence precedes any actualization in a text. Each uses to excess all the rhetorical rules of *inventio* (choice of subject), *dispositio* (internal arrangement) and *elocutio* (actual figures of rhetoric). Each insertion is in fact a real little machine for the production of a certain type of text, depending on the matrix present in the background, somewhat like a computer program. Despite their appearance of infinite diversity, the insertions are far from free. For they are in fact vignettes, purple passages, rhetorical and poetic *topoi*. Behind a verbal profusion that seems to metamorphose the world into so many *mirabilia* by kaleidoscopic and phantasmagorical effects, we soon see clichés arising.

The insertions are in fact 'clichés' in the original sense of the word ('Plate bearing in relief the reproduction of a page of type or of an image, permitting the impression of numerous copies', *Dictionnaire Petit Robert*). They are the matrices allowing the infinite reproduction of a form. In each case we are dealing with a structure, a model separable from its actualizations. In each insertion the whole series of possible actualizations proceeding from a single initial pattern looms up potentially behind each text present on the page. This virtual multiplicity points both towards the infinity of repertory and paradigm and towards the infinity of products, versions and variations of the same matrix. The text is at once a finished product and a machine whose products can be anticipated.

In this the insertions somewhat resemble the *loci memoriae* enumerated by certain ancient manuals of rhetoric specializing in mnemonics, permitting the instant recall to memory of a given piece of information.[6] These *loci* are highly differentiated, architecturalized, and narrowly compartmentalized configurations, serving to fix in each compartment an element of knowledge one wishes to retain always available for a possible recall. Just like these, the insertions are the meeting point of the abstract list and the concrete configuration. Much like the *Méthode Assimil* (which, by the way, fascinated Joyce) or Raymond Queneau's *Exercices de Style*, they partake both of the code and of its actualization, of competence and of performance.

Each insertion possesses a certain number of highly coded stylistic indicators which spring up ineluctably from the very first lines and function as varieties of signal, alerting the reader that the text belongs to a recognized genre which cannot be mistaken. Each sentence is saturated with signal-words which mark and mark over the text, designating its membership in some specific genre. The use of adjectives is particularly revealing. In the description of the giant, the nostrils are 'widewinged', the obscurity 'cavernous', the current 'powerful', the resonance 'rhythmic', the reverberations 'hale' (294/296). In the same way, in the account of the execution of the nationalist (which is a model of the genre, reminding us at the same time of the speech at the *Comices Agricoles* and Homais' newspaper article in *Madame Bovary*), we notice the abundance of clichés: 'vast throng', 'admirably rendering', 'plaintive muse', 'favourite Dublin street singers', 'considerable amusement', 'mirth-provoking fashion', 'roaring trade', 'real Irish fun', 'unexpected addition', 'excellent idea', 'instructive treat', etc. (304–5/306–7).

It is fascinating to observe at work in these insertions, be they journalistic or otherwise, this 'reification of the topic' in which Roland Barthes saw the decline of classical rhetoric.[7] The degradation is all the more striking here because of the alternation of strictly journalistic insertions and insertions in epic, oratory or poetic style. In fact there is a constant exchange between the two. The devices circulate from one text to the other (in this sense they are literally 'commonplace'). This indifferentiation, this levelling, is the mark of a radical degradation of rhetorical discourse. The society page parasitically invades the account of the natural disaster and the story of the execution of the nationalist just as much as the Zulu chief's visit to Manchester and the farewell to the great man. Turns of phrase peculiar to pseudo-scientific erudition appear as often in the account of the spiritist seance, the evocation of the canine prodigy and the description of the disaster as in the medical language of Professor Blumenduft. The oratory style becomes pomposity, the metaphor becomes 'picturesque' imagery, amplification becomes pompous officialese, epic panorama becomes nomenclature, the vignette becomes a cheap print, the *exemplum* becomes popular wisdom, the Homeric epithet becomes a commonplace, description becomes 'on-the-spot notation', the *topoi* become clichés, the eulogy becomes advertising, the portrait gallery becomes the society page.

The objective substratum behind each insertion no longer seems to be its essential feature. The text is not modelled on it. The subject is only a pretext to set in motion a whole arsenal of rhetoric. One has the impression that it is the discourse which creates the subject, that the discourse brings with it the topic that serves it best. The mechanisms deployed in the insertions imply a real division of all reality within reach, including it in advance in a factual and rhetorical typology. In the narration, on the other hand, the event, even if distorted by prejudices and partisanship, never appears to be manipulated. One could thus establish the same relationship between the story told by the Nameless One and the insertions as between the 'raw material' furnished by reporters to a newspaper for the crime page (for example, the tapes recorded on the spot — testimonies of the caretaker, the neighbours, the relatives, etc.) and the arsenal of prefabricated models at the disposal of the journalists who later transform the collected material into articles obeying the rules of journalistic writing (in fact, this activity is called 'rewriting', and the 'rewrite editor' is sometimes more important than the reporter).

Thus in juxtaposing two types of treatment of facts Joyce does more than simply induce a tension: he dissolves all possibility of a unified real underlying the fiction. In the works of Browning, Faulkner and Virginia Woolf referred to above, the real is at once the supreme absent and the supreme present. The supreme absent because the addition of all the discourses can never succeed in reconstituting a unified vision of the event. But also the supreme present, because everything is subordinate to it. If the testimonies never manage to 'cover' it, to unveil it as truth, it is because they fall short of the task, but this inadequacy never calls into question the transcendent existence of this truth. Yet it is precisely this transcendence which is dissolved in 'Cyclops'. While the speech of the Nameless One corresponds to the well-known pattern of the 'unreliable witness', the insertions function in the opposite direction: here it is no longer discourse which vainly tries to model itself on the real, it is the real which not only flows into the moulds of discourse, but loses its integrity and finds itself reduced to a pretext for rhetorical machinery to be set in motion. The insertions can only transmit a real already infected by conventions. Everything has become stereotype.

It is indeed through the irreducible faultline gap between narration and insertions that the meaning of 'Cyclops' is conveyed. This faultline is the symbol of the two discourses which pull Dublin apart: on the one hand the speech which repeats, on the other the matrix which reproduces and contaminates; here the infinite series of echoes, there the unrestrained production of the media's rhetorical machine. The whole Dublin paralysis is in this co-existence of the past of the spoken word and the present of the printed word — both transmitting nothing but alienation.

(Translated by Elizabeth Bell and the author)

Notes

1. Michel Foucault, preface to Flaubert, *La Tentation de Saint Antoine* (Paris: Livre de Poche, 1971), pp. 11–12.
2. Cf. Roland Barthes, *S/Z*, tr. Richard Miller (New York: Hill and Wang, 1974), p. 140.
3. Jacques Derrida, 'Plato's Pharmacy', in *Dissemination*, tr. Barbara Johnson (Chicago: University of Chicago Press, 1981), p. 109.
4. For the elucidation of allusions and sources I am very much indebted to two indispensable books: Weldon Thornton's *Allusions in 'Ulysses'* (Chapel Hill: University of North Carolina Press, 1968), and Don Gifford and Robert J. Seidman, *Notes for Joyce: An Annotation of James Joyce's 'Ulysses'* (New York: Dutton, 1974).
5. Mikhail Bakhtin, *Problems of Dostoevsky's Poetics*, tr. R. W. Rotsel (Ann Arbor: Ardis, 1973), p. 156.
6. Frances Yates, *The Art of Memory* (London: Routledge, 1966), ch. 1.
7. Originally, the topic is 'a network of forms, a nearly cybernetic pattern to which is submitted the material which one wants to transform into persuasive discourse'. But subsequently 'these forms soon tended to fill up [...] to carry contents which first were contingent, then repeated, reified. The topic became a stock of stereotypes.' Roland Barthes, 'L'ancienne rhétorique', in *Communications*, 16 (1970), 207.

7   Circe, regret and regression

DANIEL FERRER

Listen then. There are two things. The first is I dreamed I was killing her.
The second is when I killed her I wasn't dreaming.

Marguerite Duras, L'Amante anglaise

Moreover, if the name of the dead man happens to be the same as that of
an animal or common object, some tribes think it necessary to give these
animals or objects new names, so that the use of the former names shall not
recall the dead man to memory. This usage leads to a perpetual change of
vocabulary, which causes much difficulty to the missionaries. . .

Sigmund Freud, Totem and Taboo

What are we entering as we enter Circe, the fifteenth chapter of *Ulysses*? We
are entering, or rather re-entering, a world which is strange and yet
familiar. . . The word '*Unheimliche*' springs to mind, and we immediately
make ready to list the abundant archaic contents which present themselves.
But this will not do; it is not quite sufficient to account for everything that
is at stake in this chapter, for all the things which set it apart from all the other
chapters while it remains part of the book. Our recognition that the uncanny
lies at the heart of Circe, and that Circe is acted out at the heart of the
uncanny, can be only a first step. But it is precisely the first step which is a
problem here: can any step in Circe ever be a *first* step?

As we enter the chapter − '(*The Mabbot street entrance of nighttown*
[. . .])' − we are coming, through the entrance, into 'nighttown', the town
of the night, the red light district.[1] (But the entry occurs inside a
parenthesis.) At the opening of the chapter a topographical opening is
inscribed, and the gaping doors of the flimsy houses immediately multiply
the opening. The first words of the chapter, the first parenthesis, initiate an
entirely different typographical system (from now on, the descriptive
passages, printed in italics and set in brackets − the stage directions − will
be strictly segregated from speeches, printed in lower-case letters and always
preceded by a name printed in capital letters − the dialogue); this system,
characteristic of the drama, dramatically establishes an incongruous stage,
set, after four hundred pages, in the way of the novel's sweeping movement.
We soon realize that this break in the form is representative of a radical
change. The laws that obtain on this stage are no longer the same as those

which governed the day-time world of *Ulysses* in which we have spent the earlier chapters.

From this point only a short step is required to decide that this opening marks a break in the novel, that this strange chapter is indeed a stranger to the novel and may therefore be physically separated from it,[2] or at least should be read as a mere dream-parenthesis within a realistic whole. The red light district thus becomes a restricted scene, or the Other Scene. Critics have often said as much: 'nighttown' is quite simply dreamtown.

But, were we to take this step, we would be missing Circe. For Circe is literally inseparable from *Ulysses*. Not merely because it is impossible to study it apart, since the chapter is inevitably part of the continuum of *Ulysses*, just as 'nighttown', the brothel area, is part of the geographical and social fabric of Dublin, just as the enchantments of the witch Circe are part of the series of adventures which make up the Odyssey. But mainly because it is impossible in practice to effect such a separation, since there is no place where a cut could be made. Despite all appearances to the contrary, the initial parenthesis does not create such an opportunity; the opposite is in fact true. For, while the chapter opens with a passage between brackets (and closes in the same way), it is not, itself, contained within one greater parenthesis. '(*The Mabbot street entrance* [. . .])': it is the entrance which is thus bracketed; it is the opening which is shut in. The threshold is inscribed only to be spirited away.

Speculations

Think of a mirror: one can never enter it — not because its surface is an impenetrable obstacle, but because one cannot approach it without realizing that one is *already* in it. In the same way the reader of *Ulysses* has, without realizing it, been in Circe for a long time when he reaches chapter 15. The setting, the characters, the situations, even the vocabulary, are already familiar to him, and he cannot resist an inexorable sense of *déjà vu*. And it is important that he should *not* resist. For, just as the only way of going deeper into a mirror (or rather, of seeing one's reflection going deeper) is to back away from it, the only way of advancing into Circe is by constantly retracing one's steps.

Exploring Circe (and any other woman) is always a homecoming to familiar territory. But, inevitably, the homecoming seems uncanny. We meet familiar objects and characters, phrases and scenes, and at the same time we notice that they all undergo very strange metamorphoses. For example, hardly have we recognized the figure of Leopold Bloom than he suddenly takes on the sinister aspect of 'lovelorn longlost lugubru Booloohoom', and then at once changes into 'Jollypoldy the rixdix doldy' (428/433–4). How is this possible? Mr Bloom has, quite simply, just walked past Gillen's hairdresser's shop, and the concave and convex mirrors set up in the window have reflected him for a brief moment.

It is tempting to see in this episode a model of Circe, placed by Joyce at the opening of the chapter, a kind of variation on the model of Irish art suggested by Stephen in the first pages of the novel ('The cracked lookingglass of a servant' (13/6)). According to this model, Circe is indeed a mirror, but a distorting mirror, one of those disquieting contraptions which introduce difference in the very place where one is seeking confirmation of one's identity. Such an explanation would account for the systematic repetition of elements found earlier in the novel, and for the constant process of transformation which they undergo; it would account for the fusion, within each image, of the strange and the familiar. And yet we must not forget that the distortions created by a mirror of this type, while they seem to be random, are, in fact, always predictable, because they are based on a determined law of optics; and the knowledge of these laws enables one at any given moment to reconstitute a faithful picture of the lost reality. There is no exception to the rule that an accustomed eye can make the necessary adjustments, and therefore any sense of strangeness is rapidly dissipated. But the disquiet produced by Circe cannot be so easily dismissed. The strangeness will persist.

The first model is thus only an introduction, simplified and, indeed, over-simplified if one were to stop at this point. But we shall not stop here; we can do better than that without leaving the field of catoptrics. If we look for mirrors, there are far more diabolical reflections to be found. At the heart of Circe (508/567) is a trick which both anticipates and surpasses certain 'experiments in recreational physics'.[3] It is a mirror, placed in such a way that it shows the spectator a coat-stand made of antlers in the next room and, simultaneously, one of the spectators, thus apparently wearing an imposing pair of horns (general laughter).

The artefact has a further characteristic: the head thus seeming to be framed by this pair of horns springing from nowhere – like a real bunch of flowers in an imaginary vase – is transformed in the eye of some of the spectators, is so deformed that they see Shakespeare himself, a Shakespeare with horns, in the mirror. If we take into account that this Shakespeare is 'beardless' and suffers from facial paralysis – which does not prevent him from speaking, albeit after the manner of ventriloquists, and laughing with a capon-laugh – it will be clear that only Joyce himself (or perhaps Raymond Roussel) could give us a complete diagram of the apparatus.

Some elements of its workings will become clearer, however, if we remember that the spectators are not abstract roles but definite characters. The dramatis personae are as follows: those who see only the comic vision of a horned cuckold are Lynch (Stephen Dedalus's companion) and the prostitutes who are laughing with him; those who see Shakespeare (or rather, who see themselves as Shakespeare) in the mirror are Stephen and Bloom –

but also ourselves, spectators/readers. How can we explain this contrast? How can we explain this resemblance? What can there possibly be in common between Bloom, Stephen and ourselves?

Perhaps we should entertain the hypothesis that the same image may be produced by factors which are different for each spectator, or, more exactly, by the combination of one stable, common factor and a series of variable factors proper to each individual spectator. The stable element here is the reflection of a man crowned with horns; the variable element being each spectator's individual past, projected on to this reflection. This time there is no need to go very far back into the past. Bloom's wife has just been unfaithful to him. He has been thinking of this all day. He has even thought of the chance of being contaminated by venereal disease as a result of his wife's infidelity. Moreover, he has talked about Shakespeare several times. Stephen too has thought of Shakespeare in the course of the day. He has even talked about Shakespeare at length. For many reasons, the idea of Shakespeare is linked, for him, with the idea of his father. Because Shakespeare is the Great Begetter ('When all is said Dumas *fils* (or is it Dumas *père*?) is right. After God Shakespeare has created most' (212)). Because Shakespeare is the father of all poets. Because he played the Ghost of Hamlet's father. Perhaps also (or mostly) because Stephen believes he can demonstrate that Shakespeare was cuckolded.

This leads to the following results: Bloom, as a cuckold, replaced in his wife's bed by a more manly man, symbolically castrated and soon, perhaps, syphilitic, sees himself as Shakespeare, a horned, paralysed Shakespeare, capon-voiced and beardless; Stephen, in so far as he resembles Shakespeare (i.e. his father), sees himself as cuckolded, castrated and syphilitic. Bloom is consoling himself by identification with a great man[4] (in France the great man might be Napoleon, but Shakespeare offers the added advantage of being 'all in all' (212)). Stephen, on the contrary, is attacking his own image, and simultaneously, his father with whom he has identified. But, in attacking his father, he is digging at the roots of his own identity, for he is trying – in vain – to deny his own filiation (If my father has been cuckolded, he is not my father. But how, in that case, can I possibly look like him? I don't look like him, I look like Shakespeare. But if I don't look like him, it isn't my father who wears the horns, it's Shakespeare – or me. So my father is not a cuckold and he must be my father . . .). Every reader must continue to unfold for himself the picture of Shakespeare with horns. His own discoveries will take him closer either to Stephen or to Bloom. Their contrasted reactions are representative of two aspects of this chapter. Circe is both a magic lantern, producing phantasies whose function is to consolidate the Self, by concealing reality or filling in its flaws, without ever mingling with it, and an infernal machine which destroys identities and shatters reality.

At this point, we must check our hypothesis by applying it to a more substantial extract (more substantial because longer and more obviously important) than the minor episode of the mirrored Shakespeare. A good choice for this test is the scene in which the ghost of Stephen's mother appears, for this scene is a turning-point in the chapter and, perhaps, in the novel.

Her appearance is infinitely more dramatic than that of Shakespeare (although she is not seen by everyone, any more than was Shakespeare – we shall return to this point later). The scene is given in imposingly macabre detail, worthy of a Gothic novel in the grand manner:

(*Stephen's mother, emaciated, rises stark through the floor in leper grey with a wreath of faded orange blossoms and a torn bridal veil, her face worn and noseless, green with grave mould. Her hair is scant and lank. She fixes her bluecircled hollow eyesockets on Stephen and opens her toothless mouth uttering a silent word. A choir of virgins and confessors sing voicelessly.*)
THE CHOIR: Liliata rutilantium te confessorum. . .
                    Iubilantium te virginum. . .
(For the rest of the passage, see *U* 516–17/580–2.)

This time we are dealing with a real ghost, who fully deserves the name of revenant, for this is not the first time that it has returned. As is always the case in Circe, the event, here the appearance of the ghost, is nullified as such. An appearance can never be more than a re-appearance.

Very early in the novel, we saw Stephen remembering: 'Silently, in a dream she had come to him after her death, her wasted body within its loose brown graveclothes giving off an odour of wax and rosewood, her breath, that had bent upon him, mute, reproachful, a faint odour of wetted ashes' (11/5). And later, the same words, with minor variations, are repeated:

In a dream, silently, she had come to him, her wasted body within its loose grave-clothes giving off an odour of wax and rosewood, her breath bent over him with mute secret words, a faint odour of wetted ashes.
Her glazing eyes, staring out of death, to shake and bend my soul. On me alone. The ghostcandle to light her agony. Ghostly light on the tortured face. Her hoarse loud breath rattling in horror, while all prayed on their knees. Her eyes on me to strike me down. *Liliata rutilantium te confessorum turma circumdet: iubilantium te virginum chorus excipiat.* (16/10)

But is it indeed the same thing which re-appears on each of these three occasions, presented in similar terms? Or, more exactly, does it re-appear in the same way? The two passages from the beginning of the novel describe the memory of a dream. It is, first and foremost, a dream (the two passages are introduced by the signpost words, 'in a dream'). Nothing but a dream. A dream, moreover, which, while it retains considerable emotional significance, is not experienced directly, but seen from the vantage-point of the daytime world by being experienced as a memory. It is noticeable that the second passage suddenly changes (in the second paragraph of the quotation) into a description of the 'real' agony of the mother. The ease of the transition from dream to reality proves that the use of the past distances both experiences to the point where the remembered dream and the remembered reality merge, and the different formulations in the two passages appear as mere stylistic variations, created in the quest after a formal perfection which would fix these traumatic memories in an epiphany belonging neither to life nor to dreams, but to Art.

In contrast to these two passages, the apparition in Circe is presented in an entirely different way. Whereas the dream was described in the past tense (even in the pluperfect), the apparition is experienced in the present tense. We do not find here the hesitation between conventional narrative and interior monologue which is characteristic of the first chapter. Here we are no longer faced with subjectivity hidden behind a facade of objectivity or objectivity revealing subjectivity. From the start we are submerged in extreme subjectivity – hallucination – and in absolute objectivity – the stage directions.

These are objective since they are not interpretative, or even descriptive, but prescriptive. There is no difference of level between *Enter a ghost and hobgoblins* and *Enter the milkman*. It is left to the director (but who is the director of Circe?) to *produce* these directions and make them real. In the same way, there is no difference here between the apparition of the mother and the actions of Stephen and the other characters in Circe: they are all set on the same level of reality – or unreality. There is nothing which could make distinctions between them legitimate. On Circe's stage, the memory-narrative becomes a concrete presence. Paradoxically, the ghost makes its first appearance by re-appearing yet again.

Is the hallucination subjective? Yes, but whose subjectivity is implied? Who is having the hallucination? Should we call it Stephen's hallucination, since Bloom, Lynch and the prostitutes see nothing? But we see it too, in every detail. . . Should we therefore speak of a negative hallucination, common to all the characters except Stephen? Or is it a hallucination shared by Stephen and ourselves? When we compare this with the Shakespeare episode, we realize that the dividing line has shifted, but we, readers, are always included in the division, whichever interpretation we accept. The reader is directly concerned by the hallucination, and he cannot escape by explaining it in terms of physiology; Stephen, drunk with liquor and music, is perhaps, subjectively, dizzy, but for the spectator/reader of Circe the whole scene is whirling dizzily, and this is objective: '*Stephen whirls giddily.* **Room whirls back.** *Eyes closed, he totters.* **Red rails fly spacewards. Stars all around suns turn roundabout. Bright midges dance on wall.**' (My emphasis; 515/579) Our involvement is not accidental, it is programmed in the very form of the text. We should not forget that, in the well-known schema given by Joyce to Stuart Gilbert, this hallucination is assigned to Circe not as a theme but as a literary technique, as narration to Telemachus or monologue to Proteus. It takes a time to accustom ourselves to the idea that the hallucination is not being represented: it is a mode of representation. It is not a question of content, but of writing – and of reading.

Let us say, for the sake of the argument, that the ghost of Stephen's mother is indeed (as verisimilitude seems to require)[5] a hallucination. How can we actually share this hallucination? If the hallucination is, in fact, as was suggested in the case of the horned Shakespeare, the result of the past being projected into the frame created by the present, what form of the past can we, readers, project at this point? The answer is, as a matter of fact, included in the question: it is our own past as readers of the first fourteen chapters, since the systematic regurgitation of earlier elements which forms the very basis of Circe constantly appeals to this past experience. These elements, torn from their original context, still function within the logical framework of that context; this logic is totally foreign to the new text in which they are now set, and the conflict between two contrasted systems is what gives their second appearance its hallucinatory quality. It is thus necessary to have met earlier the ghost of Stephen's mother, in the shape of a dream or a phantasy produced by Stephen's feelings of remorse, in order to appreciate the full impact of the ghost's materialization in Circe, as simultaneously absent and present.

. . . a perpetual change of vocabulary

But we should not forget that every word in Circe has its own past and must be considered, individually, as a kind of ghost, haunting the text, returning with a whole network of associations, woven during its previous occurrences in *Ulysses*. Each sentence recalls a host of other sentences which are superimposed upon it, and which, in turn, recall yet more sentences. The ghost we are studying is, therefore, not created merely by the few lines of Circe that we have been examining. It is impossible to have any clear idea of the ghost's volume or its outlines, and, more important, it is impossible to discover the forces at work behind it and which raised it, if we do not allow the associations surrounding every word to come up freely. Let us therefore try to draw towards us, almost at random, some of the threads which make up this network.

'Stephen's mother, emaciated [. . .] *'*

The ghost of Stephen's mother is a concrete presence in Circe, but its appearance seems to betray a dearth of being. It clearly lacks flesh. This emaciation may, of course, be explained by the cancer which was the clinical cause of death. But, if we return to an earlier sentence used by Stephen, and recalled by the word 'emaciated', we shall see things from a different angle. In the earlier passage we are shown an 'omnivorous being which can masticate, deglute, digest and apparently pass through the ordinary channel with pluterperfect imperturbability such multifarious aliments as *cancrenous females emaciated by parturition*, corpulent professional gentlemen, not to speak of jaundiced politicians and chlorotic nuns [. . .].' (My italics; 416/420). Thus, for Stephen, females (but the plural hides a singular) are emaciated by parturition (and they probably suffer from cancer for the same reason). Because she has given birth, the mother has been emptied of her substance, devoured from inside. But we should note that she too has been swallowed by the great omnivorous being; swallowed, digested and 'apparently' excreted – that is, brought into the world, re-born (and this explains her return as a ghost). The question remains: what happens, in this tale, to the omnivorous being? Does he, too, become emaciated by parturition? Final question: did the mother begin by devouring the children she brings into the world? Might she not devour them again at any moment? (Stephen certainly seems convinced of this: he calls his mother a ghoul and a corpse-chewer.)

'Stephen's mother, emaciated, rises stark [. . .]*'*

'Stark' suggests the stiffness of rigor mortis, a contagious mortification which invades Stephen's own body ('his head and arms thrown back stark') just as he thinks he has got rid of the ghost. This stiffness recalls the drowned corpse described in Proteus: 'Hauled stark over the gunwale he breathes upward the stench of his green grave, his leprous nosehole snoring to the sun' (55/50).

'Stephen's mother [. . .] *rises stark through the floor in leper grey* [. . .]*, her face worn and noseless, green with grave mould.'*

Here we have the same leper grey, the same noseless face, the same green of the grave mould. The description of the drowned man suggests that these hideous mutilations are not confined to the face. We have a hint of what is taking place beneath the leper grey drapery: 'A quiver of minnows, fat of a spongy titbit, flash through the slits of his buttoned trouserfly'. In this peculiar birth, the internal devouring is clearly a form of castration. Is the noseless ghost of Stephen's mother also castrated by her offspring?

But what is a drowned man? A man who has been engulfed (devoured) by the sea, and who, after having suffered a sea-change (digestion), is thrown up by the sea.

'Our great sweet mother! Epi oinopa ponton.' (516/580).

The assimilation of sea and mother, referred to by Buck Mulligan in the very first pages of *Ulysses*, reappears in this passage. The mother is thus identified both with the sea and with the drowned man; she is devourer and devoured, container and contained. This dead sea/dead mother is also an instrument of death, but it is a pleasurable death: 'Seadeath mildest of all deaths' (55/50), because it means a return to the womb. And yet. . .

And yet Stephen fears water. He hardly ever washes himself, he never bathes in the sea and he drinks no water. But, immediately after his praise of the delights of drowning, he thinks of 'Old Father Ocean' (56/50). And the father appears too, a few lines earlier, identified with the drowned corpse, through the words of Father Shakespeare, 'Full fathom five thy father lies.'

The same ambiguities – the ambiguity of the feeling of attraction/repulsion inspired by drowning, the sexual ambiguity created by the abrupt transition from masculine to feminine – occur a little earlier: 'A drowning man. His human eyes scream to me out of horror of his death. I . . . With him together down . . . I could not save her. Waters: bitter death: lost' (51/46). It seems that Stephen would gladly go down to the bottom with him. With *her* would be another matter. The sweetness of death suddenly turns bitter.

These ambiguities recur in another passage, to which we are led by the words '*oinopa ponton*', '*Omnis caro ad te veniet*', 'death' and 'ghost': 'Tides, myriadislanded, within her, blood not mine, *oinopa ponton*, a winedark sea. [. . .] Bridebed, childbed, bed of death, ghostcandled. *Omnis caro ad te veniet*. He comes, pale vampire, through storm his eyes, his bat sails bloodying the sea, mouth to her mouth's kiss' (53/47–8). The sea, with its winedark tides, is identified with the mother, bleeding periodically from a secret wound. But the mother evokes the image of Death, and Death leads us back to the great omnivorous being.

If the mother's colour is that of wine, or of black blood, this is because she is indeed wounded in the depths of her being, eaten up by a mysterious illness. She is like the rubies (240/241), 'leprous and winedark', which Stephen sees in a jeweller's window, where, under the craftsman's 'dust darkened [. . .] toiling fingers with their vulture nails', they are assimilated to the unclean female genitalia: 'She dances in a foul gloom where gum burns with garlic. A sailorman, rustbearded, sips from a beaker rum and eyes her. A long and seafed silent rut. She dances, capers, wagging her sowish haunches and her hips, on her gross belly flapping a ruby egg', offered up to the covetousness of the great omnivorous being in a new maritime guise. The rubies conjure up an image of the interior of the mother's body, defiled and terrifying: 'Born all in the dark wormy earth, cold specks of fire, evil lights shining in the darkness. Where fallen archangels flung the stars of their brows. Muddy swinesnouts, hands, root and root, gripe and wrest them.'

But soon another shop-window attracts Stephen's gaze away from the maternal rubies. Another frame is provided for his phantasizing, this frame being the literal frame of a faded print.[6] The two people engaged with each other in the centre of this picture, under the interested gaze of a large number of spectators seen from behind, are two *men*. They are boxers, whose exchange is both hostile and affectionate: 'The heavyweights in light loincloths proposed gently each to other his bulbous fists' (241/242).

But, at some point, we must call an arbitrary halt to this flood of words and images which come forward at each fragment of the text. So we might as well confine ourselves to this small sample, and try to draw the outlines of an analysis of the ghost of Stephen's mother, based on this tangled mass of contradictory images.

Cherchez l'homme

It is necessary to distinguish between at least two levels of interpretation, which are related to the two contrasting aspects of Circe mentioned earlier. On one level, the mother is seen here as a malevolent and dangerous being, because she represents Woman.

Certainly, in *Ulysses* as a whole – setting aside the final chapter – women are presented as nuisances who spoil the friendly or even amorous brotherhood of men. We can detect, especially in Circe, an attempt to transfer to women a masculine, repressive attitude, thus putting all responsibility on to them. Bloom's masochistic phantasy paradoxically takes the form of a kind of breaking-in of Bella/Bello: the masculinization of the dominating woman is quite as important as the pseudo-feminization of the victim. The game is double-edged: on the one hand the woman is eliminated by making her adopt a masculine role; on the other hand, when the make-believe stops, she can be humiliated as a fitting punishment for the cruelty she has just displayed towards her victim (whether at his demand or simply in his imagination):

BLOOM: [. . .] Mutton dressed as lamb. Long in the tooth and superfluous hairs. A raw onion the last thing at night would benefit your complexion. And take some double chin drill. Your eyes are as vapid as the glass eyes of your stuffed fox. They have the dimensions of your other features, that's all. [. . .] Clean your nailless middle finger [. . .], the cold spunk of your bully is dripping from your cockscomb. Take a handful of hay and wipe yourself. (501–2/554)

Therefore, the most militantly anti-feminist sentiments may be expressed with a clear conscience:

As if you didn't get it on the double yourselves. No jerks and multiple mucosities all over you. I tried it. Your strength our weakness. What's our studfee? What will you pay on the nail? You fee men dancers on the Riviera, I read. [. . .] Eh! I have sixteen years of black slave labour behind me. And would a jury give me five shillings alimony tomorrow, eh? (501/553–4)

Could Bloom's odyssey not be summed up by this single detail: before leaving, he gives his wife breakfast in bed; when he comes home, returning to the natural order of things, he demands that Molly serve him in bed (at least, that is what she understands . . .)?

This gives us an insight into the dual aspect of the mother-figure, the archetype of Woman, in Circe: now a figure of fun like a music-hall clown − Bloom's mother (431/438); now a terrifying bogey ('Rawhead and bloody bones') − Stephen's mother, in the passage we have been studying. The mother is the intruder in the father and son relationship which the heroes are trying to build up. She is responsible for the prohibition which hangs over incest between father and son, a taboo whose exceptional force Stephen recalls in tones of regret (208/207).

The persecuting ghost of the mother stands between the union of father and son, taking over the function of prohibiting incest which normally belongs to the father. But the ghost also represents the father, whose forbidden love hides itself as persecution, just as Stephen's love hides itself as hate. This could explain all the sexual ambiguities we have noticed, as well as the phallic nature of the spectre, which 'rises stark' like an erect penis, which is a ghost like the Holy Ghost − who, we are re-reminded several times, got the Virgin pregnant − and which is like that other 'ghost' which appears a few pages further on as a violent emission of semen: '*He gives up the ghost. A violent erection of the hanged sends gouts of sperm spouting through his death clothes on to the cobblestones*' (523/594).

The counterpart of the masculinization of the mother, and of Woman in general, is not the assumption by the males of a truly feminine position, but the adoption of a mere disguise. The taste for female clothes found in Bloom and in Stephen ('But you were delighted when Esther Osvalt's shoe went on you: girl I knew in Paris. *Tiens, quel petit pied!* Staunch friend, a brother soul: Wilde's love that dare not speak its name' (55/49)) belongs to a fetishistic tendency: it is a denial of female castration. This form of homosexuality is a rejection of the Other, a narcissistic love of the Self. Its purpose is to reinforce identity.

Unfortunately, this reinforcement does not hold for long, as is shown here by the cataclysm on a cosmic scale which ends the ghost scene, or, throughout Circe, by the degradation suffered by characters and objects. This incestuous homosexuality is only a phase (perhaps reactional); it is not even sufficient to account for all the characteristics of the parental ghost, phallic, but castrated (lacking nose, eyes and teeth), castrating (it plunges its crab's claws into Stephen's heart, and its toothless mouth suggests its counterpart, a toothed vagina) and bisexual ('dogsbody bitchbody') − not to mention other aspects we have demonstrated to be present: cannibalism, double function as container and contents . . . To cover all these aspects we must go further, beyond the Oedipus complex, negative or positive, and look at highly archaic images, such as that of the 'combined parent-figure' or, more precisely, the mother as universal receptacle of good and bad objects.

Multitudinous mother

This return of so distant a past is less surprising when we realize that the ghost is related to much more than just the recent death of Stephen's mother. We know that the work of mourning (and this is what the theatre of Circe is all about) brings us back to a very early phase of the individual's development, forgotten, but still active. The actual loss of the beloved is never more than a repetition of a loss already suffered. As Melanie Klein has shown, 'the child goes through states of mind comparable to the mourning of the adult, or rather [. . .] this early mourning is revived whenever grief is experienced in later life'.[7] As a result of this, the adult normally reacts by setting to work the same defence mechanism which he has already used:

While it is true that the characteristic feature of normal mourning is the individual's setting up the lost object inside himself, he is not doing so for the first time but, through the work of mourning, is reinstating that object as well as all his loved *internal* objects which he feels he has lost. He is therefore *recovering* what he had already attained in childhood.[8]

Mourning is always re-gret, leading to regression. It reactivates what Melanie Klein calls the 'manic–depressive position', with its images of the mother as a complete but ambivalent object, concentrating the good and bad elements of partial objects, and carrying its weight of anxieties linked to the damage inflicted on this object by the sadism of the subject.

This is in keeping with the changing nature of the ghost, sometimes protective:

Who saved you the night you jumped into the train at Dalkey with Paddy Lee? Who had pity for you when you were sad among the strangers? [. . .] I pray for you in my other world. Get Dilly to make you that boiled rice every night after your brain work. Years and years I loved you, O my son, my firstborn, when you lay in my womb (516/581);

sometimes threatening: 'Repent! O, the fire of hell! [. . .] Beware! God's hand!'; it is also consonant with its mutilated appearance.

During the depressive phases, the subject needs constantly to compare the mother he has interiorized and the external, real mother, in order to reassure himself that she has not been wounded, that she has not been destroyed by his uncontrollable sadism, that she has not become an avenging figure. The absence of the mother (in our case by death) removes this opportunity to reassure himself by checking his phantasy against reality, and the subject is left with his interior representation of his mother; he has, in fact, made this figure suffer all kinds of cruel attacks because of his own ambivalence, and he fears its vengeance.

At this level, the hallucination may be explained as an attempt to expel into the outer world the persecutor who is threatening the subject from inside. This is a symptom of mourning which is not being carried through satisfactorily: reality-testing, which is an essential element of the normal mechanism of mourning,[9] is by-passed here by hallucination.

But this does not mean that there is here an attempt to deny the painful reality or to achieve a magic reparation of the damaged object, attitudes characteristic of the manic side of the depressive position. For the dead mother returns, but returns as a *dead* mother. There can be no question of healing her wounds. On the contrary, the hallucination leads to a new aggression, acted out by Stephen who attacks the ghost with his ashplant.

We can now see a fresh difference between the hallucinatory staging of the mother in Circe and the dreamed–narrated apparition which we met in the first chapter. The narrative neutralized the terrifying image of the dead mother, enshrining her in a well-wrought dream, trying to heal her by the use of words, of stylistic devices (the perfect or the pluperfect) of increasing perfection at each re-appearance. In Circe, by contrast, the aim is no longer perfection but destruction.

Here there is no healing of objects which would allow them to be re-incorporated, thus ensuring stable identification and structuring of the Self. We find the exact opposite: a simultaneous dislocation of the objects and of the Self — that Self which had created itself by identification with those objects (as is shown by the fact that some terms, such as 'toothless' and 'dogsbody', associated here with the ghost of the mother, are used elsewhere by Stephen to describe himself).

It would be true to say that here, beyond the mirror stage, we have a return to the original state of fragmentation, or, to continue to use Kleinian terminology, regression beyond the depressive position to the paranoid position, in which the subject, whose Self is scarcely integrated at all, is constantly being overwhelmed by his anxiety, by his fear of the persecuting 'bad object', by his own aggressive impulses, and is incapable of conceiving a 'complete' object with which he could identify.

Our ghost comes directly from this archaic phase. But it is far more than a phantasy from the past, re-appearing in isolation; it is the central core of the general regression which makes up Circe. The mother, as fundamental object, returns in an emphatic manner, but she returns as a corpse, and, worse still, in a state of decomposition. This unendurable return sets off the decomposition of the entire Universe: '*Time's livid final flame leaps and, in the following darkness, ruin of all space, shattered glass and toppling masonry*' (517/583). All things revert to primeval chaos, that is, back to the womb, considered this time as the receptacle for all partial objects, a field in which drives, and more particularly destructive drives, are freely released.

This field is the stage upon which Circe is enacted, the background against which the various figures (including that of the mother — container and contained) stand out for a moment before disintegrating, coalescing or vanishing under the impact of the destructive forces. As we have seen with the ghost, these figures do not appear in order to disguise the absence of lost objects, in an obsessive or fetishistic way, but to emphasize, to repeat their very absence, just as the young child repeats his mother's absence by the game of Fort-Da, in which Freud found evidence of a principle contrary to the pleasure principle.[10]

While this analogy affords us a glimpse of the workings of Circe, in turn Circe suggests two ideas about the Fort-Da game. Might it not be that the 'o-o-o-o's and 'Da's of the little boy correspond to *stage directions* which, rather than describing, give rise to the gesticulative part of the game (throwing the reel)?[11] Also, even if, as Freud suggests, the 'o-o-o-o' is 'not a mere interjection but represents the German word "*fort*" ', might we not conclude that this inter-jection is, however, a form of interjection,[12] that is, a direct expression (not channelled through the rudimentary system of symbols set up by the two contrasting sounds) of pulsive energy, a kind of gestic speech?

The notions of gestic speech, of gestures generated by speech, are the keys to understanding the theatricality of Circe. It was stated earlier that the stage directions which form the basis of this theatricality must be seen as totally distinct from the narrative to be found in the other chapters of *Ulysses* or in other novels. While these stage directions direct us towards external reality,[13] the mode of direction is not descriptive but prescriptive. The words used are not substitutes for pre-existing objects, but have the potential to generate images and actions which cannot thereafter be reduced to these words, or others, without loss.

Through the verbal language, another and much older language manages to intrude, a language charged with libidinal intensities, a language of gestures, in which energies are released. Stephen announced this at his first appearance in Circe: 'Gesture [. . .] would be a universal language, the gift of tongues rendering visible not the lay sense but the first entelechy, the structural rhythm' (427/432). However, although he has known it from the beginning, he has to ask his mother's ghost for the key to this language 'known to all men' (516/581), but which they have forgotten.

Each sentence should be read as a formula,[14] which is both the verbal consequence of a system of drives lying at its source, and a reservoir from which flows a series of bodily movements through channels which are those of hallucination.

. . . I wasn't dreaming

But what is a hallucination? It is a perception which comes not from the external world, but from the internal world. Freud has shown that hallucinations, like dreams, produce perception of a 'regressive' character.[15] The cathexes from the Ucs system (Unconscious) proceed backwards to the sensory end of the psychic apparatus. This *topical* regression (the transition from a system of the psychic apparatus to an anterior system) results in a predominance of visual images (see the theatrical form of Circe), which correspond to the 'ideas of things' characteristic of the Ucs system[16] which is the source of the hallucinatory cathexis.

Some 'verbal ideas', stored in the Pcs system (Preconscious), may, however, also be re-activated by unconscious cathexes and reach the conscious perception, but to do so they must go through the Ucs system by means of a topical regression and conform to the rules of the Ucs system, that is, they must undergo *formal* regression, being treated as 'ideas of things' and subjected to the primary processes. Thus, in Circe, each sentence is the consequence of other sentences which occurred earlier in the novel, and which are subjected to the mechanisms of condensation and displacement, to such an extent that the reader sometimes finds it difficult to recognize the originals. In the same way, many of the numerous tableaux, vignettes and incongruous situations are nothing more than the materialization of verbal clichés from previous chapters, made absurdly concrete.

Regression, then, in the purely rhetorical sense of the word,[17] the systematic reproduction in mirror-image of elements already present in the novel, which is the basis of the composition of Circe, is the translation on to a novelistic plane of hallucinatory regression – but only in so far as this regression is inseparable from a progression which goes on at the same time (continuation of the novel, of the odyssean adventures, of the cataloguing of organs, arts, symbols . . .).

For this is the fundamental difference between dream and hallucination. In a hallucination, the 'regressive' perceptions are not confined to another, separate, plane; they are projected directly into reality, where they mingle with ordinary perceptions. The external falls victim to the internal and can no longer extricate itself. This is what gives the hallucination its outrageous quality: it mixes what should stay apart. Was it not for this reason that Descartes, for example, in his *Meditations*, could not bring himself to identify with the lunatic who believed his body was made of glass,[18] whereas he found it easy to accept the hypothesis of the dream and even of the deceptive spirit (which is only the hyperbole of dream, not of madness)? Once the world of hallucination has been entered, nothing is certain any longer, there are no clear and distinct ideas, since everything is mixed up.

In the same way, the scene of Circe is by no means an Other Scene, a different world. Despite its phantasmagorial appearance, it is not outside reality, since the gestures generated by the words exist potentially in reality. (The theatricality makes real the hallucination, and, reciprocally, hallucinates reality.) Nor is it outside *Ulysses*, from which it is impossible (as we have already seen) to separate it. Indeed, it is this integration into the novel – an exceptional chapter in the centre of an exceptional novel – which ensures the unstable viability of Circe. It is because *Ulysses* is a world meticulously anchored to the geographical reality of Dublin and to the chronological reality of 16 June 1904, while at the same time offering itself to the reader as a perpetual referral to a host of other texts, so that it is impossible to tell where this dazzling flight of the referent may end; it is because its links with reality are both firmly stated and difficult to find, that the principle of representation is, by degrees, completely subverted by the hallucinatory technique used for Circe. It is by contrast with the narrative form of the other chapters that the dramatic form acquires its hallucinatory status. Finally, it is the extremely taut structure and the inertia of the imposing mass of *Ulysses* which prevent Circe from reaching a state of total fragmentation, and which permit a kind of balance between what we might call, to use an oversimplification, the forces of consolidation connected with the figure of Bloom, and the forces of disintegration connected with the figure of Stephen.

Circe must not be confused with those works which confine themselves to the theatre of dream or phantasy in order to copy an imaginary world, in the same way as others claim to copy the external world, both practices supporting each other. Circe is closer to those forms of fiction which Freud, while condemning them as 'not unalloyed' and productive of mystification, considers as the most efficient sources of the uncanny, because they play on several conventions, and do not allow us to discover until the very last minute whether 'their world of representation [. . .] coincides with the realities we are familiar with or departs from them'.[19] Except that here there is no very last minute. The 'world of representation' remains double. 'Or' should be replaced by 'and'.

Moreover, it is not enough for Circe, unlike these other fictions, to play on passing ambiguities in order to provoke in us uncanny feelings by showing us pictures based on ancient beliefs which we have surmounted or repressed (ghosts, for example). It is characteristic of Circe that the ghosts in it never seem really frightening as such. Whether they are purely farcical, like Bloom's grandfather, Virag, or darkly melodramatic, like Stephen's mother, we cannot take them seriously. And it is precisely this lack of credibility that makes the intrusion of these apparitions into a world which is also the real world so deeply disturbing. The constantly sustained duality of Circe shatters the stage, destroys the foundations of representation, leaving us face to face with a system of words and intensities, uncanny in the extreme, because they constantly reveal the relentless sway of the past over the present.

(Translated by Gilly Lehmann)

Notes

1. The French original gives 'le quartier réservé' for 'the red light district', for reasons which will become obvious in the following pages [Tr.].
2. This is not a gratuitous hypothesis: an attempt has, in fact, been made to turn Circe into a real play, intended for performance as a separate entity, called *Ulysses in Nighttown*.
3. This, and the subsequent reference to 'real flowers in an imaginary vase', is an allusion to the optical apparatus used by Jacques Lacan in his *Séminaire Livre I: Les Ecrits techniques de Freud* (Paris: Seuil, 1975) [Tr.].
4. As he identifies, elsewhere in the chapter, with Christ or with Parnell. It is significant that Shakespeare's face should soon be replaced in the mirror by that of Martin Cunningham, another hard-pressed husband whom Bloom greatly admires – and compares to Shakespeare (*U* 98/96).
5. Verisimilitude is, of course, purely relative. In *Macbeth*, for instance, the problem is entirely different.
6. The word 'faded' used here recalls the 'faded orange blossoms' in the description of the ghost. It is interesting to note that most of Joyce's concrete images are described as 'faded' or 'fading', as for example the photographs which Bloom keeps in his drawer. And in *Finnegans Wake*, we even find the neologism, 'fadograph' (*FW* 7.15).
7. Melanie Klein, 'Mourning and its Relation to Manic-Depressive States', in *Contributions to Psycho-Analysis 1921–1945* (London: Hogarth Press/Institute of Psycho-Analysis, 1950), p. 311.
8. Ibid., p. 330, Klein's italics.
9. Cf. Sigmund Freud, 'Mourning and Melancholia' (*Standard Edition*, vol. 14).
10. Sigmund Freud, 'Beyond the Pleasure Principle', ch. 2 (*Standard Edition*, vol. 18).
11. See the theory of rejection ('rejet' in French) by Julia Kristeva in *La Révolution du langage poétique* (Paris: Seuil, 1974).
12. Here, the author quotes the definition of the word 'interjection' taken from the *Petit Robert* dictionary: 'Mot invariable pouvant être employé isolément pour traduire une attitude affective du sujet parlant' ('A word which may be used in isolation to express an emotion of the speaking subject') [Tr.].
13. One could perfectly well say that *Ulysses never* refers to external reality, but always to other texts (see André Topia's article in this volume, pp. 103–25). If we admit this, then Circe is even more radically different from the rest of the novel. Not that references to other texts are lacking in Circe (on the contrary, they are universally present, and the whole chapter is itself a parodic reference to conventional dramatic texts), but in Circe these texts are constitutive of reality.
14. Cf. Julia Kristeva, 'L'engendrement de la formule', *Séméiotikè* (Paris: Seuil, 1971).
15. Sigmund Freud, 'The Interpretation of Dreams', ch. 7B (*Standard Edition*, vol. 5).
16. Cf. Sigmund Freud, 'A Metapsychological Supplement to the Theory of Dreams' (*Standard Edition*, vol. 14), and 'The Ego and the Id' (*Standard Edition*, vol. 19).
17. The only definition of the word given by Littré is: 'Figure de style, qui consiste à reprendre, à la fin de la phrase, les mots qui se trouvent au commencement, en les rangeant dans un ordre inverse ou en les expliquant un à un.' Compare the first two definitions given by the *Oxford English Dictionary*: (1) 'Return to a subject'; (2) Recurrence or repetition (of a word or statement)'.

18. On this subject, see the argument which opposes Jacques Derrida ('Cogito and the History of Madness', in *Writing and Difference*, tr. Alan Bass (London: Routledge, 1978)) and Michel Foucault ('My Body, This Paper, This Fire', *Oxford Literary Review* 4.1 (Autumn, 1979), 9–28.
19. Sigmund Freud, 'The Uncanny' (*Standard Edition*, vol. 17), p. 249.

8 Two words for Joyce

JACQUES DERRIDA

It is very late, it is always too late with Joyce, I shall say only two words.[1]

I do not yet know in what language, I do not know in how many languages.

How many languages can be lodged in two words by Joyce, lodged or inscribed, kept or burned, celebrated or violated?

I shall say two words, supposing that words in *Finnegans Wake* can be counted. One of Joyce's great bursts of laughter resounds through this challenge: just try to count the words and the languages I consume! I shall no doubt return to Joyce's laughter, and to his last signature. As for the languages, Jean-Michel Rabaté tells me that the experts have counted about forty.

Two words then, simply to put back into play what Hélène Cixous has just been saying: the primal scene, the complete father, the law, *jouissance* through the ear (*by the ear*, more literally, by the word ear, in the ear-mode,[2] in English, for example, and supposing that coming [*jouir*] by the ear is, for the most part, feminine . . .).

What are these two English words? They are only half English, if you will, if you will hear them, that is, do a little more than hear them: read them. I lift them from *Finnegans Wake* (258.12):

HE WAR

I spell them out: H E W A R, and sketch a first translation: HE WARS — he wages war, he declares or makes war, he is war, which can also be pronounced by babelizing a bit (it is in a particularly Babelian scene of the book that these words rise up), by Germanizing, then, in Anglo-Saxon, He war: he was — he who was ('I am he who is or who am', says YAHWE). Where it was, he was, declaring war, and it is *true*. Pushing things a bit, taking the time to draw on the vowel and to lend an ear, it will have been true, *wahr*, that's what can be kept [*garder*] or looked at [*regarder*] in truth.

He, is 'He', the 'him', the one who says I in the masculine, 'He', war declared, he who was war declared, declaring war, by declaring war, was he who was, and he who was true, the truth, he who by declaring war verified the truth that he was, he verified himself, he verified the truth of his truth by war declared, by the act of declaring, and declaring is an act of war, he declared war in language and on language and by language, which gave languages, that's the truth of Babel when YAHWE pronounced its vocable, difficult to say if it was a name. . .

I stop here provisionally, through lack of time; other transformations are possible, a great number, about which I'll say another two words later.

* *
*

Coming here, I said to myself that there are perhaps only two manners, or rather two greatnesses, in this madness of writing by which whoever writes effaces himself, leaving, only to abandon it, the archive of his own effacement. These last two words speak madness itself.

Perhaps that's an over-extreme simplification (there are certainly other 'greatnesses'), but I take the risk of saying it so as to say something of my feeling about Joyce.

I do indeed say 'my feeling': that − major − affect which, beyond all our analyses, evaluations, interpretations, controls the scene of our relationship with whoever writes. One can admire the power of a work and have, as they say, a 'bad relationship' with its signatory, at least the signatory as one projects, reconstructs, or dreams him, or when one allows oneself to be haunted by him − or by her. Our admiration for Joyce ought to have no limit, no more than should the debt owed to the singular *event* of his work (I prefer to talk here of an event rather than a work or a subject or an author). And yet I'm not sure I like Joyce. Or more exactly: I'm not sure he's liked. Except when he laughs − and you'll tell me that he's always laughing. That's true, I'll come back to it, but then everything is played out between the different tonalities of laughter, in the subtle difference which passes between several qualities of laughter. Knowing whether one likes Joyce, is that the right question? In any case, one can attempt to account for these affects, and I'm not sure that the matter is a secondary one.

I'm not sure of liking Joyce, of liking him all the time. And it's to explain this possibility that I talked of two greatnesses to measure that act of writing by which whoever writes pretends to efface himself, leaving us caught in his archive as in a spider's web.

Let us simplify outrageously. There is first of all the greatness of s/he who writes in order to give, in giving, and therefore in order to give to forget the gift and the given, what is given and the act of giving, which is the only way of giving, the only possible − and impossible − way. Even before any restitution, symbolic or real, before any gratitude, the simple memory, in truth merely the awareness of the gift, on the part of giver or receiver, annuls the very essence of the gift. The gift must be without return, without a sketch, even a symbolic one, of gratitude. Beyond any 'consciousness', of course, but also beyond any symbolic structure of the unconscious. Once the gift is received, the work having worked to the extent of changing you through and through, the scene is other and you have forgotten the gift and the giver. Then the work is loveable, and if the 'author' is not forgotten, we have for him a paradoxical gratitude, which is however the only gratitude worth its name if it is possible, a simple gratitude without ambivalence. This is what's called love, I'm not saying that it happens, perhaps it never *presents itself*, and the gift I'm describing can doubtless never make a present. One can at least dream of this possibility, and it is the idea of a writing which gives.

As for the other greatness, I shall say, with some injustice perhaps, that for me it's like Joyce's greatness, or rather that of Joyce's writing. Here the event is of such plot and scope that henceforth you have only one way out: *being in memory of him.* You're not only overcome by him, whether you know it or not, but obliged by him, and constrained to measure yourself against this overcoming. Being *in memory of him*: not necessarily to remember him, no, but to be in his memory, to inhabit his memory, which is henceforth greater than all your finite memory can, in a single instant or a single vocable, gather up of cultures, languages, mythologies, religions, philosophies, sciences, history of mind and of literatures. I don't know if you can like that, without resentment and jealousy. Can one pardon this hypermnesia which *a priori* indebts you, and in advance inscribes you in the book you are reading? One can pardon this Babelian act of war only if it happens already, from all time, with each event of writing, and if one knows it. One can pardon it only if one remembers too that Joyce himself must have endured this situation. He was its patient, and what's more that's his theme, or, as I prefer to say here, his scheme. He talks about it often enough for there to be no simple confusion between him and a sadistic demiurge, setting up a hypermnesiac machine, there in advance, decades in advance, to compute you, control you, forbid you the slightest inaugural syllable because you can say nothing that is not programmed on this 1000th generation computer — *Ulysses, Finnegans Wake* — beside which the current technology of our computers and our micro-computerified archives and our translating machines remains a *bricolage* of a prehistoric child's toys. And above all its mechanisms are of a slowness incommensurable with the quasi-infinite speed of the movements on Joyce's cables. How could you calculate the speed with which a mark, a marked piece of information, is placed in contact with another in the same word or from one end of the book to the other? For example, at what speed is the Babelian theme or the word 'Babel', in each of their components (but how could you count them?), co-ordinated with *all* the phonemes, semes, mythemes, etc. of *Finnegans Wake*? Counting these connections, calculating the speed of these communications, would be impossible, at least *de facto*, so long as we have not constructed the machine capable of integrating all the variables, all the quantitative or qualitative factors. This won't happen tomorrow, and in any case this machine would only be the double or the simulation of the event 'Joyce', the name of Joyce, the signed work, the Joyce software today, joyceware.

It is with this sentiment, or one should say this resentment, that I must have been reading Joyce for a long time. And no doubt I'm not the only one. Ellmann has recently quoted the avowals of so many writers, critics, artists, all admirers or friends of Joyce, who expressed something of this malaise. But I'm not sure that one can say 'reading Joyce' as I just have. Of course, one can do nothing but that, whether one knows it or not. But the utterances 'I am reading Joyce', 'read Joyce', 'have you read Joyce?' produce an irresistible effect of naivety, irresistibly comical. What exactly do you mean by 'read Joyce'? Who can pride himself on having 'read' Joyce?

With this admiring resentment, you stay on the edge of reading Joyce — for me this has been going on for twenty-five or thirty years — and the endless plunge throws you back onto the river-bank, on the brink of another possible immersion, *ad infinitum*. Is this true to the same extent of all works? In any case, I have the feeling that I haven't yet begun to read Joyce, and this 'not having begun to read' is sometimes the most singular and active relationship I have with this work.

That is why I've never dared to write *on* Joyce. At most I've tried to mark (you were kind enough to recall this a while ago) in what I wrote of Joyce's scores [*portées*], Joyce's *reaches* [*portées*].[3] Beyond the musical measure that can be recognized in this word *portée*, which speaks too of the proliferating generous multitude of the animal [*portée* as 'litter'], you can also hear this in it: such and such a text *carries* [*porte*] in truth the signature of Joyce, it *carries* Joyce and lets itself be carried by him, or even carried off [*déporter*] in advance. Paradoxical logic of this relationship between two texts, two programmes or two literary 'softwares': whatever the difference between them, even if, as in the present case, it is immense and even incommensurable, the 'second' text, the one which, fatally, refers to the other, quotes it, exploits it, parasites it and deciphers it, is no doubt the minute parcel *detached* from the other, the metonymic dwarf, the jester of the great anterior text which would have declared war on it in languages; and yet it is also another set, quite other, bigger and more powerful than the all-powerful which it drags off and reinscribes elsewhere in order to defy its ascendancy. Each writing is at once the detached fragment of a software and a software more powerful than the other, a part larger than the whole of which it is a part.

This is already what *Finnegans Wake* represents with respect to all the culture, all the history and all the languages it condenses, puts in fusion and fission by each of its forgeries, at the heart of each lexical or syntactic unit, according to each phrase that it forges, stamping invention there. In the simulacrum of this forgery, in the ruse of the invented word, the greatest possible memory is stamped and smelted. *Finnegans Wake* is a little, a little what?, a little son, a little grandson of Western culture in its circular, encyclopedic, Ulyssean and more than Ulyssean totality. And then it is, simultaneously, much bigger than even this odyssey, it comprehends it, and this prevents it, dragging it outside itself in an entirely singular adventure, from closing in on itself and on this event. The future is reserved in it. The 'situation' of *Finnegans Wake* is also, because of this, our own situation with respect to this immense text. In this war of languages, everything we can say after it looks in advance like a minute self-commentary with which this work accompanies itself. It is already comprehended by it. And yet the new marks carry off, enlarge and project elsewhere — one never knows where in advance — a programme which appeared to constrain them. This is our only chance, minuscule and completely open.

So, yes (I'm replying to your suggestion), every time I write, and even in the most academic pieces of work, Joyce's ghost is always coming on board. Twenty years ago, in the *Introduction to 'The Origin of Geometry'*,[4] at the very centre of the book, I compared the strategies of Husserl and of Joyce: two great models, two paradigms with respect to thought, but also with respect to a certain 'operation' of the relationship between language and history. Both try to grasp a pure historicity. To do this, Husserl proposes to render language as transparent as possible, univocal, limited to that which, by being transmittable or able to be placed in tradition, thereby constitutes the only condition of a possible historicity; and from this point of view, it is necessary that some minimal readability, an element of univocity or an analysable equivocality, resist the Joycean overload and condensation for there to be a reading, and the work's legacy; something of the meaning of *He war* must cross the threshold of intelligibility, through the thousand and one meanings of the expression, for a history to take place, if at least it is to take place, and at least the history of the work. The other great paradigm would be the Joyce of *Finnegans Wake*. He repeats and mobilizes and babelizes the (asymptotic) totality of the equivocal, he makes this his theme and his operation, he tries to make outcrop, with the greatest possible synchrony, at great speed, the greatest power of the meanings buried in each syllabic fragment, subjecting each atom of writing to fission in order to overload the unconscious with the whole memory of man: mythologies, religion, philosophies, sciences, psychoanalysis, literatures. This generalized equivocality of writing does not translate one language into another on the basis of common nuclei of meaning (*Introduction to 'The Origin of Geometry'*, pp. 103ff); it talks several languages at once, parasiting them as in the example *He war* to which I shall turn in a moment. For there will remain the question of knowing what one should think of the possibility of writing several languages at once.

A few years later, I had the feeling that without too much difficulty one could have presented *La Pharmacie de Platon*[5] as a sort of indirect reading of *Finnegans Wake*, which mimes, between Shem and Shaun, between the penman and the postman, down to the finest and most finely ironized detail, the whole scene of the pharmakos, the pharmakon, the various functions of Thoth, th'other, etc. I cannot here reconstitute the extreme complexity of this network. I had to be content with playing, in a single note (*Dissemination*, p. 88), at recalling that, of course, 'as will quickly have been understood', the whole of *La Pharmacie de Platon* was only 'a reading of *Finnegans Wake*'. This double genitive implied that this modest essay was read in advance by *Finnegans Wake*, in its wake or its lineage, at the very moment that *La Pharmacie de Platon* was itself presenting itself as a reading-head or principle of decipherment (in short another software) for a possible understanding of *Finnegans Wake*. There again there is a paradoxical metonymy: the most modest, the most miserable descendant of a corpus, its sample in another language, can appear to be *more capacious* than what it allows to be read.

I pass quickly over *Scribble*,[6] the title of my introduction to the *Essai sur les hiéroglyphes*, a partial translation of Warburton's essay, where, beyond even the title and the quotations, I constantly refer to *Scribbledehobble: The Ur-Workbook for Finnegans Wake* (1961). And I pass quickly over *Glas*[7] which is also a sort of wake.

Above all, ten years later, *La Carte postale*[8] is haunted by Joyce, whose funerary statue stands at the centre of the *Envois* (the visit to the cemetery in Zurich). This haunting invades the book, a shadow on every page, whence the resentment, sincere and acted, always mimed, of the signatory. He sometimes confides his impatience in his addressee, whom, in the first words of the book, two years earlier, he had conceded was right ('Yes, you were right . . .'):

. . . You are also right about Joyce, once is enough. It's so strong that in the end nothing can resist it, whence the feeling of facility, however deceitful it may be. One wonders what he ended up doing, that guy, and what made him tick. After him, don't start again, draw the veil and let everything happen behind the curtains of language which can't do anything about it. But there's a coincidence; for this seminar on translation I followed all the babelian indications in *Finnegans Wake* and yesterday I wanted to take the plane to Zurich and read out loud sitting on his knees, from the beginning (Babel, the fall, and the finno-phoenician motif, 'The fall (bababadalgh [. . .]. The great fall of the offwall entailed at such short notice the pftjschute of Finnegan [. . .] Phall if you but will, rise you must: and none so soon either shall the pharce for the nunce come to a setdown secular phoenish [. . .]') up to the passage on Gigglotte's Hill and Babbyl Market near the end, passing through 'The babbelers with their thangas vain have been (confusium hold them!) [. . .] Who ails tongue coddeau, aspace of dumbillsilly? And they fell upong one another: and themselves they have fallen . . .' and through 'This battering babel allower the door and sideposts . . .' and the whole page up to 'Filons, filoosh! *Cherchons la flamme*! Fammfamm!

Fammfamm!', through this passage which you know better than anyone (*FW* 164) and in which I suddenly find 'the babbling pumpt of platinism', through this other passage about 'the turrace of Babbel', the whole Anna Livia Plurabelle passage, where you will find absolutely amazing things; and then everything that comes around 'A and aa ab ad abu abiad. A babbel men dub gulch of tears.', or 'And shall not Babel be with Lebab? And he war. And he shall open his mouth and answer: I hear, O Ismael . . . And he deed . . .', up to 'O Loud . . . Loud . . . Ha he hi ho hu. Mummum.' I run through the text, as they say of actors, at least up until '*Usque! Usque! Usque!* Lignum in . . . Is the strays world moving mound or what static babel is this, tell us?' (*La Carte postale*, pp. 257–8)

Elsewhere, in front of Joyce's funerary monument: 'He's read us all − and pillaged us, that guy. I imagined him looking at himself posed there − by his zealous descendants, I suppose' (*La Carte postale*, p. 161). Read and pillaged in advance, then. The whole (scriptural and postal) scenography of *Finnegans Wake* is put back into play, starting with the couple Shem/Shaun, the penman/the postman, up to the war over the invention of the postage stamp and the penny post which is to be found deposited in Joyce's book (*La Carte postale*, pp. 151, 155). With a whole family of James, Jacques, Giacomo, the *Giacomo Joyce* scans all the *Envois* which are sealed, near the end, by the *Envoy* of G. C.: 'Envoy: love me love my umbrella.' '*11 August 1979* (. . .) James (the two, the three), Jacques, Giacomo Joyce − your counterfeit works wonders, this pendant to the invoice: "Envoy: love me love my umbrella." (. . .) I was forgetting, Giacomo also has seven letters. Love my shadow, it − not me. "Do you love me?" And you, say "me" ' (*La Carte postale*, p. 255).[9]

But I repeat, it is above all the Babelian motif which obsesses the *Envois*, and this is where we get back to the *He war* to which I should like to return in conclusion. If you will permit, I shall read first a fragment of the card which quotes the 'he war':

no my love that's my wake. The day when I was talking about all these pp (private *picture postcard* and *penny post*), I was first struck by this: prepayment institutes a general equivalent which regulates the tax according to the size and weight of the *support* and not the number, tenor or quality of the 'marks', even less on what they call the meaning. It's unjust and stupid, it's barbarous, even, but immensely important [*d'une immense portée*]. Whether you put one word or one hundred in a letter, a hundred-letter word or one hundred seven-letter words, it's the same price; it's incomprehensible, but this principle is capable of accounting for everything. Let's leave it there. Writing *penny post*, I had also the premonition in my memory that Jean the postman (Shaun, John *the postman*) was not very far away, and nor was his twin brother Shem *the penman*. Another pp fraternal couple at war with each other, *the penman and the postman*. The writer, Shem, is the legatee of H.C.E., Here Comes Everybody, which I translate into my idiom as 'Here comes whoever will have loved me in my body'. So I looked for two hours for the *penny post* and here it is, at least one you could link to an all-powerful 'he war' (YHWH declaring war by decreeing dishemination, deconstructing the tower, saying to those who wanted to make a name for themselves, the shemites, and to impose their particular language as a universal language, saying to them 'Babel', I call myself and I impose my father-name, which you understand confusedly as 'Confusion', try, I beg of you, to translate but I hope you won't be able to, it's my double bind), passing through '*his penisolate war*' and the 'sosie sesthers' of the first page. Here then, on page 307 of *Finnegans Wake*: 'Visit to Guinness' Brewery, Clubs, Advantages of the Penny Post, When is a Pun not a Pun?'. Across, in the margin in italics, the names, you know. Here: 'Noah. Plato. Horace. Isaac. Tiresias'. On the preceding page, I pull out only this, for later: 'A Place for Everything and Everything in its Place, Is the Pen mightier than the Sword?' which pulls the following thread for example (p. 211): 'a sunless map of the month, including the sword and stamps, for Shemus O'Shaun the Post . . .'. Read the sequel round about 'Elletrouvetout' and 'Where-is-he?; whatever you like . . .' etc. Look at them, Sword/Pen.

I've just phoned you, it was impossible, you understood, you have to be naked on the phone. But at the same time it's enough for you to undress for me to see myself naked. Our story is also a twin progeny, a procession of Sosie/sosie, Atrée/Thyeste, Shem/Shaun, S/p, p/p, (*penman/postman*) and more and more I metempsychose myself of you, I am with others as you are with me (for better but also, I see clearly, for the worst, I play the same tricks on them). Never have I imitated anyone so irresistibly. I'm trying to shake myself out of it because if I love you infinitely I don't love the whole of you I mean these inhabitants of you with their little hats the uniquely each time I love: beyond all that is, you are the one − and therefore the other. (*La Carte postale*, pp. 154–5)

*   *

*

'He war', then. How to read these two words? Are there two of them? More or less? How to hear them? How to pronounce them and pronounce on their subject? The question 'how to hear them' multiplies itself, moreover, and echoes in the whole passage from which I extract these two words with the unjustifiable violence which the situation imposes on us, the little time at our disposal. How to hear them? Everything around speaks to the ear and of the ear: what speaking means but first what *listening* means: lending one's ear (*e ar, he ar*) and obeying the father who raises his voice, the lord who talks loud. What rises so high is laud. This audiophonic dimension of the divine law and its sublime height is announced in the English syllabification of *he (w)ar*, is doubled in the *w* and disseminates, for the seme and the form, on the whole page.[10] The rhythm of Biblical writing is mimed by the 'And . . .' of 'And he war . . .'. I read very aloud:

And let Nek Nekulon extol Mak Makal and let him say unto him: Immi ammi Semmi. And shall not Babel be with Lebab? And he war. And he shall open his mouth and answer: I hear, O Ismael, how they laud is only as my loud is one. If Nekulon shall be havonfalled surely Makal haven hevens. Go to, let us extell Makal, yea, let us exceedingly extell. Though you have lien amung your posspots my excellency is over Ismael. Great is him whom is over Ismael and he shall mekanek of Mak Nakulon. And he deed.

Uplouderamainagain!

For the Clearer of the Air from on high has spoken in tumbuldum tambaldam to his tembledim tombaldoom worrild and, moguphonoised by that phonemanon, the unhappitents of the earth have terrerumbled from fimament unto fundament and from tweedledeedumms down to twiddledeedees.

Loud, hear us!

Loud, graciously hear us!

Now have thy children entered into their habitations. And nationglad, camp meeting over, to shin it, Gov be thanked! Thou hast closed the portals of the habitations of thy children and thou hast set thy guards thereby, even Garda Didymus and Garda Domas, that thy children may read in the book of the opening of the mind to light and err not in the darkness which is the afterthought of thy nomatter by the guardiance of those guards which are thy bodemen, the cheeryboyum chirryboth with the kerrybommers in their krubeems, Pray-your-Prayers Timothy and Back-to-Bunk Tom.

Till tree from tree, tree among trees, tree over tree become stone to stone, stone between stones, stone under stone for ever.

O Loud, hear the wee beseech of thees of each of these they unlitten ones! Grant sleep in hour's time, O Loud!

That they take no chill. That they do ming no merder. That they shall not gomeet madhowiatrees.

Loud, heap miseries upon us yet entwine our arts with laughters low!

Ha he hi ho hu.

Mummum.   (258.11–259.10)

Let us leave to one side, given the lack of time, numerous intersecting motifs, accumulated or condensed in the immediate context of 'he war' (Fall – 'Byfall'; the curtain drops, applause – 'Uploud!', 'Uplouderamainagain!' – after the *Götterdämmerung* – 'gttrdmmrng'; the double: Garda Didymus and Garda Domas, the two policemen; Vico's ghost everywhere, the children's prayer . . . (257–8)), and let us limit ourselves, if one can say this, to all that passes through the voice and the phenomenon, the phenomenon as phoneme: at the centre of the sequence, hear the 'phonemanon'.

It reflects, in a state of extreme concentration, the whole Babelian adventure of the book, or rather its Babelian underside: 'And shall not babel be with Lebab'. This palindrome which overturns the tower of Babel also speaks of the book, and Philippe Lavergne recalls the two Irish words *leaba*, the bed, and *leabhar*, the book.

A few examples among others: 'The babbelers with their thangas vain have been (confusium hold them!) they were and went; thigging thugs were and houhnhymn songtoms were and comely norgels were and pollyfool fiansees. [. . .] And they fell upong one another: and themselves they have fallen' (15.12–19); or again: 'and we list, as she bibs us, by the waters of babalong' (103.10–11), 'the babbling pumpt of platinism' (164.11), 'the turrace of Babel' (199.31), 'Is the strays world moving mound or what static babel is this, tell us?' (499.33–4), 'to my reputation on Babbyl Malket for daughters-in-trade being lightly clad' (532.24–6), etc. . . .

In the landscape immediately surrounding the 'he war', we are, if such a present is possible, and this place, at Babel: at the moment when YAHWEH declares war, HE WAR (exchange of the final R and the central H in the anagram's throat), and punishes the Shem, those who, according to Genesis, declare their intention of building the tower in order to make a name for themselves. Now they bear the name 'name' (Shem). And the Lord, the Most High, be he blessed (*Lord, loud, laud* . . .), declares war on them by interrupting the construction of the tower, he deconstructs by speaking the vocable of his choice, the name of confusion, which in the hearing, could be confused with a word indeed signifying 'confusion'. Once this war is declared, he was it (*war*) by being himself this act of war which consisted in declaring, as he did, that he was the one he was (*war*). The God of fire assigns to the Shem the necessary, fatal and impossible translation of his name, of the vocable with which he signs his act of war, of himself. The palindrome ('And shall not Babel be with Lebab? And he war . . .') overthrows the tower but plays too with the meaning and the letter, the meaning of being and the letters of being, of 'being',[11] BE,EB (baBEl/lEBab), as it does with the meaning and the letter of the name of God, EL,LE. The names of the father (*Dad, Bab*) are moreover dispersed on the same page, along with those of the Lord and of an Anglo-Saxon god (*Go to* − twice, *Gov*) which can spread out elsewhere into governor and scape*goat*.

This act of war is not necessarily anything other than an election, an act of love. We would have to reread here the prodigious pages around this 'paleoparisien schola of tinkers and spanglers who say I'm wrong *parcequeue* . . .' (151.9–10), where we would find the following: '. . . for aught I care for the contrary, the all is *where* in love as war and the plane where . . .' (151.36–152.1). And as in Ponge's *Le Soleil placé en abîme*, the redhead whore is not far from the father, in his very bed she becomes one with him: '*In my Lord's Bed by One Whore* . . .' (105.34). This is in the great catalogue introduced by 'Thus we hear of . . .' (104.5). But I break off this reconstruction here.

So what happens when one tries to translate this 'he war'? It is impossible not to want to do it, to want violently − and reading itself consists, from its very first movement, in sketching out translation. 'He War' calls for translation, both orders and forbids transposition into the other language. Change me (into yourself) and above all do not touch me, read and do not read, say and do not say otherwise what I have said and which will have been: in two words *which was*. For the 'he war' also tells of the irreplaceability of the event that it is, which is that it is, and which is also unchangeable because it has already been, a past without appeal which, before being, was. So that's war declared: before being, that is being a present, it was: was *he*, the late god of fire.[12] And the call to translate rejects you: thou shalt not translate me. Which will also perhaps be translated in the banning of translation (as 'representation', 'image', 'statue', 'imitation', so many inadequate translations of 'temunah')[13] which immediately follows the moment at which YHWH names himself ('Me, YHWH, your Elohim . . .'). The law enounced in the performative dimension is thus also the ban on the very principle of translation, the ban *in* the very principle of translation, inter-translation as one and the same experience of language: of the one language as one God. And transgression (just as impossible) consists, among other things, in translating that, and, already, in perverting into a description or a constatation (*he war*) a first-person performative, the performative of the first person or rather of the first word.

So what happens − I repeat the same question − when one attempts to translate this 'he war'? Nothing, everything. Beyond immense difficulties, a limit remains essential. The difficulties: is it possible to make heard (*hear*) *all* the semantic, phonic, graphic virtualities which communicate with the *he war* in the totality of the book and elsewhere? The essential limit (a repetition of Babel's act of war declared − and not declared! − which Joyce reprints here) pertains to the graft (and without any possible rejection) of one language onto the body of another. In two words of which each is the head, the capital or, if you prefer, the principal member. Imagine the most powerful and refined translation-machines, the most able translation teams. Their very success cannot but take the form of a failure. Even if, in an improbable hypothesis, they had translated *everything*, they would by that very fact fail to translate the multiplicity of languages. They would erase the following simple fact: a multiplicity of idioms, not only of meanings but of idioms, must have structured this event of writing which henceforth stands as law, and will have laid down the law *about itself*. It *was* written *simultaneously* in both English and German. Two words in one (*war*), and thus a double noun, a double verb, a noun and a verb which are divided in the beginning. *War* is a noun in English, a verb in German, it resembles an adjective (*wahr*) in that same language, and the truth of this multiplicity returns, from the attributes (the verb is also an attribute), towards the subject, *he*, who is divided by it right from the origin. In the beginning, difference, that's what happens, that's what has already taken place, that's what was when language was act, and the tongue [*la langue*] writing. Where it was, *He* was.[14]

The German *war* will only have been true in declaring war on English, and in making war on it in English. The *fact* of the multiplicity of languages, what *was done* as confusion of languages can no longer let itself be translated into *one* language, nor even (I'll come to this in a moment) into *language* [*la langue*]. To translate 'he war' into the system of a single language − as has just been tried in French ('Et il en fut ainsi') − is to erase the event of the mark, not only what is said in it but its very saying and writing, the mark of its law and the law of its mark. The current concept of translation is still regulated according to the *twice one*, the operation of passing from one language into another, each of them forming an organism or a system the rigorous integrity of which remains at the level of supposition, like that of a body proper. The translation of a Babelism involving at least two languages would demand an equivalent which would restore not only all the semantic and formal potentialities of the hapax 'he war', but also the multiplicity of languages in it, the *coition* of that event, in truth its very number, its numerous essence. You can always try. It is not only *Finnegans Wake* which here resembles a too-powerful, outsize calculator incommensurable with any translating machine conceivable today, but already the event which the book translates or mimes, before which it, *Finnegans Wake*, will have presented itself.

For a little while, I've been speaking out loud. In proffering 'he war', I entrust myself to this truth, so often recalled: in this book, in this event worked on by the confusion of languages, multiplicity remains controlled by a dominant language, English. Now despite the need to 'phonetize', despite this book's appeal for reading out loud, for song and for timbre, something essential in it passes the understanding as well as the hearing:[15] a graphic or literal dimension, a muteness which one should never pass over in silence. You can't economize on it, and this book could not be read without it. For the Babelian confusion between the English *war* and the German *war* cannot fail to disappear − in becoming determined − when listened to. It is erased when pronounced. One is constrained to *say* it either in English *or else* in German, it cannot therefore be received as such by the ear. But it can be read. The homography retains the effect of confusion, it shelters the Babelism which here, then, plays between speech and writing. This Anglo-Saxon commerce, these exchanges of a piece of merchandise (*ware*) in two languages, must pass through acts of writing. The event is linked to the spacing of its archive and would not take place without it, without being put into letters and pages. Erase the typeface, mute the graphic percussion, subordinate the spacing, that is, the divisibility of the letter, and you would again reappropriate *Finnegans Wake* into a monolingualism, or at least subjugate it to the hegemony of a single language. Of course this hegemony remains indisputable, but its law only appears *as such* in the course of a *war* through which English tries to erase the other language or languages, to colonize them, to domesticate them, to present them for reading from only one angle. But one must also read the resistance to this commonwealth, not only pronounce oneself but also write oneself against it. Against Him. And this is indeed what happens. Between islands of language, across each island. Ireland and England would only be emblems of this. What matters is the contamination of the language of the master by the language he claims to subjugate, on which he has declared war. In doing so he locks himself in a double bind from which YHWH himself will not have escaped. If it is impossible to sing in German and English at one and the same time, the written form retains polyglossia by placing the tongue at risk.

He war, God's signature. As quotation replays the whole of the world's memory, in *Finnegans Wake*, one can only quote − 'mention', the speech-act theorists would say, rather than 'use' − the 'I' which thenceforth becomes 'he', Him, or the 'he', a pronoun cited rather than a 'real' subject, aimed at by some direct reference. 'He' and not 'she', he who was he in declaring war. He resounds, he gives himself to be heard, he articulates himself and makes himself heard right up to the end: in opposition to the 'Mummum', to the last murmur which closes the sequence, a maternal inarticulated syllabification which falls as close as can be to to the 'hush' [*chut*] or the fall [*chute*] after the last vocalization, the series of expiring vowels, voices out of breath:

> Ha he hi ho hu
> Mummum.

These are the last 'words', the last word of the sequence. In the series of vowels, the 'he' reappears, a simple second place in the sequence of a general hubbub. And if the page is turned, after a broad blank there is the beginning of Book II, Chapter 2 (I content myself here with letting read and resound):

As we there are where are we are we there   UNDE ET UBI
from tomtittot to teetootomtotalitarian. Tea
tea too oo.   (260.01–03)

The final 'Mummum', maternal syllable right near the end, could, if one so wished, be made to resound with the feminine 'yes' in the last line of *Ulysses*, the 'yes' of Mrs Bloom, of ALP, or of any 'wee' girl, as has been noted, Eve, Mary, Isis, etc. The Great Mother on the side of the creation and the fall. In William York Tindall's book on *Finnegans Wake* I came across the following sentence where the word 'hill' plays more or less innocently with the French personal pronoun 'il', to say nothing of the 'île': 'As he [HCE] is the hill in Joyce's familial geography, so she is the river [. . .]. This "wee" (or *oui*) girl is Eve, Mary, Isis, any woman you can think of, and a *poule* − at once a riverpool, a whore, and a little hen.'[16]

* *
*

'I'm not sure I like Joyce . . . I'm not sure he is liked . . . except when he laughs . . . he's always laughing . . . everything is played out in the difference between several tonalities of laughter': that is what I suggested as I started. The question would be this: why does laughter here traverse the whole of the experience which refers us to *Finnegans Wake*, thus not letting itself be reduced to any of the other modalities, apprehensions, affections, whatever their richness, their heterogeneity, their overdetermination? And what does this writing teach us of the essence of laughter if it recalls that laughter to the limits of the calculable and the incalculable, when the whole of the calculable is outplayed by a writing about which it is no longer possible to decide if it still calculates, calculates better and more, or if it transcends the very order of calculable economy, or even of an incalculable or an undecidable which would still be homogeneous with the world of calculation? A certain quality of laughter would supply something like the affect (but this word itself remains to be determined) to this beyond of calculation, and of all calculable literature.

It is perhaps (perhaps) this quality of laughter, and none other, which resounds, very loud or very soft, I don't know, through the prayer which immediately precedes the 'Ha he hi ho hu. Mummum.' at the end:

Loud, heap miseries upon us yet entwine our arts with laughters low![17]

Laugh down low of the signature, calm the crazy laughter and the anguish of the proper name in the murmured prayer, forgive God by asking him to let us perform the gesture of giving according to art, and the art of laughter.

At the beginning I spoke of resentment. Always possible with respect to Joyce's signature. But it was a way of considering, on a small scale, Joyce's revenge with respect to the God of Babel. But the God of Babel had already tortured his own signature; he was this torment: resentment *a priori* with respect to any possible translator. I order you and forbid you to translate me, to interfere with my name, to give a body of writing to its vocalization. And through this double command he signs. The signature does not come after the law, it is the divided act of the law: revenge, resentment, reprisal, revendication *as* signature. But also as gift and gift of languages. And God lets himself be prayed to, he condescends, he leans over (Loud/low), prayer and laughter absolve perhaps the pain of signature, the act of war with which everything will have begun. This is art, Joyce's art, the space given for his signature made into the work. *He war*, it's a counter-signature, it confirms and contradicts, effaces by subscribing. It says 'we' and 'yes' in the end to the Father or to the Lord who speaks loud, there is scarcely anyone but Him, but it leaves the last word to the woman who in her turn will have said 'we' and 'yes'. Countersigned God, God who countersigneth thyself, God who signeth thyself in us, let us laugh, amen.

(Translated by Geoff Bennington)

Notes

1. What follows is a transcription of a more or less extemporary talk given at the Centre Georges Pompidou, Paris, in November 1982. Jacques Derrida has preferred to mark the circumstantial nature of the talk by retaining in this printed version references to a talk given by Hélène Cixous on the same occasion [Tr.].

2. The French text plays here on the homophony of 'le mode oreille' and 'le mot d'oreille' [Tr.].

3. Derrida plays here and in the following sentence on three senses of the word 'portée': (1) range, reach, or scope; (2) musical staff or stave; (3) litter in the veterinary sense [Tr.].

4. *Introduction to 'The Origin of Geometry'*, tr. Edward Leavey (Hassocks: Harvester, 1978), pp. 103ff.

5. 'Plato's Pharmacy', in *Dissemination*, tr. Barbara Johnson (Chicago: University of Chicago Press, 1981), pp. 61–171.

6. 'Scribble (writing-power)', *Yale French Studies*, 58 (1979), 116–47.

7. *Glas* (Paris: Galilée, 1974).

8. *La Carte postale de Socrate à Freud et au-delà* (Paris: Aubier–Flammarion, 1980).

9. 'Et toi, dis moi': the absence of the hyphen between 'dis' and 'moi' dictates the translation, but also calls up, by graphic difference, the possibility: 'And you, tell me' [Tr.].

10. Along with the sense of 'war', the signalling of the recourse to German, etc., this audiophonic dimension of *he war* is one of the very numerous things which must go by the board in the nonetheless very commendable translation of *Finnegans Wake* by Philippe Lavergne (Paris: Gallimard, 1982), which I did not know when I gave this talk. 'And he war' is 'rendered' by 'Et il en fut ainsi' (p. 278). But let us never malign translations, especially this one. . .

11. 'joue aussi avec le sens et la lettre, le sens de l'être et les lettres de l'être, de "être" ': playing on the homophony 'lettre(s)'/'l'être' [Tr.].

12. 'feu le dieu de feu': 'feu' placed before the noun means 'late' in the sense of 'deceased' [Tr.].

13. See Michal Govrine, 'Jewish Ritual as a Genre of Sacred Theatre', *Conservative Judaism*, 36.3 (1983).

14. 'Là où c'était, *Il* fut': troping against Freud's famous 'Wo es war, soll Ich werden' [Tr.].

15. 'quelque chose d'essentiel y passe l'entendement aussi bien que l'écoute': the connotation of hearing (*entendre*) in 'entendement' (understanding) is carried over in the translation to cover 'écoute' (listening) too [Tr.].

16. William York Tindall, *A Reader's Guide to 'Finnegans Wake'* (London: Thames and Hudson, 1969), p. 4.

17. I do not know if 'laughters low' can be translated, as Lavergne does, by 'sourire discret'. But how to translate — for example the opposition of the first and last word of the prayer, 'Loud'/'low'? And must one translate? On what criteria will one rely to decide that here one must translate, or at least try, and here not? For example: should one, or should one not, translate 'Ha he hi ho hu', where the 'he' is also the homophone of a 'real' word in the language? But again, does not the question 'must one translate' arrive too late, always too late? It cannot be the object of a deliberate decision. Translation has begun with the first reading, and even — this is the thesis of these two words — before reading. There is scarcely anything but writing in translation, as Genesis tells us. And Babel is also the difference of pitch [*hauteur*] in the voice (loud/low) as well as in space. The erection of the tower is interrupted by the *He War*: 'Let's go! Let's get down! Let's confuse their lips there, man will no longer hear his neighbour's lip' (Genesis 11: 7–8; translated from André Chouraqui's French translation).

Contributors

DEREK ATTRIDGE is Professor of English Studies at the University of Strathclyde. He is the author of *Well-weighed Syllables* (Cambridge: Cambridge University Press, 1974) and *The Rhythms of English Poetry* (London: Longman, 1982), and articles on Joyce, Racine, and the language of literature.

JACQUES AUBERT is Professor of English at the University of Lyon II. He is the author of *Introduction à l'esthétique de James Joyce* (Paris: Didier, 1973) and the editor of the first volume in the Pléiade edition of Joyce's works (Paris: Gallimard, 1982); he organized the 1975 International James Joyce Symposium in Paris and, with Maria Jolas, edited the proceedings (Paris: C.N.R.S., 1979).

HÉLÈNE CIXOUS is Professor of English at the University of Paris VIII. She is the author of *L'Exil de James Joyce* (Paris: Grasset, 1968), translated as *The Exile of James Joyce* (New York: David Lewis, 1972), and *Prénoms de personne* (Paris: Seuil, 1974), as well as numerous books on literary and feminist theory and many novels and other literary works.

JACQUES DERRIDA is Directeur d'Etudes, Ecole des Hautes Etudes en Sciences Sociales. His publications include *L'Écriture et la différence* (Paris: Seuil, 1967), translated as *Writing and Difference* (Chicago: University of Chicago Press, 1978); *De la grammatologie* (Paris: Minuit, 1967), translated as *Of Grammatology* (Baltimore: Johns Hopkins University Press, 1976); *La voix et le phénomène* (Paris: P.U.F., 1967), translated as *Speech and Phenomena* (Evanston: Northwestern University Press, 1973); *La Dissémination* (Paris: Seuil, 1972), translated as *Dissemination* (Chicago: University of Chicago Press, 1981); *Marges de la Philosophie* (Paris: Minuit, 1972), translated as *Margins of Philosophy* (Chicago: University of Chicago Press, 1982); *Glas* (Paris: Galilée, 1974); and *La Carte postale* (Paris: Flammarion, 1980). He was recently invited by the French government to set up the *Collège International de Philosophie* in Paris.

DANIEL FERRER is Maître-Assistant in English at the University of Besançon. He has published articles on Joyce, Virginia Woolf, William Faulkner, American painting, Hogarth and Stravinsky, and literary theory, and is co-author of *Genèse de Babel: James Joyce et la création de 'Finnegans Wake'*, to be published by Éditions du C.N.R.S.

STEPHEN HEATH is a Fellow of Jesus College, Cambridge, and a University Lecturer in English. Among his many publications are *The Nouveau Roman* (London: Elek, 1974), *Vertige du déplacement: Lecture de Barthes* (Paris: Fayard, 1974), *Image-Music-Text* (London: Collins, 1977), and *The Sexual Fix* (London: Macmillan, 1982).

JEAN-MICHEL RABATÉ is Professor of English at the University of Dijon. His books include *James Joyce: Portrait de l'auteur en autre lecteur* (Petit-Roeulx: Cistre, 1984) and *Language, Sexuality and Ideology in Ezra Pound's 'Cantos'* (London: Macmillan, 1984), and he is the editor of *Beckett avant Beckett* (Paris: P.E.N.S., 1984); he has also published essays on Joyce, Pound, and Hermann Broch.

ANDRÉ TOPIA is Maître-Assistant at the University of Paris X. He has published essays on Joyce, Beckett, Flann O'Brien, David Mercer, and Raymond Queneau.